V.S. Naipaul

V.S. Naipaul

Editors

Dr. A.A. Khan

Umesh Chandra Joshi

SHREE PUBLISHERS & DISTRIBUTORS

NEW DELHI-110 002

Edition : 2012

Published by :
SHREE PUBLISHERS & DISTRIBUTORS
22/4735 Prakash Deep Building,
Ansari Road, Darya Ganj,
New Delhi–110 002

ISBN : 978–81–8329–491–1

Printed by :
D.G. Printers
Delhi–110 094

Preface

English for Indians, is not an alien language now. This international language is essential for all the students in universities and for others, who may be aspiring for different competitions and various positions, in the corporate and government setup. Beyond the learning of the language, a thorough study of English Literature is helpful in understanding life better and knowing society, further, in a rational manner. Hence, there is always a need for good books to attain knowledge in this regard. Notably, English literature is the literature, written in the English language, including the literature, composed in English by writers, not necessarily from England.

English literature is as diverse as the varieties and dialects of English, spoken around the world. For instance, Robert Burns was Scottish, James Joyce was Irish, Joseph Conrad was Ukrainian, Dylan Thomas was Welsh, Edgar Allan Poe was American, Vladimir Nabokov was Russian and V.S. Naipaul has been born in Trinidad and Salman Rushdi is of Indian origin. Mulk Raj Anand and R.K. Narayan are from India, but all of them are considered significant writers in the history of English literature.

These books have been designed and prepared, within the parameters of the courses for the post-graduate students in various universities of the country. These books, on different topics, are in accordance with the requirements of various courses for the M.A. Examination. All these books have very strictly been shaped as per the prescribed syllabus, on a point to point basis. Therefore, it can be ascertained that these books would be able to fulfil all needs of the students, who are, in fact, our targeted readers. These books would expectedly be accepted by students and acknowledged by teachers, who in turn may recommend these reader-friendly books to their pupils.

We are indebted to all scholars, authors and compilers, whose valuable contributions, we have benefited from, while preparing these books. We are also thankful to the publishers and website operators, whose works, we have referred to, during the compilation of these books. And last but not the least, the undersigned express a wholehearted gratitude to all the associates, who extended their full cooperation in shaping and finalising these books.

These books have covered the whole gamut of English Literature, from the earliest era, through medieval and modern periods to the current age. This particular book is on: ***V.S. Naipaul.*** Enlightening advisory notes and esteemed remarks are solicited from all concerned circles.

— Dr. A.A. Khan
Umesh Chandra Joshi

Contents

1 Life and Times

Profile

Naipaul is a noted author in modern English Literature. Sir Vidiadhar Surajprasad—"V. S." Naipaul, (born 17 August 1932) is a Nobel prize-winning Trinidadian-British writer, who is known for his novels focusing on the legacy of the British Empire's colonialism. He has also written works of non-fiction, such as travel writing and essays.

Naipaul has been called "a master of modern English prose" in *The New York Review of Books* and has been awarded numerous literary prizes including the John Llewellyn Rhys Prize (1958), the Somerset Maugham Award (1960), the Hawthornden Prize (1964), the W. H. Smith Literary Award (1968), the Booker Prize (1971), the Jerusalem Prize (1983) and the David Cohen Prize for a lifetime's achievement in British Literature (1993). In 2001, he won the Nobel Prize for Literature. In 2008, *The Times* ranked Naipaul seventh on their list of "The 50 greatest British writers since 1945".

Early Life

Naipaul was born in Chaguanas, Trinidad and Tobago, to parents of Indian descent. He is the son, elder brother, uncle, and cousin of published authors Seepersad Naipaul, Shiva Naipaul, Neil Bissoondath, and Vahni

Capildeo, respectively. His current wife is Nadira Naipaul, a former Pakistani journalist.

Naipaul was married to Englishwoman Patricia Hale for 41 years, until her death due to cancer in 1996. According to an authorised biography by Patrick French, the two shared a close relationship when it came to Naipaul's work—Pat was a sort of unofficial editor for Naipaul—but the marriage was not a happy one in other respects. Naipaul regularly visited prostitutes in London, and later had a long-term abusive affair with another married woman, Margaret Gooding, which his wife was aware of.

Prior to Hale's death, Naipaul proposed to Nadira Naipaul, a divorced Pakistani journalist, born Nadira Khannum Alvi. They were married two months after Hale's death, at which point Naipaul also abruptly ended his affair with Gooding. Nadira Naipaul had worked as a journalist for the Pakistani newspaper, *The Nation*, for ten years before meeting Naipaul. She was divorced twice before her marriage to Naipaul and has two children from a previous marriage, Maliha Naipaul and Nadir.

She is the sister of Maj. Gen. (Retd.) Amir Faisal Alvi, a former chief of the Special Service Group, Pakistan Army, who was later assassinated during the War in North-West Pakistan.

Family Background

Vidia Naipaul's grandfather came from India as an indentured labourer. He spoke very little English and made little attempt to learn the language that his children spoke. This grave, Hindi-speaking grandfather, like Naipaul's gold-teeth *nanee* [maternal grandmother] and mustached babu , recreated the eastern Indian state of Uttar Pradesh in his homeland in Chaguanas, Central Trinidad. For them, the basic difference between Trinidad and India was simply a change in geographical location; their entire culture was transported whole with them. They had abandoned that "area of darkness" but they also denied Trinidad, so much so that they refused to participate in anything that did not belong to their world. If Edward Brathwaite identifies and explores the remaining fragments of African culture in The African Presence in the West Indies , Naipaul seeks to do the same in "A Resting Place for the Imagination," in An Area of Darkness.

Naipaul identifies what remains of India in Trinidad with the old generation's attitudes and ways of thinking and seeing, pieces of furniture, musical instruments, household articles, religious ingredients, food preparations, taboos and housing designs. Naipaul was born in the Lion House (a stark symbol of the Indian world), Chaguanas, on August 17, 1932 where he lived until he was about eight years old. The great house, reproduced almost exactly in A House for Mr. Biswas, as Hanuman House, was built by his grandfather, Pundit Capildeo Maharaj, in 1920.

> When (my grandfather) built his house, he ignored every colonial style he might have found in Trinidad and put up a heavy, flat-roofed oddity, whose image I was to see again and again in the small, ramshackle towns of Uttar Pradesh. (An Area of Darkness 33)

It is said that Mr. Capildeo brought a builder from India to construct the house. The description of the house, however, is not as important as the images it conjures. As already mentioned, it is an Indian artifact in Trinidad. Naipaul's novel describes the house as an alien white fortress, having no windows, with walls of uneven thickness. With cobwebs and darkness, the house becomes a prison in which Seepersad, Naipaul's father, and Mr. Biswas are trapped. (This is one piece of evidence to suggest that there is a biological link between Mr. Biswas and Seepersad Naipaul). The House can also represent the Commonwealth Empire into which Mr. Biswas was colonised and subordinated, very much like the old Dowager's house in Lamming's Water with Berries. It is also a symbol of the Great House during the slave-master's reign.

Seepersad Naipaul, author of The Adventures of Gurudeva (and Other Stories), possessing no land, came from Longdenville to marry into the rich Capildeo family in 1929. He married one of the seven Capildeo girls, Draupati, commonly called Bhola—prototype of Shama in Mr. Biswas's story. The Capildeos were among the Seereerams, Seepersads, and the Seths, who were renowned landowners in Central Trinidad. Seepersad was confronted by some traumatic issues upon marriage into this family. Having no house of his own, Seepersad lived at his wife's parents' home where he was constantly reminded that he had come from an impoverished family. There was the inevitable conflict between the rich and the poor, subordination and insubordination , strong and weak, individual and establishment. It was the long and bitter struggle of a man who refused to submit to a system, who refused to lose his identity in a clan, and who refused to be colonised in order to establish his own independence. It was in the midst of such turbulence that the young Naipaul grew up.

Seepersad, as a young married man, voluntarily joined the Arya Samaj , a reformist Hindu movement. This conversion was contradictory to the established doctrines of the Capildeos, and rumour has it that he was threatened to be beaten if he did not make a public apology in the newspapers. According to Naipaul, that had made Seepersad unhappy and he was almost on the verge of a breakdown.

Seepersad Naipaul, now deceased, is described by acquaintances today as "broad-minded," although he was bitter against his in-laws who attempted to subjugate him at every turn. Seepersad was not concerned about becoming rich. He enjoyed reading, and as a young man he could tell stories whenever he was in a group. He was serious about making a career in writing. Living in the Lion House, however, with his wife and his first child, Naipaul, was like living in the lion's mouth. He felt that the rights belonging to the family unit were being encroached upon. A poor man, Seepersad was determined to sever any dependence upon the powerful Capildeo clan by setting up his own house. This movement away from the phantom Capildeo presence affected Naipaul's childhood:

> I suppose this is the essential feature of my childhood: In my memory it is extremely disordered, and I think this is because between my birth and the age of seven, we lived in about seven or eight different houses ... This is interesting, because most of them in fact, were in a very small area ... they are probably within about a mile or so of one another. *(The Listener 306)*

Although Naipaul uses the term "we lived," he in fact spent most of his time at the Lion House while his family was in Chaguanas. Again, Seepersad is slighted for not having a close relationship with his son whom he wanted to raise in his own manner. This situation is very much like Mr. Biswas's at Arwacas.

Seepersad was separated intermittently from his wife and children. It was considered convenient for Vidia to stay at the "Monkey House" while he attended the Canadian Mission School, which he did for a little under two years. When the family moved to Port of Spain , Vidia continued to stay with his uncle Capildeo at 17 Luis Street in Woodbrook.

In Port of Spain, Seepersad was able to secure a job with the Trinidad Guardian . Seepersad's parents had wanted him to become a pundit and he was actually, as a boy, apprenticed to a Pundit Sahadeo. Residing in the capital of the island, Seepersad made relative material improvements, but his wealth could not overshadow the Capildeo's presence. After years of struggle and humiliation, Seepersad acquired a red Prefect car and a house at 26 Nepaul Street in St. James. The house still stands today as "a huge and squat sentry-box; tall, square two-storeyed, with a pyramidal roof of iron" (A House for Mr. Biswas 572). After laying his claim to his portion of the earth and finally separating himself from the Capildeo establishment, Seepersad died in 1953 of a heart attack while Naipaul was still pursuing his Bachelor of Arts degree at Oxford University in England.

Childhood

Growing up in a devout, orthodox family where the Hindu way of life was stressed, Naipaul became acutely conscious of the kind of food he ate. William Walsh writes in his book, V.S. Naipaul: "The family were Brahmins, the modes and forms of life at home profoundly Indian, and Naipaul has retained to this day characteristic Brahmin delicacies and repugnancies" (1). At the age of thirty-two on a journey by airplane to Paris, Naipaul announced to the steward: "I am sorry ... But I don't eat meat ... but you must have an egg or some fish or something" (The Overcrowded Barracoon 34). This sensitivity to food is characteristic of Naipaul. It caused disturbance at home many times when his mother had cooked food that Naipaul avoided. Even when he was among the star section of the exhibition class at Queen's Royal College he perpetually refused to drink milk (unlike Anand Biswas who made daily trips to the dairies). The food that he relished had to be carefully cooked, otherwise he would complain of an upset stomach. Like Ganesh Ramsumair, Naipaul recoiled from food offered by strangers:

> [Mr. Stewart] had taken a lot of trouble to prepare tea. There were sandwiches of three sorts, biscuits, and cakes. And although Ganesh was beginning to like Mr. Stewart

> and wanted to eat his food, all his Hindu instincts rose high and he was nauseated to bite into a cold egg-and-cress sandwich. *(The Mystic Masseur)*

It is this nausea over food and flesh based on Brahmin taboos that characterises Ralph Kripalsingh as a nihilist , absurd anti-hero in The Mimic Men (1967). As a child, Naipaul began developing a strong sensitivity to anything that came into contact with his body. He was obsessed with the fear of being contaminated: "It horrified me at school to see boys sharing Popsicles and Palates, local iced lollies; as it horrifies me to see women sipping from ladles with which they stir their pots" (An Area of Darkness 33).

As part of his study of the West Indian islands in The Middle Passage, V.S. Naipaul analysed the typical Trinidadian response to cinema. It was one activity in which he was an active participant. He tells us briefly of one of his trips: "It was my French master who urged me to go to see Brief Encounter, and there were two of us in the cinema, he in the balcony, and I in the pit".

Vidia discloses his brief experience, as a patron, in the cinema. But there is more to it than he wishes to divulge. As a boy, among boys, he frequented the Rivolto cinema (after converted to Galleria Shopping Gallery). He would buy his ticket and stand outside, waiting for the music of the soundtrack to begin, waiting for the lights to turn off. Then he would dash into the pit to see his film. He could not bear the humiliation of being seen in the pit because that section of the cinema carried a stigma. The pit, house and balcony of the cinema represented, in a rigid way, the triangular three-class structure of the society. To be seen in the pit was to be automatically categorised into the lowest social stratum of society. But the tunnel to pit was the only available avenue to cinematic entertainment for the poor. This can be understood simply by observing the cinema fans' behaviour in A House for Mr. Biswas. Naipaul describes the patrons entering the pit, among them, Anand and Biswas who are pushed and jostled as if in a crowded Sunday morning market:

> Mr. Biswas and Anand arrived to find the mouth of the tunnel blocked by a turbulent, unaccommodating mob. They lost control of their hands and feet. Anand, wedged between tall men, shut off from light and air, could only

> allow himself to be carried along ... The pressure of Anand increased; he feared he would be crushed against the angle of wall and tunnel. *(456)*

It was mainly through films in the cinema that Naipaul got insights into the outside world. Films were complements to his books. He mentions various films, actors and actresses in the Trinidad section of The Middle Passage. On the screen he saw, among other things, American and British men and women in their native country. A substantial amount of American films were running on the Rivolto screen at that time, but Naipaul felt the Trinidadian could respond only to the Hollywood formula. For them nothing outside America was worth considering. So until the time British films acquired an American gloss, they played to empty houses. Although Naipaul frequented the cinema as a boy, he was critical of the American cowboys. He told his childhood friend, Roy, whom I had interviewed: "Those cowboys are dirty creatures, man. They round up cattle all day and they don't even bathe. On the whole, Americans are a cruel people. Nasty and cruel."

Even here, Naipaul, like many of Swift's characters, reveals his hypersensitivity to dirt and an obsession for cleanliness. But Naipaul paid reverence to the British.

Once asked: "Why do you prefer the British to the Americans?" The young Naipaul replied: "If you question an American soldier in civilian clothes about his profession, he would say, 'I am a colonel.' The Britisher would say, 'I am in the army.'"

Here Naipaul hints at his concern for nationalist feeling in a land of various races, religion, sets and cliques. But what is more revealing in his reply is his attitude towards the British as ideal. Trapped as a Trinidad orthodox Hindu in an educational system where the British way of life was stressed, Naipaul was torn between two worlds.

"Who is the greatest cricketer in the world?" The question was asked by a Negro teacher in a General Knowledge test when Naipaul was a fourth-standard pupil at the Tranquillity Boys' School. The question was at once a springboard for a long discourse on cricket in the West Indies. As a boy, Naipaul was fascinated by the game and he turned out to be a good left-armed spin bowler . But being a participant in the game, he was careful not to have his clothes smeared with the ball—an early characteristic of his nihilistic tendencies (like a young Kripalsingh). On weekends and on school holidays, he would play with a group of neighbours on the road on Luis Street. It is this street with all its characters (the live Topee becomes the fictional Hat) and incidents that are reproduced in Miguel Street. Also, Naipaul was so attracted to cricket that his mother remembers him becoming quite enraged whenever his school team was defeated in matches. He told a friend that a cricketer's performance—such panache—was short-lived and he did not want to become a sportsman. Soon, he became a literary critic , cricket commentator, and a joint scorer with Jesse Noel during the cricket season for the QRC First Eleven in 1950.

Even Naipaul's mother saw that the social environment in Trinidad was not suited for her son's growth and development. She was becoming particularly concerned not only with the quality of his associates but also the places to which they went. When Naipaul came home late two or three nights with the sent of liquor on his breath she became worried. At his own request, his friends took him to a club on Independence Square where they sat at a bar and drank. The I-narrator of Miguel Street describes the bar with more accuracy.

> A small crowded room lit by green bulbs. The green lights seemed as thick as jelly. There were many women all about the room, just waiting and looking. A big sign said: Obscene Language Forbidden. *(216)*

Naipaul knew what was required of him but, instead, he interviewed the young prostitutes who were predominantly Indian girls. It was what he had come to the club to do. Just after this encounter, he felt disgusted. It is the same disgust which permeates Kripalsingh's experience when he frequents prostitutes: "But there was skin, there was the smell of skin. There were bumps and scratches, there were a dozen little things that could positively enrage me" (65). Naipaul mentions nothing about prostitution in his non-fiction, and, when he refers to "night clubs" in The Middle Passage, it is only an allusion to what modernity means in Trinidad.

Accidents and Encounters

One Saturday night Naipaul and a friend found themselves strolling along the sidewalk in San Juan . The town was bustling with activity. There were the usual wayside vendors peddling oranges, cigarettes and confectioneries, coconuts, oysters, nuts pudding, and boiled and roasted corn. People were moving in all directions and the taxi drivers were doing good business. Naipaul bought a few oysters from a flambeau-lit stall. He and his friend were walking away from the stall when they were confronted by a young man of African descent. "Indian, give me a cigarette, dey," the man said. Though he knew that his friend had just bought a packet of cigarettes, Naipaul declared instantly that they had none. The man remained fixed; he was doubtful about the genuineness of Naipaul's reply. There was probably something in Naipaul's voice which betrayed his pretension . The instant reply might have suggested that the speaker had no intention of sharing his possession. Naipaul was about to step forward but the man's stern, accusing stare held him fixed. His friend, sensing that this confrontation might end in a physical exchange of some sort, steered his hand into his trouser pocket and delivered his cigarette to the man. Naipaul and his friend continued their walk safely. But Naipaul was angry. "You shouldn't give him, man," he told his friend. "You encouraging these people to beg. Let him go and work."

Mohan Biswas, working as a journalist for the Sentinel, confronts a similar situation. His job involves travelling on a bicycle to collect harrowing details of "Deserving Destitutes." It is the real boyhood experience of Naipaul, infused into the character of Biswas, which is described here:

> He was sometimes accosted by burly Negroes, pictures of health and strength; "Indian, give me some money." Occasionally, exact sums were demanded: "Indian, give me a shilling." He had been used to such threatening requests from healthy Negroes outside the larger cinemas, but there the bright lights and the watchful police had given him the confidence to refuse. (A House for Mr. Biswas 463)

Both Biswas and Naipaul refuse to share what they believe comes from work and sweat. But their refusal grows out of quite different reasons. Vidia's refusal to share can be accounted for in many ways: the alert policeman on a Saturday night beat, wandering Trinidadians searching for excitement, the unusual small stature of the Negro, or the ally of his friend. Naipaul in San Juan assumes the proportion of a hero while Biswas, the "hero," is diminished into the submissive Indian.

The similarities between Vidia Naipaul and Ganesh Ramsumair are too numerous to pass unnoticed: they both considered themselves to be orthodox Hindus, they did not play games at school, they were branded as real creamers, they had momentary experiences as teachers, they attended Queen's Royal College, they were later to become authors, they allowed the idea of travel to enter (their) minds, they emerged victorious at examinations, and their advent to the city started a feeling of self-consciousness. But the biographical link between Ganesh's childhood and Naipaul's is even more pointed. It was during the *janayew* or thread initiation ceremony that Naipaul's head was shaved. His was among the three shaved heads to enter the QRC compound that morning; his two cousins, Premchand and Capildeo, were also initiated into becoming Brahmins. Their schoolmates tormented them. They even took turns caressing the young boys' shaved heads to further humiliate them. The Capildeo boy was quite upset; he began to cry. Premchand was big-bodied; he challenged a fight. Naipaul was near to sobbing. It was a dramatic confrontation between the insulated Hindu world and the open Creole society which must be encountered; and yet it wasn't—anyone who had just cut his hair got "tapped" at school. The confrontation is repeated in The MysticMasseur with Ganesh as a student of QRC.

> His head was still practically bald when he went back to school, and the boys laughed so much that the principal called him and said, "Ramsumair, you are creating a disturbance in the school. Wear something on your head." So Ganesh wore his khaki topee in the classroom until his hair grew again.

But Naipaul paints a mild confrontation of the scene involving Ganesh. To rewrite the incident as it actually happened would have been to relive that humiliation, to experience again that open assault in the city. Naipaul was again to be affected after the *katha* [family prayer ceremony] was held under a *pipal*/banyan tree in the Botanical Gardens, over which his mother presided. The older generation stood in its self-contained world where it not only refused to see, but also ceased to hear and feel. But it was the young generation that had to interact with the Creole society which had realised time and time again that this was Trinidad and not India. Naipaul recollects that katha in the Botanical Gardens and the janayew when he writes that "for those of us at school at the time, the public ceremony had been a strain. We were becoming self-conscious, self-assessing: our secret world was shrinking fast" (An Area of Darkness).

As a boy, Naipaul liked swimming in the sea at Carenage and Blue Basin. The boys in Nepaul Street sometimes organised a walking race in which Naipaul participated with the finishing line ending at Carenage Beach. He was among a group of cyclists who made frequent excursions to bathing places. It was on one such excursion that he came into confrontation with the police. It was dusk when two policemen stopped him on his bicycle demanding to see either a license plate or receipt. Naipaul had neither. The licence for the bicycle had been paid but the evidence was at home. Naipaul was detained as one of his friends cycled home for the receipt. It was brought and Naipaul was released. Of all of Naipaul's characters, the one who comes into contact with the Trinidad police is the I-narrator of Miguel Street. His offence was riding in the dark without a light to report an attempted suicide.

> Before I had cycled to Ariapita Avenue I had met not one but two policemen. One of them was a sergeant. He said, "You thinking of going far, eh?" I said, "Is you I was coming to find."

The other policeman laughed.

> The sergeant said to him, "He smart, eh? I feel the magistrate go like that excuse. Is a new one and even me like it."
>
> I said. "Come quick, Edward wife try to kill sheself again."
>
> The constable said, "He really smart, you know."
>
> The sergeant said, "Yes. We leave him here and go find somebody who try to kill sheself. Cut out this nonsense, boy. Where your bicycle license?" *(193)*

Alone, Naipaul escapes from the clutches of the law by the urgency of his mission. It is worth noting here that Naipaul is referred to as a "smart" boy (although the word suggests "cunning" in this context). It is the same remark (though different in suggestion from the first) that a mason is to make to Mrs. Naipaul on hearing the young Naipaul talk. Naipaul himself claims, in an interview with Nigel Bingham, that his "school career was precocious" and that he "became very bright" (306).

Father-Son Relationship

Naipaul considers his relationship with his father, Seepersad Naipaul, to be a crucial aspect of his childhood. And whenever he is talking or writing about his personal life in Trinidad, it is almost certain that he would make mention of him. In fact, he states that what he has become is because of that close relationship with his father. He says, "My father was a defeated man: I think that contempt was all that he could teach. I was contaminated by this" (The Listener 306). Naipaul also feels that his sense of isolation goes back to, among other things, that father-son relationship. Anand, a character in A House for Mr. Biswas, is based largely on Naipaul's own childhood experiences. In this brilliant work, Naipaul attempts to recreate that intimacy with his father. Naipaul writes of Anand:

> Anand was among the strong. His satirical sense kept him aloof. At first this was only a pose, an imitation of his father. But satire led to contempt, and at Shorthills contempt, quick, deep, inclusive, became part of his nature. It led to inadequacies, to self-awareness and a lasting loneliness. But it made him unassailable.
>
> *(A House for Mr. Biswas 412-413)*

Some of the attributes referred to may be true of Naipaul the youth, but not of Naipaul the novelist. As a novelist, Naipaul is distinguished among other West Indian writers by his keen sense of satire. Anand's contempt is an intensification of Naipaul's sense of satire and is not injected directly by his father. In writing, Naipaul did not attempt the contempt taught to him by his father, or if he did, it does not reveal itself poignantly in his earlier works. Contempt, and a sense of universal futility, is quite pronounced in his work since The Mimic Men.

In 1943, when Naipaul was eleven years old, his father published a small collection of short stories. The printing was done, slowly, by the Guardian Commercial Printery; my father brought the proofs home bit by bit in his jacket pocket; and I shared his hysteria when the linetypists, falling into everyday ways, set—permanently, as it turned out—two of the stories in narrow, newspaper-style columns (The Adventures of Gurudeva 7).

Naipaul's father dedicated his collection of short stories to his son, Vidia. Naipaul also feels that a lot of the spirit of his own earlier work is meant to be dedicated to his deceased father. One must understand the mutual concern between father and son. The common ground between these two individuals is their preoccupation with the written word. Seepersad Naipaul's story ends with the publication of The Adventures of Gurudeva and Other Stories. Vidia Naipaul, in 1961, would resurrect Seepersad Naipaul's aborted story and enliven it to the point of his father's death in Sikkim Street, St. James. Naipaul really begins where Seepersad ends in more ways than one. (Works written before A House for Mr. Biswas can be seen merely as introductory pieces towards the making of this 1961 classic). Seepersad introduced his son to the written word by teaching him to read, and also by urging him to write.

Thirty-three years later, the resurrection of The Adventures of Gurudeva was made possible by Naipaul through his contacts with Andre Deutsch, an established London publisher. Even after his death, Seepersad's dream came true: his work was finally published by a London firm. But what these stories tell, in themselves, is not as important as what they meant for Naipaul:

> I remember the passion that preceded the writing ...I remember taking down, at my father's direction, a page or two of a version of this sketch.
>
> *(The Adventures of Gurudeva)*

Through his father, Naipaul got firsthand insight into the expression of life on paper; words as facilitators of expression and self-exile, which define a writer's life. In short, Naipaul was given an introduction into the craft of novel writing by his father.

Dialogue between Biswas and Anand, Seepersad and Naipaul, arises out of the particular concern each has for the welfare of the other. Seepersad, a defeated man, found refuge in satire and contempt. Mr. Biswas finds solace in the grotesques of Dickens where traumas were ridiculed and diminished. But these were only forms of retreat which one day would collapse. Writing became a form of exorcism , a divulgence of distaste, for Seepersad and later for Naipaul when he became a novelist. Biswas shared his discovery of the power of the written word with Anand by making Anand write out and learn the meanings of difficult words. At that moment of training, Biswas declares to his son that he doesn't want Anand to be like him, thus insinuating that he does not want his son to become the poverty-stricken man he has become.

However, he is also hinting, implicitly, that they must have the same profession of creating with the written word. Biswas is teaching his son to write just as Seepersad prepared Naipaul for his entrance into elementary school . Both characters, and persons, feel a sense of responsibility for each other. In A House for Mr. Biswas, Naipaul writes of Biswas and Anand:

> Father and son, each saw the other as weak and vulnerable, and each felt a responsibility for each other, a responsibility which in times of particular pain, was disguised by exaggerated authority on the one side, exaggerated respect on the other. (374)

Escape Motif

Vidia Naipaul has an early memory of himself when he was two years old: "My first memory is of waking up in a hospital room and finding myself strapped to a bed" (The Listener). He had contracted pneumonia and refused to be confined in the ward. He kept crying and made many attempts to escape. The hospital authorities had to strap him down. This might well be an epigraph for the escape motif in Naipaul's childhood and, by extension, his adulthood. What he would have said then about the hospital room is what he says about Trinidad in September 1960, when he examines this fear, this nightmare of Trinidad in The Middle Passage: "I find this place frightening. I think this is a very sinister place".

Later Life

Strange Luck

'No-one comes close to V.S. Naipaul. He has reached such a pitch of authority that even if you disagree with what he is saying, you have to acknowledge his intellect and astonishing mastery of style' — Philip Hensher in the Guardian's recent survey of the greatest living writers in English.

This is the first time that Sir Vidia Naipaul has agreed to a comprehensive documentary being made about his life and work. He has not been the subject of a film of any kind for almost twenty years — long before he was knighted (1992) and awarded the Nobel Prize in Literature

(2001) – so this is a unique opportunity to get close to our greatest living novelist.

> "I could never become vain, because I know there's been a large element of luck– but probably everyone has these bits of luck in his life, don't you think? Everyone who does something, who achieves something, has had his own stations of luck. It's not all a Calvary."

The Strange Luck of V.S. Naipaul interweaves the strands of his life in the three most significant places in his experience as a writer: Trinidad, India and Wiltshire.

Dairy Cottage Wiltshire

Scribes have visited Naipaul at home in rural Wiltshire, charting the seasons in his beloved garden, talking to him about his life, work and inspirations – and his precious cat, Augustus. He has lived in Wiltshire for thirty years and acquired all the attributes of an English gentleman of letters. They ask: what is the source of his enormous industry and creativity, and why has he become one of the most forthright and controversial of English writers? "The press have created a myth about me... they see me as Reactionary, Right Wing and Racial'". They hear how Naipaul counters these accusations, and what he thinks about himself.

Sir Vidia told them that he would like the film to be 'as personal as possible'. He agreed to be filmed both in public and in private, and to be interviewed on any subject. The film has been shot over nearly a year, recording the details of his life, and allowing him to talk freely about his development as a writer. His second wife Nadira, his agent Gillon Aitken, his first editor Diana Athill (whose recent book, 'Somewhere Towards The End' has been widely acclaimed), also appear in this intimate portrait, but the central character is Naipaul himself, who remains, at the age of seventy-five, as vital a presence and as incisive a mind as ever.

Visit to Trinidad

In May 2007, Naipaul made his first visit for over a decade to Trinidad, the island where he was born and grew up, but which he has since dismissed as a "plantation society". One scribe accompanied him, his wife Nadira, and his long-term agent Gillon Aitken to film his trip. They saw the neighbourhood that inspired his first book, Miguel Street, the family home that he transformed into his masterpiece, A House for Mr. Biswas, and other significant places in and around Port-of-Spain, as well as a pugnacious encounter with local press, some of whom have never forgiven him for failing to mention Trinidad when he was awarded the Nobel Prize. They also saw his encounters with Trinidadian dignitaries (including the President), old boys from Queen's Royal College (the school from which he won an island scholarship to Oxford University in 1948) and local journalists (he did not suffer the fools gladly).

Visit to New Delhi

In October 2007, the same scribe went with Naipaul and his wife to India (the country his grandparents came from, with which he has a passionate and often turbulent relationship). He said that he might not visit India again, and wanted to see certain things of significance to him, which he felt we might like to film. He was with him in New Delhi when he visited Humayan's Tomb (the second Emperor in the Mughal dynasty – about which he has controversial opinions and whom he regards as "Muslim invaders"), the collection of Hindu bronzes in the National Museum of India (which he thinks are some of the finest in all Art), a vast Hindu drama in a sports stadium (which reminds him of pageants he saw as a child in Trinidad), a curious animal sanctuary ("I've become a fanatic about animals – I love them all") and the offices of India's radical current affairs magazine, Tehelka (which he helped save from extinction by the right-wing government). He also filmed him and his wife at private parties in Delhi, and travelling on the spanking new Metro (an example of India's recent transformation and booming economy).

Life at a Glance

1932: Naipaul is born in Chaguanas, Trinidad, August 17.

1948: "Liza of Lambeth." Queen's Royal College Chronicle (Port of Spain) 23 (1948): 42-43.

1950: Leaves Trinidad to study English at University College, Oxford.

1953: Naipaul's father, Seepersad Naipaul, dies. Awarded Oxford degree in English.

1955: Marries Patricia Ann Hale, 10 January. BBC Caribbean Service, part-time

1956: "Honesty Needed in West Indian Writing." Trinidad Guardian (1956): 29.

1957: The Mystic Masseur. London: Andre Deutsch, 1957.

1958: Awarded the John Llewellyn Rhys Memorial Prize for The Mystic Masseur

— "Where the Rum Comes From." New Statesman (1958): 20-21.

— "Seven Ages of Humour: Young Men Forget." Punch 234 (1958): 734-36.

— "A Letter to Maria." New Statesman 56 (1958): 14.

— The Suffrage of Elvira. London: Andre Deutsch, 1958.

1959: Miguel Street. London: Andre Deutsch, 1959.

1960: Returns to Trinidad (September) on a scholarship granted by the government of Trinidad & Tobago; researches (travel from end of December 1960 through April 1961)

1961: Receives the Somerset Maugham Award for Miguel Street

— "The Little More." The Times (1961): 13.

— "Living Like a Millionaire." Vogue 138 (1961): 93-93, 144, 147.

— A House for Mr. Biswas. London: Andre Deutsch, 1961.

1962: "Trollope in the West Indies." The Listener 67. (March 15 1962): 461.

— "Tea With an Author." Bim 9 (1962): 79-81.

— "The Immigrants: Lo! The Poor West Indian." Punch 242 (1962): 124-26.

— Begins in February a yearlong tour (via Greece and Egypt) of India during which he gathers material for An Area of Darkness. While travelling in Kashmir during the spring-summer he writes Mr. Stone and the Knights Companion.

— The Middle Passage. London: Andre Deutsch, 1962.

1963: "India's Cast-Off Revolution." Sunday Times (1963): 17.

— "Sporting Life Beyond a Boundary." Encounter 21 (1963): 73-75.

— "Black Man's Burden." The New York Review of Books 1.5 (1963).

— Mr. Stone and the Knights Companion. London: Andre Deutsch, 1963.

1964: Receives the Hawthornden Prize for Mr. Stone and the Knights Companion.

— An Area of Darkness. London: Andre Deutsch, 1964.

— "Critics and Criticism." Bim 10.38 (1964): 74-77.

— "Speaking of Writing." The Times (1964): 11.

— "Trinidad." Mademoiselle 59 (1964): 187-88.

— "Words on Their Own." Times Literary Supplement (1964): 472.

1965: "They Are Staring at Me." Saturday Evening Post (1965): 82-84.

— "A West Indian Culture?" Illustrated Weekly of India 86 (1965): 23.

— Buys London house in the Stockwell district in early 1965 Travels in East Africa from December 1965 through September 1966.

1966: "The Last of the Aryans." Encounter 26 (1966): 61-66.

— Acts as Judge of the Duff Cooper Prize. University of Kampala, Uganda.

1967: The Mimic Men. London: Andre Deutsch, 1967.

— "What's Wrong With Being a Snob?" Saturday Evening Post (1967): 12, 18.

— A Flag on the Island. London: Andre Deutsch, 1967.

1968: Receives the W.H. Smith Prize for The Mimic Men. Sells Stockwell house in September. Travels in the Carribean, Central America, and the US until September 1969

— "Biafra's Rights." The Times (1968): 11.

— "I Don't Consider Myself a West Indian." Guyana Graphic (1968).

1969: The Loss of El Dorado. London: Andre Deutsch, 1969.

— "Anguilla: The Shipwrecked 6000." The New York Review of Books 12.8 (1969).

— "St. Kitts: Papa and the Power Set." The New York Review of Books 12.9 (1969): 23-27.

— "Et in America Ego." The Listener 82 (1969): 302-04.

— "Books of the Year: A Personal Choice." Observer (1969): 17.

1970: Moves to a cottage in Wiltshire.

— "New Year Predictions." The Listener 83 (1970): 17.

— "Power to the Caribbean People." The New York Review of Books 15.4 (1970).

1971: Early in year, travels to India and Mauritius for about ten weeks. Awarded Booker Prize. From November 1971-April 1972 visits Trinidad.

— "One Out of Many." Atlantic Monthly 227.4 (1971): 71-82.

— "The Election in Ajmer." Sunday Times Magazine (1971): 8, 17.

— "The Circus at Luxor: Epilogue to a Novel." The New York Review of Books 17.7 (1971): 8-12.

— "Escape From the Puritan Ethic." Daily Telegraph Magazine (1971): 38.

— In a Free State. London: Andre Deutsch, 1971.

1972: "Without a Dog's Chance." The New York Review of Books 18.9 (1972): 29-31.

— "Mauritius: the Overcrowded Barracoon." Sunday Times Magazine (1972): 4-38.

— "The King Over the Water: Juan Peron." Sunday Times (1972): 29-30.

— "The Corpse at the Iron Gate." The New York Review of Books 19.2 (1972).

— "Comprehending Borges." The New York Review of Books 19.6 (1972).

— "It Is Not Easy to Be Famous in a Small Town." Daily Telegraph (1972): 37.

— The Overcrowded Barracoon. London: Andre Deutsch, 1972.

1972/74: During this period, works with many themes and ideas in addition to several journalism projects. Travels to Argentina, New Zealand, and elsewhere. Publishes various articles in NYRB and Sunday Times Magazine dealing with his travels and observations; mostly journalistic pieces.

1974: "A Country Dying on Its Feet." The New York Review of Books 21.5 (1974).

— "The Killings in Trinidad: Part One." Sunday Times Magazine (1974): 16-35.

— "The Killings in Trinidad: Part Two." Sunday Times Magazine (1974): 24-41.

— "Argentina: The Brothels Behind the Graveyard." The New York Review of Books 21.14 (1974).

— "Conrad's Darkness." The New York Review of Books 21.16 (1974).

— "The Reality and the Romance." Sunday Times Magazine (1974): 56-66.

— "The Secret Agent." The New York Review of Books 21. 19 (1974).

1975: Guerrillas. London: Andre Deutsch, 1975.

— Early in the year, travels to the Congo. Writes the foreword to Seepersad Naipaul's stories. Travels to India during August-November.

— "A New King for the Congo." The New York Review of Books 22.11 (1975): 19-25.

1976: "India: A Wounded Civilization." The New York Review of Books 23.7 (1976).

— "The Wounds of India." The New York Review of Books 23.8 (1976).

— "Bombay: The Skyscrapers and the Chawls." The New York Review of Books 23.10 (1976).

— "India: New Claim on the Land." The New York Review of Books 23.11 (1976): 11-18.

— "India: A Defect of Vision." The New York Review of Books 23.13 (1976): 14-19.

— "India: Synthesis and Mimicry." The New York Review of Books 23.14 (1976): 14-19.

— "India: Paradise Lost." The New York Review of Books 23.17 (1976): 10, 12, 14-19.

1977: "India: Renaissance or Continuity." The New York Review of Books 23.21-22 (1977).

— India: A Wounded Civilization. London: Andre Deutsch, 1977.

1978-79: Distinguished Writer in Residence at Wesleyan College, Conneticut.

1979: A Bend in the River. London: Andre Deutsch, 1979.

— "Indian Art and Its Illusions." The New York Review of Books 26.4 (1979).

— "The Flight From the Fire." The New York Review of Books 26.7 (1979).

— "Argentine Terror: A Memoir." The New York Review of Books 26.15 (1979).

— Travels from August 1979 to February 1980 in Iran and other Muslim countries.

1980: The Return of Eva Peron, With The Killings in Trinidad. London: Andre Deutsch, 1980.

— Receives Bennett Award (Hudson Review).

1981: Among the Believers: An Islamic Journey. London: Andre Deutsch, 1981.

— "Tehran Winter." The New York Review of Books 28.15 (1981).

1982: "A Note on a Borrowing by Conrad." The New York Review of Books 29.20 (1982): 37-38.

1983: "Writing A House for Mr. Biswas." The New York Review of Books 30.18 (1983): 22-23.

— Receives Jerusalem Prize.

1984: Finding the Centre: Two Narratives. London: Andre Deutsch, 1984.

— "Heavy Manners in Grenada." Sunday Times Colour Magazine (1984): 23-31.

— "An Island Betrayed." Harper's Magazine 268 (1984): 61-72.

— "Among the Republicans." The New York Review of Books 31.16 (1984): 5-17.

— Attends the Republican Convention in Dallas; report appears in New York Review of Books.

1986: "Reflections of a Reluctant Gardener." House and Garden 158 (1986): 118-19.

— "The Enigma of Arrival." New Yorker (1986): 26-62.

— Awarded Ingersoll Prize.

1987: "My Brother's Tragic Sense." Spectator 258 (1987): 22-23.

— "The Ceremony of Farewell." The New York Review of Books 34.2 (1987).

— "On Being a Writer." The New York Review of Books 34.7 (1987).

— "Some Thoughts on Being a Writer." Chronicles: A Magazine of American Culture 11.5 (1987): 13-15.

— Tours the Southern United States to study its culture.

— The Enigma of Arrival. London: Andre Deutsch, 1987.

1988: "Rednecks." The New York Review of Books 35.20 (1988).

1989: "A Turn in Atlanta." The New York Review of Books 35.21-22 (1989).

— A Turn in the South. London: Andre Deutsch, 1989.

1990: Awarded Trinity Cross, Trinidad & Tobago's highest honour.

— "The Shadow of the Guru." The New York Review of Books 37.20 (1990).

— India: A Million Mutinies Now. London: Heinemann, 1990.

1991: "Our Universal Civilization." The New York Review of Books 38.3 (1991): 22-25.

— "A Handful of Dust: Return to Guiana." The New York Review of Books 38.7 (1991): 15-20.

1992: "Argentina: Living With Cruelty." The New York Review of Books 39.3 (1992).

— "The End of Peronism? " The New York Review of Books 39.4 (1992).

1993: Receives first David Cohen Prize for life-time achievement. Archive acquired by the U. of Tulsa.

1994: "A Way in the World." The New York Review of Books 41.9 (1994).

— A Way in the World. London: Heinemann, 1994.

1995: "Acceptance Speech of the First David Cohen British Literature Prize." Wasafiri 21 (1995): 7-8.

— "Letters to a Young Writer." New Yorker 71.18 (1995): 144-53.

1996: Patricia Naipaul (married in 1955) dies on 3 February. Marries Nadira Alvi, 18 April.

1998: Beyond Belief: Islamic Excursions Among the Converted Peoples. London: Little Brown, 1998.

— "Indonesia: The Man of the Moment." The New York Review of Books 45.10 (1998).

1999: Letters Between a Father and Son. London: Little, Brown and Co., 1999.

— "Reading & Writing." The New York Review of Books 46.3 (1999).

— "The Writer and India." The New York Review of Books 46.4 (1999).

— "Memento Mori." New Statesman 128.4467 (1999): 126.

2000: Reading & Writing: A Personal Account. New York: New York Review of Books, 2000.

2001: Half a Life. London: Picador, 2001.

— "Bohemia." The New Yorker (2001): 66-71. a story Receives Nobel Prize in Literature on October 11, 2001

2002: The Writer and the World. New York: Alfred A. Knopf, 2002.

2003: Literary Occasions: Essays. New York: Alfred A. Knopf, 2003.

2004: "Suckers." The New Yorker (2004): 76-85. [a story]

— Magic Seeds. London: Picador, 2004.

2 Literary Career

Among the Readers and Learners

Naipaul found a kind of solace in reading ("I went to books for a special sort of participation"). He found that he could not be satisfactorily successful as an athlete, so he was determined to excel intellectually. His father, a journalist with the Trinidad Guardian, had taught him to read even before he attended school. "The memory of my father teaching me is really a curious memory of us just being together, alone" (The Listener).

Beginning to Read Widely

Unlike the residents and boarders in A House for Mr. Biswas, Naipaul never had to be forced to do schoolwork at home. Read and learn became a mantra in Naipaul's childhood; he never had to be urged by the whip. On the contrary, Naipaul's mother would complain about his long hours of studying throughout the night and into the emerging morning. The light of the naked electric bulb disturbed her sleep.

His neighbour, an old woman now, has an image of Naipaul fixed in her mind. It is the only image of him she possesses. In a personal interview with this neighbour (whose name has been withheld on request), she says: "All the time Vidoo only reading book. He hardly playing, he hardly going out." She opened her hands and studies her palms. "Vidoo only reading book" (January 21, 1980).

The fact that Naipaul was a serious "book-beater" is verified by many of his schoolmates. His mother remembers very little of his childhood outside the ritual of studying at home and school. In a personal interview with her on January 20, 1980, she describes his childhood as "a school's life." Kamla, Anand's sister in A House for Mr. Biswas, claims astounding scholastic achievements for her brother: "My brother read more books than all of you put together".

> Anand lived a life of pure work. Private lessons were given in the morning for half an hour before school; private lessons were given for an hour after school; private lessons were given for the whole of Saturday morning. Then in addition to all these private lessons from his class teacher, Anand began to take private lessons from the headmaster, at the headmaster's house, from five to six. He went from school to the Diaries to school again; then he went to the headmaster's, where Savi waited for him with sandwiches and lukewarm Ovaltine. Leaving home at seven in the morning, he returned at half past six. He ate. Then he did his school homework; then he prepared for all his private lessons. (A House for Mr. Biswas 463)

Naipaul attempts to evoke humour in this passage through repetition. Time and place of activity are given special attention. Savi's function as a provider of fuel to the busy student invites us to associate Anand with a contestant in a race. This is the West Indian race to grab education as a means of social mobility. Though the passage is treated with exaggeration, it more or less gives us a pattern of Naipaul's activities as a child.

At an early age, Naipaul was discovering with wonder the things that could be contained within a book. He became an avid reader, collecting a store of books in his household. But his marvel and reverence for books went beyond what the printed words expressed. Like Ganesh Ramsumair, he would relish the smell and feel of it even before reading it.

> Left alone, Ganesh began taking surreptious sniffs at the paper, and, closing his eyes, passes his hands over many papers, the better to savour their texture.
>
> *(The Mystic Masseur)*

The gesture performed both by Ganesh and Naipaul suggests that bond between their preoccupations and the appreciation of bookmaking. Both the man and the character have a strong desire to write on paper. Early drafts of Miguel Street were written in exercise books, and Ganesh's passion for writing finds expression in personally manufactured notebooks.

Even as early as Queen's Royal College, Naipaul was manifesting his potential both as writer and critic. He wrote a critical approach to Somerset Maughan's first novel Liza of Lamberth which was published in the school's magazine. "It is not difficult to see why Naipaul should have been drawn to the novel. Liza's fate turns on the clash between her desire for beauty and romance and the sordid circumstances of her slum-life—a theme of his early work" (White). Still at school, Naipaul wrote an early draft of "My Aunt Gold Teeth" which aroused anger from his aunt upon whom the story was based.

Then he wrote another composition on an actual incident which took place in Green Street. A fat man was pushing his car just outside his house. The car rolled faster and faster until the man lost control and there was no one inside to steer. The fat man ran behind the car, waving and shouting. It is the mechanical genius, Uncle Bhaku, in Miguel Street, who repeats this incident, though it is altered slightly. The boys of the street, eagerly awaiting the new-bought car, begin to wave and cheer when they see it approaching. Bhaku, the driver also waves his left hand:

> The car came nearer and Hat said, "Jump, boys! Run for your life. Like he gat mad."
>
> It was a rare thing. The car just raced past the house and we stopped cheering.
>
> Hat said, "The car out of control. It go have a accident, if something don't happen quick."
>
> He [Bhaku] wasn't waving with his left hand. He was trying to warn people off.
>
> By miracle, it stopped just before Ariapita Avenue.

Bhaku complains that the brakes are malfunctioning. In both incidents, comedy is derived from the situation. But it is the story of "Bogart" and not "The Mechanical Genius" that Naipaul claims to have been his first. "Bogart" was written "without pausing" one afternoon in 1955 at the Langman Hotel in England. After two or three false starts he had "discovered the trick of writing" and went on to include other stories in the Miguel Street collection (The Times). "The Mechanical Genius" was sketched at his Woodbrook home in Trinidad while Naipaul was still at QRC.

Vidia's mother was zealous about her son's performance at school. She was one of many parents who realised that education was the only avenue for social mobility. In a personal interview with her on January 20, 1980, she had said, "Education was strictly for the poor." She was keen about the friends with whom he associated, and the atmosphere in which he studied. She complained to her neighbour one night that the noise emanating from a cricket club meeting was affecting her son's concentration. Parents' attitude towards education is one factor that contributes towards a child's academic performance at school. Vidia grew to become an outstanding pupil which won him much recognition at school:

> Mr. Hinds never beat me. He never made me clean the blackboard. He never made me shine his shoes with the duster. He even called me by my first name, Vidiadhar.
>
> *(A Flag on the Island)*

At Tranquillity Boy's School, Naipaul was brilliant enough to be selected as a candidate for the prestigious exhibition examination. In 1942 under the legendary teacher, Mr. O. E. Romilly, Naipaul emerged as a third-place winner out of the twenty-one exhibitions offered in the island. He was thus able to acquire a free place at Queen's Royal College from January 1943 to April 1949.

It was at Queen's Royal College that this young educated Hindu came into confrontation with other ethnic communities. It was not a dramatic confrontation between opposed worlds: he came into contact with Africans and Whites, but interaction operated only at an academic level. At the end of the school day, each boy retreated to his private world at home—a world in which he felt secure. Naipaul's detachment from those separate worlds is expressed in his treatment of the young Negro, Browne, as a stereotyped, cartoon figure. Browne, the performer on stage "wore a straw hat and a proper suit with a bow tie" (The Mimic Men 92). But confrontation was inevitable even in the classroom. Jeers emanated uncontrollably from his African classmates when the name Vidiadhar Surajprasad Naipaul was announced. Whenever possible, he did like Choonilal in his "Christmas Story" and suppressed the first two names behind the blank initials V.S. Ramjit Kirpalsingh, Ganesh Ramsumair and others also altered their names to an English version because "the Negro makes less effort than the average English person to pronounce Indian names correctly" (An Area of Darkness 35). The alteration of names indicates that sense of loss which all West Indian writers explore. At school in the science class, a beaker with a tube was passed from boy to boy, so that each might suck and make observations.

> I let the beaker pass me. I thought I hadn't been seen, but an Indian boy in the row behind, a Port of Spain boy, a recognised class tough, whispered, "Real Brahmin." His tone was approving. (An Area of Darkness)

The incident saddens Vidia because of the sense of loss of caste differences made explicit in the boy's open declaration. Furthermore, the incident reveals Naipaul's fears of contamination with anything alien, even miscegenation , resulting in recoiling into himself as Santosh did in "One Out of Many" (In a Free State).

Naipaul spent five years as a student at QRC at the end of which the Island Scholarship examination had to be taken. Through an oversight, Naipaul omitted fulfilling a requirement on the registration form for the examination. He gained astounding marks in French and Spanish, as the results revealed, but he was not awarded a scholarship. Controversy raged until a decision was finally reached. The principal at QRC sat with members of the Education Board and a special scholarship was created for Naipaul. On April 22, 1949 the Trinidad Guardian carried a photograph of Naipaul alongside an article about his award:

> The Trinidad Government on the recommendation of the Education Board has decided to grant a special scholarship to Vidia S. Naipaul, 16, of QRC who got two distinctions in French, and Spanish in the Modern Studies

Group in last year's Cambridge Higher School Certificate Examination, but whose marks were not approved by Cambridge.

Naipaul returned to Queen's Royal College in January 1950 to teach English as a substitute for an indisposed master. Students of his class were startled by his wealth of knowledge and his command over the English Language . He remained a student teacher at QRC for six months and then flew to take up his place at the University College, Oxford.

Short Fiction

Naipaul has produced three volumes of short stories. In 1959 he published *Miguel Street,* a collection of character sketches he had finished writing several years earlier while working as a writer for "Caribbean Voices." All the *Miguel Street* stories take place in Port of Spain, Trinidad, and are told from the perspective of a West Indian child who, like Naipaul, finally leaves the island to study abroad. Each short story (or chapter of what some commentators take to be a novella) tells the comic tale of an assortment of Trinidadian oddballs and misfits who desperately struggle to make their lives meaningful, but whose efforts are ultimately crushed by their own narrow connection to their environment and because of the chaos and squalor that surround them. The humorous dimensions of the stories, which reveal Naipaul's early sympathy with those struggling to fit into a world made miserable by ignorance and cultural depravity, are intensified with dramatic use of Caribbean dialect that masterfully brings the characters to life.

A Flag on the Island (1967), Naipaul's second volume of short stories, was collected from pieces written between 1950 and 1962; some had been published previously in English and American periodicals. Like the *Miguel Street* tales, most of the stories of *A Flag on the Island* take place in Trinidad and typically deal with a clash of values as local Trinidadians of Indian descent try in vain to structure their lives around a culture that is now far away and only dimly remembered. Other stories deal with the latent terror underlying seemingly ordinary lives of immigrants in London. While this collection again uses comic effect to intensify themes of alienation, failure, and racial discrimination, the general tone of the collection is much more bitter and pessimistic than that in *Miguel Street.*

In 1971 Naipaul attracted worldwide attention as well as heavy censure for his book *In a Free State*, which combined two autobiographical travel narratives based on experiences in Africa and the Caribbean with two short stories and a novella. The work treats the lives of immigrants as they try to assimilate to new environments, exploring the problems that arise because of their own limitations as well as larger societal trends of racial discrimination and cruelty. One short story, "One out of Many" tells of a domestic servant from Bombay who moves with his master to the United States but whose hopes of freedom and opportunity in the new land are dashed as he finds himself even more alone and imprisoned than he had been in India.

The second short story, "Tell Me Who to Kill," is about a Trinidadian man who lives in London and whose goal in life is to see that his younger brother does not have to endure the indignities that he himself has suffered. This objective is thwarted when the younger brother squanders the money the elder brother has saved for his education, leaves school, and marries a white woman. The title novella in the volume, "In a Free State," tells of a white couple touring Africa who discover that behind the veneer of civilization is a culture ripped apart by despotic brutality and tribal savagery. Naipaul won the Booker Prize for this unusual treatise about cultural detachment and alienation, but many commentators denounced the work because of its portrayal of Third World cultures as essentially hopeless.

Themes and Form

In "Reading and Writing," Naipaul recalls "one day, deep in my almost fixed depression, I began to see what my material might be: the city street from whose mixed life we had held aloof, and the country life before that, with the ways and manners of a remembered India. It seemed easy and obvious when it had been found; but it had taken me four years to see it. Almost at the same time came the language, the tone, the voice for that material. It was as if voice and matter and form were part of one another."

Naipaul's first books are set in Trinidad. A House for Mr. Biswas, his first major novel, is an imaginative account of the Indian experience in Trinidad—his father's life and his own youth. A few years after its publication he went to India, finding only disappointment in the recognition that colonialism and the new world had stripped him of the capability of contentment there. This realisation is the subject of An Area of Darkness.

His work went in a new direction in the early 1960s, beginning with Mr. Stone and the Knights Companion—the setting is England and the tone is more serious and philosophical. Naipaul's feelings of alienation, his disdain for both England and Trinidad, and his sense of responsibility as a post-colonial writer weighed heavily on him, culminating in The Mimic Men.

A few years later, after the publication of The Loss of El Dorado, which examined the early history of Trinidad in light of the surrounding world affairs, Naipaul attempted to return to Trinidad. But he soon retreated to England, unable to find happiness there. During this period, his work broadened. "Fiction, which had once liberated me and enlightened me, now seemed to be pushing me towards being simpler than I really was." In a Free State, which was awarded the Booker Prize, transcended the boundaries of genre. It consists of short stories, a novella, and two excerpts from a travel diary. The only common thread is the concern with issues of freedom for the individual and the decolonised world. Naipaul's position as a social and political critic grew with the publication of his next few books, all of which treated the issues surrounding colonisation.

Beginning with Finding the Centre, Naipaul's writing moved away from critical analysis of the problems of freedom. Instead, he embraced the people and places he visited, withholding judgement and a seeing beauty where he once saw futility. The synthesis of autobiography and fiction continued, and even became subject matter in The Enigma of Arrival. In "Reading and Writing," Naipaul explains, "So, as my world widened, beyond the immediate personal circumstances that bred fiction, and as my comprehension widened, the literary forms I practised flowed together and supported one another; and I couldn't say that one form was higher than another." Travel and autobiographical books followed. In India: A Million Mutinies, Naipaul's views of his family's homeland are reconsidered and adjusted. And in A Way in the World, Naipaul further demonstrated the improvement in his view of humanity. He continues to write, and will continue to be a prominent writer, be it "post-colonial" or not. Themes of alienation, mistrust, rootlessness, mockery, and self-deception will certainly continue to pervade throughout his work.

Naipaul's experiments with form are perhaps his greatest achievements. Of this, he wrote: "Literature, like all living art, is always on the move. It is part of its life that its dominant form should constantly change."

Fiction versus Documentary

Theme: In examining the structure of the novels, Naipaul's early works and Half a Life, it becomes apparent that there are three distinct leitmotifs, which are interwoven with a number of smaller side themes such as houses, gardens, professions, even attempts at writing. This interdependent grid of themes illustrates the realm and personality of the characters. V.S. Naipaul is focused on the people living within a post-colonial environment. The remaining effects colonialism has on culture and society trickle down to the individual. The human being lives with a feeling of displacement, insecurity, and disorientation due to a social environment, which is half-developed and half-eradicated. These are the leitmotifs that carry through the characters of Miguel Street, A House for Mr. Biswas, The Mystic Masseur, and Half a Life. Titus Hoyt's desperate search for recognition; Man-man's religious sacrifice that wasn't meant to be taken serious after all; Mr. Biswas' non-existent self-confidence; Pundit Ganesh's contradictory existence without meaning; Willie's constant and aimless flight from his birthplace – these characters drift through life following imaginary metaphysical clues, other people's paths, or mere coincident, but at the core are displacement, insecurity, and disorientation.

His documentary works are based on encounters and experiences – some planned, some coincidental – and in the "Postscript: Our Universal Civilization," from The Writer and the World, he claims that "[he] has no unifying theory of things. To [him] situations and people are always specific, always themselves. That is why one travels and writes: to find out". However, the environments he exposes himself to have one similarity: he examines the post-colonial life of individuals. He talks to people of all social classes and professions, and visits urban, as well as rural areas. In this venture, he finds idiosyncratic themes of people living in a sphere torn between native and foreign cultural significance, indigenous and imported religious values, and the interests of individuals with and without power. The only leitmotif is Naipaul's interest in cause and effect In the essay "Argentina and the Ghost of Eva Peron," the roles are for once reversed and it is the foreign population (since the native has been nearly eradicated) that is "...hanging on by their fingertips". "And the poor, who are Argentines, the sons and grandsons of those recent immigrants, will now have to stay. Now a larger faith is needed, some knowledge of a sheltering divinity. Without faith these abandoned Spaniards and Italians will go mad"

Naipaul, genuinely interested in the state of the post-colonial experience, finds the Ivory Coast split in two separate worlds. Night and day, French and African; the realities of these Ying and Yang halves are fully understandable to someone with an open mind and a neutral position. "She [Arlette] spoke of the two worlds, the world of the day and the world of the night, the two ideas of reality that made Africans so apparently indifferent to their material circumstances. She had seen it in the Ivory Coast, she said. Men of wealth and position could return easily to their villages at the weekend, could easily resume the hut life, could welcome that life. That was the way it was in the upper world. The inner world, the other world, continued whole. And that was what mattered.

Tone

The tone with which V.S. Naipaul describes his fictional subjects is a realistic and harsh sincerity, without losing the level of neutrality, which allows him to remain out of the picture. The descriptions are simple and to the point, leaving the reader with a caricature-like image of individuals. Within the works, there is a slight distinction between his early works and Half a Life. He maintains his critical tone, however, the subjects of denigration have changed and he uses the voice of characters to describe certain individuals. Most of the time, it is the characters that give themselves a "bad" image through their opinions or ideas. Ramlogan's scheming and pathetic character is displayed when he tries to convince Ganesh to help him keep the dowry low in The Mystic Masseur: Is the shame, sahib, that eating me up everybody go see what I give you, and they go say, 'look, a boy with a college education, this is all the man giving.' Is that what eating me up, sahib. I know that for you, educated and reading books night and day, it wouldn't mean much, but for me, sahib, what about my cha'acter and sensa values?

In Miguel Street, though maybe comedic, or satiric, the condescension couldn't be clearer. Through the narrator, Naipaul's voice comes through "I suppose Laura holds a world record. Laura had eight children. There is nothing surprising in that. These eight children had seven fathers. Beat that! It was Laura that gave me my first lesson in Biology." At the social gathering for the maudlin editor in Roger's house, the international partygoers, after an intimate prelude from the host, turn out to be caricatures similar to those living on Miguel Street, merely with a distinction of financial means or social class. The bedroom Marxist mingles with Serafina, who is in search for a rich, white male. Marcus, in hope to regress his African heritage with his insatiable sex drive, ignores the lonesome, sobbing editor.

In his documentary writings, V.S. Naipaul carries the same, critical tone. His images are to the point and with the descriptiveness of a news reporter. Although, he has his own voice and lets us into his realm of personal impressions, his personality does not distract or protrude too much, for it is truth he writes.

"The leader [Malik], the unique spokesman of Negroes dangerous with a just hatred of the white man; but the crowds at this trial were good-humoured, even gay. No one jeered; he was a martyr to no cause, Naipaul states in "Michael X and the Black Power Killings in Trinidad," from The Writer and the World, To the Trinidad crowds Malik had become a 'character,' a Carnival figure, a dummy Judas to be beaten through the streets on Good Friday. Which was all that he had been in London, even in the great days of his newspaper fame as the X: the militant who was only an entertainer, the leader who had no followers, the Black Power man who was neither powerful nor black. He wasn't even black; he was 'a fair skin man,' half-white. That, in the Trinidad phrase, was the sweetest part of the joke.

Naipaul has the ability to remain neutral. He sees the overall picture and exposes all, who need to be exposed. He writes: that section of he middle class that knows only that it is secure, has no views, only reflexes and scattered irritations, and sometimes indulges in play: the people who keep up with the 'revolution' as with the theatre, the revolutionaries who visit centres of revolution, but with return air tickets, the people for whom Malik's kind of Black Power was an exotic but safe brothel. His critique goes out to the people who deserve criticism. These two excerpts display his strongest attacks. In Beyond Belief, he describes the Ivory Coast's neighbouring countries' conditions: "All around was chaos and nullity,' but before one can become offended, he explains the forces that lead to these circumstances in a rational and well-researched manner. In a similar approach, but with this new input of his personality, he introduces the reader to academically controversial Niangoran-Bouah. We share the skepticism, for "...if he was a world expert on Drummology it was because he had started the subject and had in fact invented the word. [...] Some people doubted whether Drummology or African philosophy existed". But judgement is not passed until we finally meet the man and learn more about him and his ambition, which is "to offer proof of African civilization".

In analysing the works of fiction and documentary of V.S. Naipaul, the true brilliance of the writer comes to the forefront. It is apparent that there is a vast difference between the substance and incorporation of themes, when examining the novels and the various essays. Miguel Street, A House for Mr. Biswas, The Mystic Masseur, and Half a Life are strenuously built and organised. The leitmotifs — displacement, insecurity, and disorientation – are incorporated through the drifting existence of the protagonists. The sub-themes are features woven into the plot and account to the realism. In the travel essays, Naipaul tells us about life as well, but with the curiosity of a neutral writer. His purpose is to inform and to explain. The themes, as he travels the globe and interviews individuals from all backgrounds, are merely relayed to us.

The tone Naipaul's voice carries, whether through a narrator or himself, is virtually the same. He never loses his neutrality and objectivity, though he adds moral criticism when applicable. Murder is murder; bigotry is bigotry; and absurdity, no matter rich or poor, is just that. The writer does show that he has changed his world-view, gradually expanding the scope with time and experience. Where he is very critical towards the native population of Trinidad in his early works, he shows a deeper understanding of circumstances and cause and effect, as he begins to grasp the forces that be. He shifts his focus on the impeding powers, explains the thought process and social, as well as financial and religious pressures, and then, in his true neutral stance, lets us make up our own mind. Excellent evaluation with insightful illustrations.

Love for Controversy

With the overdue settling of one frayed-around-the-edges feud, it was surely time for Sir Vidia Naipaul to upset someone else. "If a writer doesn't generate hostility, he is dead," the eminent novelist declared a few years ago. "Writers should provoke disagreement." Indeed. So why not go for broke and insult half the planet?

Sir Vidia's claim last week that women writers were doomed to inferiority by their "sentimental" attitudes and "narrow view of the world" certainly did the trick. But only to the extent that at 78 – a cranky old man grown out of an even crankier young one – it was almost expected of him. He boasted that the works of the greatest female novelists were "unequal" to his own efforts, and dismissed his celebrated former publisher – the saintly nonagenarian Diana Athill – as a writer of "feminine tosh".

Loud, outraged and wholly predictable was the squawking that resulted. Newspapers were ablaze with words like "delusional", "narcissistic" and "arrogant". And that was just The Guardian. Yet Naipaul's putting down of potential rivals and extravagant praising of himself was fully in keeping with a literary tradition that goes back to the time of Shakespeare and Marlowe. The self-regard of an author is to be expected. It's everything else about Sir Vidia that frightens his admirers.

Among whom we can now re-include the travel writer Paul Theroux, a one-time protege of the Nobel Prize-winner, who ended their 15-year falling-out with a handshake at last week's Telegraph Hay Festival. Naipaul had, apparently, suspected Theroux of trying to seduce his first wife, and Theroux had retaliated by writing a savage memoir – Sir Vidia's Shadow – detailing the supposed deficiencies of the older man's character.

As Theroux saw it, Naipaul was "a grouch, a skinflint, tantrum-prone, with race on the brain. He was then, and continued to be, an excellent candidate for anger-management classes, sensitivity training, psychotherapy, marriage guidance, grief counselling and driving lessons – none of which he pursued."

Bad as all this sounded, there was plenty worse that Theroux – thanks to his publisher's lawyers – wasn't able to put in his book. "I wanted to write about his cruelty to his wife," he recalled later, "his crazed domination of his mistress that lasted almost 25 years, his screaming fits, his depressions, his absurd contention that he was the greatest writer in the English language."

But even this pasting came to look like flattery when Patrick French's authorised biography of Naipaul was published three years ago. Drawn from lengthy interviews and unrestricted access to the novelist's papers, it gave a hair-raising account of Naipaul's sexually unfulfilled, 41-year marriage to Pat Hale, a shy, lower-middle class history undergraduate he met at Oxford University. For much of their troubled time together, Naipaul found his thrills among prostitutes and, even more readily, through the intense, sadomasochistic relationship he maintained with his Argentinian mistress, Margaret Gooding. "Margaret was Vidia's ideal woman," writes French.

> "A woman of a kind that had previously existed only in his fantasy life. He could string her along and mistreat her with her abject consent. She said she had done things to Vido that would have made her sick with anyone else, and yet she longed for the time when she could do them again."

Back in the reality of their childless marriage, Naipaul would tell Pat: "You are the only woman I know who has no skill. You behave like the wife of a clerk who has risen above her station." By the time Pat died of cancer in 1996, having apparently forgone chemotherapy in order not to be an inconvenience, the novelist already had a new love in the wings, Pakistani journalist Nadira Khanum Alvi, the current Lady Naipaul.

Thus does a man get stuck with a reputation. And, in Vidia's case, not for being the greatest novelist in the English language. While today's cultural orthodoxy is to maintain a polite distinction between artistic achievement and private behaviour – the Roman Polanski syndrome – Naipaul has pushed the limits further than most.

In doing so, he has presented the overwhelmingly liberal-minded literary establishment with a particularly painful dilemma. Born into relative poverty in Trinidad, the son of expatriate Indian parents, Vidia should be one of those Third World supernovas – proof that greatness can arise from anywhere, and a rebuke to the lingering snootiness of those who associate the best writing with white chaps in wing-collars.

Instead, many of Naipaul's pronouncements smack of an Evelyn Waugh-style reactionary bufferishness that specialises in puncturing liberal pieties. He has been accused of racism ("Africans need to be kicked, that's the only thing they understand"), and being a Tory stooge (the New Labour years he portrays as a plot to impose a "plebeian culture" on Britain), while fellow-novelist Robert Harris has described him as "toxic" and "a fascist".

The truth, as it tends to be, is more complicated. Virtually every serious critic sees in Vidia's writings – which include A Bend in the River and A House for Mr. Biswas – a kind of rootlessness, born of a desperation to escape. His father, a psychologically fragile journalist with the Trinidad Guardian, transferred to his son the idea of a greater, better world beyond the island. Naipaul would later dismiss his homeland as "unimportant, uncreative, cynical, a dot on the map".

The need to move on took him to Oxford in the early 1950s, but England's hallowed seat of learning failed to meet his expectations. "There were a lot of working-class people who'd been given special grants," he complained. "They were not all fine. Some were, most were not."

From all this grew the writer who, knighted in 1990, went on to win the Nobel Prize for Literature. The Academy's citation compared him to Joseph Conrad, "as the annalist of Empires in the moral sense; what they do to human beings".

Happily, the recognition – like the criticism – has done nothing to mellow him, or to shake his conviction that he's top of the pile, and that no woman is going to push him off it.

Acknowledgement

In awarding Naipaul the Nobel Prize for Literature in 2001, the Swedish Academy praised his work "for having united perceptive narrative and incorruptible scrutiny in works that compel us to see the presence of suppressed histories." The Committee added, "Naipaul is a modern *philosophe* carrying on the tradition that started originally with *Lettres persanes* and *Candide*. In a vigilant style, which has been deservedly admired, he transforms rage into precision and allows events to speak with their own inherent irony." The Committee also noted Naipaul's affinity with the novelist Joseph Conrad:

Naipaul is Conrad's heir as the annalist of the destinies of Empires in the moral sense: what they do to human beings. His authority as a narrator is grounded in the memory of what others have forgotten, the history of the vanquished.

His fiction and especially his travel writing have been criticised for their allegedly unsympathetic portrayal of the Third World. Literary critic Edward Said, for example, argues that Naipaul "allowed himself quite consciously to be turned into a witness for the Western prosecution", promoting what Said classifies as "colonial mythologies about wogs and darkies". Said believes that Naipaul's worldview may be most salient in the author's book-length essay *The Middle Passage*, which Naipaul composed after returning to the Caribbean after ten years of exile in England, and the work *An Area of Darkness.*

Writing in the *New York Review of Books* about Naipaul, Joan Didion offers the following portrayal of the writer: The actual world has for Naipaul a radiance that diminishes all ideas of it. The pink haze of the bauxite dust on the first page of *Guerrillas* tells us what we need to know about the history and social organisation of the unnamed island on which the action takes place, tells us in one image who runs the island and for whose profit the island is run and at what cost to the life of the island this profit has historically been obtained, but all of this implicit information pales in the presence of the physical fact, the dust itself... The world Naipaul sees is of course no void at all: it is a world dense with physical and social phenomena, brutally alive with the complications and contradictions of actual human endeavour... This world of Naipaul's is in fact charged with what can only be described as a romantic view of reality, an almost unbearable tension between the idea and the physical fact...

Naipaul has mentioned some negative aspects of Islam in his works, such as nihilism among fundamentalists. He has been quoted describing the bringing down of the Babri Mosque as a "creative passion," and the invasion of Babur in the 16th century as a "mortal wound." He views Vijayanagar, which fell in 1565, as the 'last bastion of native Hindu civilization'. He bitingly condemned Pakistan in *Among the Believers.*

He was elected a Foreign Honorary Member of the American Academy of Arts and Sciences in 1990. In 1993 Naipaul was awarded the British David Cohen Prize for Literature.

In 1998 a controversial memoir by Naipaul's sometime protege Paul Theroux was published. The book provides a personal, though occasionally caustic portrait of Naipaul. The memoir, entitled *Sir Vidia's*

Shadow, was precipitated by a falling-out between the two men a few years earlier. Theroux supposedly blamed Naipaul's second wife, Nadira Naipaul, for driving the two apart.

In early 2007, V. S. Naipaul made a long-awaited return to his homeland of Trinidad. He urged citizens to shrug off the notions of "Indian" and "African" and to concentrate on being "Trinidadian". In 2008, writer Patrick French released the first authorised biography of Naipaul, which was serialised in *The Daily Telegraph.*

Critical Reception

Naipaul's three collections of short stories are seen by critics as some of the finest expressions of the dilemmas and struggles of colonised people striving to make both their individual and social lives meaningful in a post-colonial context. *Miguel Street* drew almost universal praise for its comic irony and colourful dialect used to illustrate the author's own need to flee his home and family to establish himself in a culture of perceived high traditions and customs. While some of the short stories in *A Flag on the Island* received critical attention, the book was generally dismissed as a collection of minor works by an author who had much better to offer. *In a Free State* was quickly recognised as an important new collection of short stories, and Naipaul's fellow travel writer and friend, Paul Theroux, called the work a "masterpiece in the fiction of rootlessness." While nearly all critics have praised the charming prose style and delicate humour of the stories, many commentators, most often from the developing world, have charged that even in the early works Naipaul paints pictures of Third World people as culturally inferior. The criticism that Naipaul is only able to find fault with the individuals and societies he describes persists as he continues to record, without apology, his impressions of the alienation and inhumanity he considers to be the enduring legacies of colonialism.

Criticism

Naipaul, a novelist, short story writer, essayist, and author of travel books, born in Trinidad and lived in England since 1950 is the winner of several important awards for his fiction, he writes with precision, confidence, and a fine wry humour.

A travel book by an author of little personality is likely to be plain dull; a travel book by an author with a pronounced personality (like Mr. Naipaul) is likely to tell us more about the author than about the country. Heads, the country loses; tails, the author wins.

Mr. Naipaul's earlier book on the West Indies hinted pretty strongly at its author's prickly, susceptible nature, the rawness of his nerves, his thinness of skin. In *The Middle Passage* it was the noise, especially in Trinidad, which most obviously tormented him. In *An Area of Darkness* it is the public defecation.... There are moments in both books when the reader fears that the author (who has a gift for drawing the reader too into his orbit) is about to be badly beaten up. Mr. Naipaul loses his temper with an Indian, and then loses his temper with himself for losing his temper. And, such is the author's absorptive power, somehow the reader feels partly to blame for it. His quick exasperation is tied up with his artist's openness and vulnerability, and unhappily in *An Area of Darkness* (a generalising title!) he is mostly open to spectacles of human degradation or double-think or colossal inefficiency. The sight of a beggar, a human ruin, or 'the starved child defecating at the roadside while the mangy dog waited to eat the excrement', this arouses pity. But what use is pity?—it soon yields to contempt. Contempt must be fought down—but how, except by learning to feel nothing? And out of feeling nothing, nothing can come.

Mr Naipaul agrees with Malcolm Muggeridge (and a number of other Englishmen) that almost the last true Englishmen are Indians. The epigram flatters neither race. Certainly in his sense of personal outrage when, say, someone is trying to cheat him, Mr. Naipaul is very much the Englishman, especially the Englishman during his first few days in the mysterious East....

The determination to remain what he was, to preserve his face, is plain and strong throughout *An Area of Darkness*, and sometimes, I suspect, it prevents him from seeing other people for what they were. 'All things uncomely and broken, all things worn out and old....' Mr. Naipaul is something of an aesthete, an aristocrat, he has the sensibility of a Brahmin, but not the supporting beliefs—or complacency—or callousness. His puritanical honesty, his refusal to be taken in by talk of Indian spirituality, afflicts him like an ingrowing nail. He is hardly ever out of pain. The reader suffers with him. Perhaps that is all we can do in the face of such colossal suffering—suffer a little ourselves, for a very little it will be, relatively.

> *D. J. Enright, "The Sensibility of V. S. Naipaul" (1964), in his* Man Is An Onion: Reviews and Essays *(1972 by D. J. Enright; reprinted by permission of Open Court Publishing Co. and Chatto & Windus), Chatto & Windus.*

V.S. Naipaul is by now recognised as the most talented of those West Indian novelists who have appeared on the literary scene since the publication, in 1949, of V. S. Reid's *New Day*. Yet Naipaul's true literary stature, and the magnitude of his achievement, are generally obscured by the ultra-traditional guise of his writing, with its Victorian ease and lack of stylistic innovation, and by his reputation as a purveyor of whimsy and patronising satire....

He does not seek to produce documentary propaganda, but nevertheless sees the act of literary creation as being deeply involved with the desire to produce observations of a quasi sociological nature. C. L. R. James, the West Indian historian, has drawn attention to such a phenomenon in a different context by talking of a particular feature of West Indian life—the non-political writer devoted to the analysis and expression of West Indian society. Naipaul seems to be cast in this mold....

Naipaul's finest achievement is undoubtedly *A House for Mr. Biswas* (1961). It is the story of one man's effort to overcome the wasteland, the derelict land of Trinidad's East Indian community.... The writer's attitude is tender but ironic; there is the inner, sardonic toughness of phrases like "futile with asthma." The impact is attenuated and diluted, yet the tragic undertone to the comic cameo is apparent.

> *David Ormerod, "In a Derelict Land: The Novels of V. S. Naipaul," in* Contemporary Literature *(1968 by the Regents of the University of Wisconsin), Vol. 9, No. 1, Winter, 1968.*

The position of the ironist in colonial society is indeed a delicate one. [George] Lamming [in *The Pleasures of Exile*] can see little that is risible in a society whose history is one of underprivileged. One appreciates his point. The early Naipaul is at times the irresponsible ironist, subtle, but lacking in a sensitive participation in the life he anatomises. If one says that the exercise of irony precludes sympathy, one is merely defining the limitations of irony, and the limitations of any of Naipaul's work which depends solely on irony. So far one agrees with Lamming.

Satire is the sensitive measure of a society's departure from a norm inherent in itself. Since Naipaul starts with the conviction that such a norm is absent from his society, his task as satirist becomes doubly difficult. Not only must he recreate experience, but also simultaneously create the standards against which this experience is to be judged. This explains the mixture of farce and social consciousness which occurs in [*The Mystic Masseur* and *The Suffrage of Elvira*].

If in the early farces an absurd world is presented as real, in *The Middle Passage* a real world is presented as tragically futile and absurd. The deeper implication of the first two books is that West Indian society, emerging from ignorance and superstition, is peculiarly susceptible to depredation by the fraud and the politician, and by all opportunists who are prepared to exploit the social unease for their personal ends. That Ganesh and Harbans are treated so genially conceals Naipaul's seriousness of purpose. Ganesh, who poses as the defender of Hinduism while it is politic and profitable to do so, completely rejects Indian dress and changes his name to G. Ramsay Muir once he becomes a successful politician. This change of name and dress is always used by Naipaul to symbolise the acculturation of the East Indian to pseudo-western patterns of life, which is something he writes of with bitterness, despair and regret. One should not be misled by his genial tone to overestimate his admiration for Ganesh, the successful fraud.

If the impulse behind *Miguel Street* is similar to that behind *The Mystic Masseur*, the whole tone is more serious. The farce has become a nightmare. Here one finds it difficult to accept Lamming's description of Naipaul's satire as a refuge and escape from experience. If satire is a means of running away, it is equally a means of fighting: an act of bravery, not cowardice; the confrontation of a nightmare, not the seeking of a refuge.

Sometimes one wonders at Naipaul's hypersensitivity and asks oneself whether the neurosis is completely controlled by the irony. Is not this complete acquiescence with Froude that there are "No people there in the true sense of the world," a formula for evading the complex sympathy which the West Indian experience seems to demand? I stated above that what appears to Lamming as a conscious struggle on Naipaul's part to adopt the standards of a "superior" metropolitan culture, is explicable as a too easy acquiescence with European historians; they assumed that the "native" was an inferior animal and consequently failed to look for positives in his society. Perhaps it is easier to see Trinidad as an historical rubbish-heap and a sociological abstraction; easier to see evidence in every observed and carefully chosen detail of some deep-seated social malaise which justifies one's neurosis; easier than to see the country as a vast Miguel Street of individuals, people in a truer sense of the word than Froude seems to have been aware of, each making demands on one's imaginative sympathy, because of the unique history which each has endured.

[Although] one accepts Naipaul's point that protest literature can become a sterile and stereotyped posturing in the name of blackness, one also realises that protest against the past is a vital transitional stage in the reconstruction of a sense of personality. Naipaul does not realise that in treating the theme of East Indian acculturation, and the reconstruction of the Indian personality in the New World, he is at one with Negro writers who are also trying to reconstruct personality, and is writing a most vital portion of the sensitive history of the West Indies. Naipaul's Mr. Biswas rebels because his society denies him personality and forces him to live with an inferiority complex and a sense of nonentity. Negro writers, in the Caribbean or America, protest because their society annihilated identity. Both in the case of Mr. Biswas and the Negro of the New World, underprivileged is struggling to build its symbolic house against overwhelming odds.

A House for Mr. Biswas is more profound than anything else Naipaul has written because, for the first time, he is able to feel his own history not merely as a squalid farce, but as an adventure in sensibility.

The Middle Passage relates to the problem of West Indian creative writing, as well as to the writing of West Indian history as an academic pursuit. West Indian history can never be satisfactorily told, he says, because nothing was created in the West Indies, where there is neither achievement, nor a tradition of accepted values. Yet in *Miguel Street* and *A House for Mr. Biswas* he tells a vital part of West Indian history, for the books are a sensitive presentation of the history of underprivileged. The worth of his irony is that it enables him to examine his past without any sentimental self-indulgence. We see Biswas as a full human being who is as weak and contemptible as he is forceful and admirable. Irony enables Naipaul to get down to the bare humanity beneath his history. Because he is dealing with his own personal past, his irony does not preclude sympathy but reinforces it. He is able to answer in terms of creative sensibility a question to which he could find no satisfactory academic answer.

> *Gordon Rohlehr, "The Ironic Approach: The Novels of V. S. Naipaul," in* The Islands in Between: Essays in West Indian Literature, *edited by Louis James (1968 by Oxford University Press; reprinted by permission of Oxford University Press, Inc.), Oxford University Press, 1968.*

I have always believed that a writer writes one book all his life: whether consciously so or not, his work is of a piece. For this reason the writer is entitled to present as the provisional entity between two covers, which is what any single book is, any combination of writing that *he* sees as that entity. V. S. Naipaul's grouping together of a short novel, two stories and two fragments of a travel diary [*In a Free State*] is not a collection of "occasional" pieces but an entity; and I approach it as contiguous with a personal vision that blazed forth in his magnificent novel "A House For Mr. Biswas" a few years ago.

The free state of the title that Naipaul's people seek is, needless to say, an inner kingdom. But they seek it in their various ways, through the poor, crude, ridiculous instruments which are all that daily life has to offer in the various societies they find themselves in....

To borrow a description from another of V. S. Naipaul's novels (The Mimic Men), the black people he writes of are doomed to be "mimic men." They try to find meaning for themselves in the values of a foreign popular culture and are gradually imbued with embarrassment for their own identity, since others fail to understand it.

In the brilliant and shocking funny story in this volume, "One Out of Many"—shocking because what one is seeing is the disintegration of personality, Naipaul is past master of the difficult art of making you laugh and then feel shame at your laughter....

We know of no other contemporary novelist who can deal so devastatingly, yet quietly, with the sensation and terror at the core of ordinary encounters.

This book is not his best work; but it is part of an achievement that we believe in the end will show him to have been a great writer. His limitations? They are perhaps unconsciously expressed in a reflection, in the epilogue to this book, on the unknown tomb artist of Egypt: "Perhaps that had been the only pure time, at the beginning, when the ancient artist knowing no other land, learned to look at his own and had seen it as complete."

> *Nadine Gordimer, in* The New York Times Book Review *(1971 by The New York Times Company; reprinted by permission), October 17, 1971.*

Many critics have commented on Naipaul's unique gifts, but they have said little about his unique condition. He is, in his own words, "without a past, without ancestors," "without a tradition," "a little ridiculous and unlikely." His homelessness has produced in him a capacity to create characters of tremendous diversity. This is an age of the national writer; it is very unusual to come across a writer who has no national identity, a stateless artist.

Naipaul's concerns remain constant. He writes of fantasy, slavery, power, Empire, exile. The condition of rootlessness, a motif in his *Area of Darkness*, is a frequent theme in his fiction; and it is the subject of *In a Free State*. Some of the territory here is new. For the first time, he is writing of an Indian in America; of West Indians in London; British people in Africa. Framed by two personal anecdotes, which serve as prologue and epilogue, the three stories—incidents in three countries—form a sequence and make a large statement about freedom and homelessness, dependency and belonging. The book is Naipaul's most ambitious work, a story-sequence brilliant in conception, masterly in execution, and terrifying in effect—the chronicles of a half-a-dozen self-exiled people who have become lost souls.

Having abandoned their own countries (countries they were scarcely aware of belonging to), they have found themselves in strange places, without friends, with few loyalties, and with the feeling that they are trespassing. Worse, their lives have been totally altered; for them there is no going back; they have fled, each to his separate limbo, and their existence is like that of souls in a classical underworld....

The subject of displacement is one few writers have touched upon. Camus has written of it. But Naipaul is much superior to Camus, and his achievement—a steady advance through eleven volumes—is as disturbing as it is original. *In a Free State* is a masterpiece in the fiction of rootlessness. France claimed the Algerian Camus. No country can claim Naipaul. It is a demonstration of the odds against him, but certain evidence of the uniqueness of his vision.

Paul Theroux, "To be Without Roots," in Book World (The Washington Post), *December 5, 1971.*

["In a Free State"] is an extraordinarily penetrating book and a disturbing one....

Naipaul writes about the many psychic realities of exile in our contemporary world with far more bite and dramatic havoc than Joyce brought to that stage Jew Leopold Bloom.

In this new book, one of his very best, he has sharpened and tuned, on five different examples of contemporary wandering, his already prodigious sense of fiction. No one else around today, not even Nabokov, seems able to employ prose fiction so deeply as the very voice of exile. If "our" fiction began with the raw merchants settling into their overstuffed interiors, the brilliance of fiction today would seem to depend on a sense of displacement which so many smart American novelists who have never been put to the actual test have already played with in their more theoretical novels.

What makes Naipaul hurt so much more than other novelists of contemporary exodus is his major image—the tenuousness of man's hold on the earth. The doubly unsettling effect he creates—for the prose is British-chatty, proper yet bitter—also comes from the many characters in a book like this who don't "belong" in the countries they are touring or working in, who wouldn't "belong" any longer in the countries they come from, and from the endless moving about of contemporary life have acquired a feeling of their own unreality in the "free state" of endlessly moving about. All travel is an adoptive consciousness—only Ulysses was transported in his sleep. And it is so *much* consciousness, "raised" yet unavailing, that makes one's motion and freedom clash with so many other too conscious egos forever crazily on the move. There is a peculiarly contemporary despair in seeing so much exertion of the will mocked by the lack of tradition, assurance, and moral comfort in which we travel....

Naipaul has never encompassed so much, and with such brilliant economy, with such a patent though lighthanded ominousness of manner, as in ["In a Free State"]. The volume of detail is extraordinary, and so is the sequence of action parodying the fretful trip by car as Bobby confesses his dream of returning, somewhere, out of the rain, to a warm lighted house....

The sinuous conjunction of the talk between the unloving couple in the car with the sudden sharp treacheries of the road and the weather, and above all the dramatic movement, line by line of landscape and action duplicating the mingled ease, boredom, and anxiety of a long trip by car—all this gives "In a Free State" an amazing tense fullness in all it takes in and suggests of the African landscape, the old "settler mentality," the educated African politicians whom Bobby and Linda discuss and whom we never see, the sheer sweating fear of the English and blacks towards each other....

I suppose one criticism of Naipaul might well be that he covers too much ground, has too many representative types, and that he has an obvious desolation about homelessness, migration, the final placelessness of those who have seen too much, which he tends to turn into a mysterious accusation. Though he is a marvellous technician, there is something finally modest, personal, openly committed about his fiction, a frankness of personal reference, that removes him from the godlike impersonality of the novelist so often praised by Joyce—and so much cherished by novelists like Nabokov who angrily deny that *they* use themselves. Naipaul belongs to a different generation, to a more openly tragic outlook for humanity itself. He does not want to play God, even in a novel. He has associated himself with "history," and does not expect better treatment.

> *Alfred Kazin, "Displaced Person," in* The New York Review of Books *(reprinted with permission from* The New York Review of Books; *1971 by NYREV, Inc.), December 30, 1971.*

The sad figure of Mr. Biswas lends itself to a vulgar and comic principle of classification of things and people which gives [*A House for Mr. Biswas*] a conventional centre. In the first place Naipaul's world is one which is devoid of phenomenal and therefore corrosive sensibility. He builds his chronicle around a traditional Hindu family in Trinidad and therefore persuades his readers to identify with an assumption of individual status, of historical context. The inner and outer poverty of Naipaul's characters—while achieving at times memorable pathos—never erupts into a revolutionary or alien question of spirit, but serves ultimately to consolidate one's preconception of humanity, the comedy of pathos and the pathos of comedy. It is this "common picture of humanity" so-called on which Naipaul's work rests. The novel for him, as for many contemporary readers and writers, restricts the open and original ground of choice, the vision and stress of transplantation in the person out of one world into another, the necessity for epic beyond its present framework, or tragedy within its present framework, since the assumption remains to the end a contemporary and limited one of burial and classification, a persuasion of singular and pathetic enlightenment rather than a tragic centrality or a capacity for plural forms of profound identity.

Wilson Harris, in Modern Black Novelists: A Collection of Critical Essays, *edited by Michael G. Cooke, Prentice-Hall, Inc., 1971.*

Wholly original, [Naipaul] may be the only writer today in whom there are no echoes of influences.

The act of writing, the capacity for creation, separates those of Naipaul's characters with an active imagination from those who fantasise.

Creation, in Naipaul's terms, involves perception. The ability to assess oneself in one's setting is necessary if a person is to write well or make anything new; detail must be seen, judgements questioned. With these perceptions, the experience of something sighted, arrives a specific calmness which is resolution. In this calmness is the confident detachment which can result in creation: this still moment, which the creator occupies, makes it possible for the experience to be written about, or painted, or sculpted, given its true shape....

The release that true creation offers in completing a man is a point that is often made in Naipaul's work.

Naipaul's heroes are extremely private souls, sensitive about revealing anything of themselves, even to people who are close, to wives and children.

Imagination helps a man to become whole. Fantasy, which is the expression of a perverse hunger, destroys and degrades a man. This idea occurs, with various illustration, in every one of Naipaul's books. It is related to Naipaul's ideas of grief and religion, ritual, Empire, slavery and dependency.

The fact of death stuns various of Naipaul's characters into a mechanical bewilderment which is more fantasy than grief. It is almost as if grief is beyond them; they are not whole enough to experience true loss. Their sadness is compulsive utterance.

Rebellion, flight, danger, homelessness, dependency, fame: they are linked concepts in Naipaul's work, and he gives elaborate expression to them in his essays, travel books and novels. Apart from the concept of fame—a significant omission—these are the themes in his most recent novel, *In a Free State.* But the people in this book are quite different from Naipaul's other fictional characters: they do not rise; they are uncreative, vulnerable, terrified, dependent, as unlike the rebellious heroes as it is possible to be. It is a book about rebellion's absence, about resignation, a statement about surrender, with a personal, uncompromising act of assertion—Naipaul's own—in the Epilogue.

In a Free State extends Naipaul's ideas of rootlessness and rebellion and the paradox of freedom. The title itself suggests continual aimless movement. The factual Prologue and Epilogue, Naipaul's personal experiences, a traveller's tales, seem to contain a reply to the degradation he dramatises in the stories.

The action in the Epilogue—it helps to know what Naipaul has seen in *The Middle Passage* and *An Area of Darkness* to understand how huge a gesture it is—indicates that he hasn't surrendered himself; but symbolic action is not enough relief, and temperamentally Naipaul is so different from these characters that it is really impossible for his behaviour to serve as a model for them or to draw any conclusion other than, urged by conscience, a man can still make himself a rebel by acting.

In a Free State is the first book of Naipaul's in which a fear of death and a preoccupation with failure are considered as being final. In his other fiction—*Mr. Stone* is a good example—thoughts of death and failure produce a moment of vision by feeding the imagination with a means of escape. What confounds and isolates the characters in *In a Free State,* liberates and involves Mr. Stone. It is his most disturbing book.

What is Naipaul's style? Is it those short single sentences of *Miguel Street*? Can it be found in the long luxuriant paragraphs of *Mr. Biswas*, or the lucid short paragraphs of *Mr. Stone*, or the heavily-punctuated regrets of Ralph Singh?... In each instance Naipaul is making a direct response to his subject, allowing his material to determine his tone.

Compression is Naipaul's forte.... [He] is a writer who places little value on coincidence or suspense. He conceals nothing; his ingenuousness, his avoidance of sarcasm, and his humour—a delight that no essay can do justice to—make him very special among writers; there is no one like him writing today. He is odd in other respects: he has no feeling for the theatre; he has never written a play or a poem or an autobiographical novel; he has neither pandered to the popular taste nor offered the cheap comfort of fictional simplicities. It is evidence of the uniqueness of his vision, but a demonstration of the odds against him, that no country can claim him.

> *Paul Theroux, in his* V. S. Naipaul: An Introduction to His Work, *(copyright 1972 by Paul Theroux; published by Africana Publishing Company, a Division of Holmes & Meier Publishers, Inc. and reprinted by permission), Africana, 1972.*

Miguel Street's slum dwellers lack education, tradition, culture, and sometimes enough food—but not pride, vitality, humour, freewheeling imagination, and tenacity. Fortunately Naipaul does not sentimentalise them; they are folk realists about whom he is realistic....

The Suffrage of Elvira (1958),... [one] of his slighter novels, without any well-developed characters or especial richness of theme,... has engagingly idiosyncratic figures, ample comic inventiveness, and the pointed, deadpan humour through dialogue which is one of Naipaul's most effective and characteristic satirical strategies.... *The Suffrage* is a farce, not a realistic novel....

With its amiably unprincipled hero Ganesh in inventive quest of success and its ingenuously admiring narrator, Naipaul's first published novel, *The Mystic Masseur* (1957), is his most delightful effort in pursuit of truth.... Naipaul's indefatigable Ganesh from Trinidad is a successful man because he is shrewd enough to know how to turn "fate" to his advantage. Forever proclaiming that destiny has preordained his successes, he is meanwhile creating them for himself.

But Ganesh is very much of our times in not taking personal responsibility for his actions. That is really why the narrator follows his career with such interest....

His concern with how men dodge and face responsibility reappears in *A House for Mr. Biswas* (1961), a good companion piece to the success story of Ganesh. This is Naipaul's longest novel, an almost painfully specific account of the struggles of a poor Trinidadian to make himself matter. And given every possible disadvantage, from an ill-omened birth into a superstitious, impoverished Hindu family, to a scrawny physique and an ill-advised marriage, to a dangerous naivete about the ways of the world and apparently irremediable poverty, Mr. Biswas succeeds. He achieves nothing without pain and acquires nothing without flaws, but he continues to struggle and manages to die content, at forty-six, in his own house. A symbolic house for Biswas and the reader, the house is mortgaged and badly designed and constructed, but Biswas has achieved possession of it and—as Naipaul is really saying, of himself—justified his existence....

The narrator of his *Miguel Street* (1959) is describing all Naipaul's novels when he says, we "saw our street as a world, where everybody was quite different from everybody else." Naipaul's five novels are peopled by quite singular characters who dwell on a street with universal boundaries. He transmutes the vagaries and quotidian confusions of modern anti-heroes into energetic, universalised fiction in the precisely phrased, deftly ironic novels—*The Mystic Masseur* (1957), *The Suffrage of Elvira* (1958), *A House for Mr. Biswas* (1961), *Mr. Stone and the Knights Companion* (1963), and *The Mimic Men* (1967)—which have earned him his impressive list of awards and honours....

Because, except for *Mr. Stone and the Knights Companion,* his novels are set wholly or partly in Trinidad, and he has written two non-fiction books about the Caribbean area, he has gained some reputation as a West Indian writer. Yet Naipaul does not see himself as one. He objects to West Indian writers as inclined to choose "too special" situations, meaningful only to compatriots: any other reader "is excluded; he is invited to witness; he cannot participate."...

Granted the particularity of Naipaul's Caribbean descriptions and the vitality of his dialect, seeing him only as a skilful local colourist or regional sociologist underestimates him. Naipaul's novels are about contemporary man and how he manages to survive and sometimes almost flourish. His books are not confined within their local settings nor, for all their explicitly precise detail, are they tied to literal realism: he finds metaphor more expressive. The local settings are convenient to his ideational purposes. As a society "continually growing and changing, never settling into any pattern" ..., Trinidad invites themes of instability and flux, and as a colonial and emergent nation it provides a good setting for problems of dependency and freedom. The narrator of *Mimic Men* aptly says, "It has happened in twenty countries."... The dominant pressures in Naipaul's fictional world derive from man's precarious existence. He has not only to contend with psychic conflict and cultural fragmentation but to exist in a hard world within an indifferent universe.... At their best, Naipaul's characters are resilient, managing to transcend nonentity by their stubbornness. Naipaul may not willingly suffer people's pretensions, deceptions, and illogicalities, but he can admire their refusal to be the counters of fate or circumstance....

The elusive narrator [of *The Mimic Men*], whose opinions keep changing under the pressure of his recapturing the past, is a more intellectually and emotionally sophisticated character than Naipaul has created before. His account is not a simple flashback but a process of sorting and regrouping the psychic freight of roughly five periods in his life.... Naipaul thus asks far more of his reader with this book than with earlier ones. Singh [the protagonist] being essentially a humourless man, he also dispenses with truly comic effects (in any case, these were diminishing with each succeeding book). Yet one recognises a familiar Naipaul....

Singh accepts essentially Naipaul's perspective, according to which we neither come from nor return to a universal scheme of wholeness and harmony and should not plan on finding restorative magical light anywhere. We cannot pretend to any sort of mythic consciousness; its time has long since passed. On the other hand, individual cells can and do clump. Even men in cities, as Singh discovers ..., manage to form meaningful units and, more important, manage to grow into operatively unitary personalities, assimilating change as it comes. Real men, Naipaul says once again, can manage with what is given.... Pursuing illusions of a better world on earth is a game for mimic men.

One may take an insistence on confronting reality as (provisionally) Naipaul's final stand as a novelist. It does accord with his belief in, and skilful practice of, the novel as an expression of "concern with the condition of men" and "a response to the here and now."...

Harriet Blodgett, "Beyond Trinidad: Five Novels by V. S. Naipaul," in South Atlantic Quarterly *(reprinted by permission of the Publisher; copyright 1974 by Duke University Press, Durham, North Carolina), Summer, 1974.*

Significant Works

Fiction:

- The Mystic Masseur – (1957) (film version: The Mystic Masseur (2001))
- The Suffrage of Elvira – (1958)
- Miguel Street – (1959)
- A House for Mr. Biswas – (1961)
- Mr. Stone and the Knights Companion – (1963)
- The Mimic Men – (1967)
- A Flag on the Island – (1967)
- In a Free State – (1971): Booker prize
- Guerrillas – (1975)
- A Bend in the River – (1979)
- Finding the Centre – (1984)
- The Enigma of Arrival – (1987)
- A Way in the World – (1994)
- Half a Life – (2001)
- Magic Seeds – (2004)

Non-fiction:

- The Middle Passage: Impressions of Five Societies – British, French and Dutch in the West Indies and South America (1962)
- An Area of Darkness (1964)

- The Loss of El Dorado – (1969)
- The Overcrowded Barracoon and Other Articles (1972)
- India: A Wounded Civilization (1977)
- A Congo Diary (1980)
- The Return of Eva Perón and the Killings in Trinidad (1980)
- Among the Believers: An Islamic Journey (1981)
- A Turn in the South (1989)
- India: A Million Mutinies Now (1990)
- Homeless by Choice (1992, with R. Jhabvala and Salman Rushdie)
- Bombay (1994, with Raghubir Singh)
- Beyond Belief: Islamic Excursions among the Converted Peoples (1998)
- Between Father and Son: Family Letters (1999, edited by Gillon Aitken)
- Reading & Writing: A Personal Account (2000)
- The Writer and the World: Essays – (2002)
- Literary Occasions: Essays (2003, by Pankaj Mishra)
- A Writer's People: Ways of Looking and Feeling (2007)
- The Masque of Africa: Glimpses of African Belief (2010)

3 Thoughts and Ideology

Views

On Politics

Naipaul insists that his writing transcends any particular ideological outlook, remarking that "to have a political view is to be prejudiced. I don't have a political view." His supporters often perceive him as offering a mordant critique of many left-liberal pieties while his detractors, such as critic Edward Said and poet Derek Walcott accuse him of being a neo-colonial apologist. He has also excoriated Tony Blair as a "pirate" at the head of "a socialist revolution", a man who was "destroying the idea of civilization in this country" and had created "a plebeian culture".

In his book dealing with the influence of Islam on non-Arab Muslims, *Beyond Belief: Islamic excursions among the converted peoples*, Naipaul states the following about Islam:

The cruelty of Islamic fundamentalism is that it allows to only one people – the Arabs, the original people of the Prophet – a past, and sacred places, pilgrimages and earth reverences. These sacred Arab places have to be the sacred places of all the converted peoples. Converted peoples have to strip themselves of their past; of converted peoples nothing is required but the purest faith (if such a thing can be arrived at), Islam, submission. It is the most uncompromising kind of imperialism.

On Female Writers

Naipaul attracted media controversy with statements about women he made in a May 2011 interview at the Royal Geographic Society, expressing his view that women's writing was inferior to men's, and that there was no female writer whom he would consider his equal.

Naipaul stated that women's writing was "quite different", reflecting women's "sentimentality, the narrow view of the world". He had previously criticised leading female Indian authors writing about the legacy of colonialism for the "banality" of their work.

Insight into his Escape

"Bogart," the first story in the collection Miguel Street may well give us an insight into why Naipaul wished to escape from Trinidad where he spent his childhood. Bogart, uncreative, playing Patience all day, had a habit of drawing ring, on the pavement with his fingers; rings that could mean imprisonment , continuation and sameness.

He is imprisoned within the lowest class structure of society and plays Patience to pass the time. Man-man is to make a similar gesture by writing several Os, and later, by depositing blobs of excrement in a cafe.

These patterns may represent the islands on which they are figuratively shipwrecked. In fact, Hat is imprisoned in Carerra, a blob of an island, for inflicting bodily harm on a woman. This continuation, implicit in the circle motif, pervades the entire book and is to be remarked upon when Naipaul revisits the island in 1960:

> But driving now through Port of Spain, seeing the groups lounging at corners, around flambeau-lit stalls and coconut carts, I missed this thrill, and was distressed, not so much by the familiarity, as by the feeling of continuation. (The Middle Passage)

Miguel Street is considered to be semi-autobiographical. In it, as has been pointed out in Commonwealth Short Stories, Naipaul's "boyhood experiences have been looked at in retrospect with the wisdom of the adult" (199). It would be worthwhile to spend some time here. The characters in this third novel are disillusioned by the quality of life available to them.

They live in a colonial system which is closed, devoid of any history, and their future is without any glimmer of hope. They constantly seek to escape from their condition by creating fantasies of themselves.

In a society which denied itself heroes, the characters of Miguel Street become Bogarts of the film world with which they are fascinated; or eccentrics like Man-man, who isn't mad. Growing up in Trinidad, the I-narrator of the novel reveals himself as a heavy drinker, and in reply to his mother says: "What else anybody can do here except drink?" This scathing remark finds echo in Naipaul's analysis of the island in 1960:

> It was a place where the stories were never stories of success but of failure: brilliant men, scholarship winners, who had died young, gone mad, or taken to drink; cricketers of promise whose careers had been ruined by disagreements with the authorities. (The Middle Passage)

The I-narrator escapes from the island by being endowed with a government scholarship to study drugs. Education is seen as a means of escape from the lowest class, the poor, who were invariably black. Those who are not fortunate enough to secure an education remain stagnant in their condition. Naipaul's instincts—even to the very end of the novel—and that of those of the lowest class in the society are imprisoned within the confines of the circle motif.

Naipaul's sense of continuation in the island is restated here.

> And back in Miguel Street the first person I saw was Hat. He was strolling flat-footed back from the cafe, with a paper under his arm. I waved and shouted at him.
>
> All he said was, "I thought you was in the air by this time." I was disappointed. Not only by Hat's cool reception.

> Disappointed because although I had been away, destined to be gone for good, everything was going on just as before, with nothing to indicate my absence. (The Mystic Masseur)

Flight from the island forms a pattern throughout Naipaul's work: at the end of The Mystic Masseur the narrator is at an English University; Harbans disappears from the eyes of his electors by the end of The Suffrage of Elvira; the I-narrator is destined for London in Miguel Street; and Mr. Biswas escapes in death while Anand flies to England in A House for Mr. Biswas. On the latter, Ramchand writes: "One suspects that the world of A House for Mr. Biswas is one modelled upon a society from which the author has himself wished to escape".

The escape motif continues in the rest of Naipaul's works. Shifting from one address to another is characteristic of Naipaul's life. His restlessness begins at the Lion House in Trinidad and follows him to various places and houses in England.

As an adult, Naipaul claims to have never lived in any house for more than about three-and-a-half years. His restlessness is felt even in his non-fiction works like An Area of Darkness where escape is sought in "Flight" from which the title of this section is taken.

B. Wordsworth, the poet-calypsonian in Miguel Street, is invented mainly to show Naipaul's own predicament at home as a West Indian artist (Omerod). The man who peddles his poems lives in exile from his community.

The fulfilment he receives from writing literature is equally matched by his feeling of insignificance in his society: The poet's poems are not selling; he is treated without importance in his community; his pastoral landscape is destroyed and his life, like the poem he was writing, is incomplete. It is the very dilemma which Naipaul faced as a boy (note that the poet tells the I-narrator: "You're as good as me.").

Like George Lamming, Naipaul, at an early age, had set for himself the career of writing; he wanted to write as his father did and not like his maternal uncles who were in the legal profession. As an adult, like B. Wordsworth, he knew that he could not survive in Trinidad as the only professions to choose from were law and medicine, because there was no need for any other. Escape from the West Indies, from the continuation implicit in the circle motif, was the only solution: "I had never wanted to stay in Trinidad. When I was in the fourth form I wrote a vow on the endpaper of my Kennedy's Revised Latin Primer to leave within five years. I left after six" (The Middle Passage).

Nobel Lecture

'Two Worlds'

This is unusual for me. I have given readings and not lectures. I have told people who ask for lectures that I have no lecture to give. And that is true. It might seem strange that a man who has dealt in words and emotions and ideas for nearly fifty years shouldn't have a few to spare, so to speak.

But everything of value about me is in my books. Whatever extra there is in me at any given moment isn't fully formed. I am hardly aware of it; it awaits the next book. It will — with luck — come to me during the actual writing, and it will take me by surprise. That element of surprise is what I look for when I am writing. It is my way of judging what I am doing — which is never an easy thing to do.

Proust has written with great penetration of the difference between the writer as writer and the writer as a social being. You will find his thoughts in some of his essays in Against Sainte-Beuve, a book reconstituted from his early papers. The nineteenth-century French critic Sainte-Beuve believed that to understand a writer it was necessary to know as much as possible about the exterior man, the details of his life. It is a beguiling method, using the man to illuminate the work. It might seem unassailable.

But Proust is able very convincingly to pick it apart. "This method of Sainte-Beuve," Proust writes, "ignores what a very slight degree of self-acquaintance teaches us: that a book is the product of a different self from the self we manifest in our habits, in our social life, in our vices. If we would try to understand that particular self, it is by searching our own bosoms, and trying to reconstruct it there, that we may arrive at it."

Those words of Proust should be with us whenever we are reading the biography of a writer — or the biography of anyone who depends on what can be called inspiration.

All the details of the life and the quirks and the friendships can be laid out for us, but the mystery of the writing will remain. No amount of documentation, however fascinating, can take us there. The biography of a writer — or even the autobiography — will always have this incompleteness.

4 Miguel Street

Miguel Street," by V. S. Naipaul, is a beguiling book about growing up in the West Indies. The sketches are written lightly, so that tragedy is understated and comedy is overstated, yet the ring of truth always prevails.

A comparison with "Porgy and Bess" has been suggested. The parallel has at least the merit of reminding us that the whole world is one. In that hospitable mood we might also remember Mark Twain's tales of life on the Mississippi. But Miguel Street, in Trinidad, is not really very much like Catfish Row, nor are reminders of nineteenth-century Missouri prevalent. What is true and, if you will, significant about Mr. Naipaul's book is that it presents a world of its own excellently.

The time of that world is the late Nineteen Thirties and most of the Nineteen Forties on a sunny slum street in Port of Spain. Here the young narrator of the story and his Hindu relatives live in a community as heterogeneous as, say, that of Manhattan Island.

Introduction

Based on a fabled Port of Spain resident whose Messianic tale is captured by The Mighty Wonder's calypso "Follow Me Children," Man-man is the "mad-man" of Miguel Street whose descent into religious fantasy results in a mock (and failed) crucifixion and, thereafter, permanent incarceration. Man-man's identity, his very name, expresses the dialectic of "Man"—capitalised and universal—a supposedly homogenous collective, and "man"—uncapitalised and singular—a sometimes lonely and socially isolated being. In The Crucifixion (1987) Ismith Khan also employs the story of the preacher's self crucifixion while Lovelace recreates the motif of Christ-like sacrifice in Taffy and then Bolo, and even resurrects Man Man (no hyphen) as the martyred leader of a secret African society in the opening lines of Salt (1997). In all these cases the heroic and/or mock heroic martyr is part of the ongoing and concurrent construction and interrogation of the self sacrificing leader—the man whose "man-ness" will lead the people to freedom, liberty and, crucially, Nationhood.

In attempting to write Cricket into the dust of Miguel Street, Man-man reaches Crick before his inscription and his story stutter at the letter E; a letter that obviously evokes England and his surprisingly English accent. Man-man repeatedly carves E's into the landscape of Trinidad, into the poverty of Port of Spain, until Naipaul's young narrator returns from his out-of-sight cricket game. Only then can Man-man mark the final letter T. Much like Alford's repetition of A's and his eventual arrival at C in Lovelace's Salt, Man-man's linguistic stutter is part of a wider concern with literacy and mimicry that reflects a coming into language, an obsession with the word and a faltering relationship with the old colonial master whose imposition of English and cricket coincide in his inscription. It is in the context of Man-man's story that this discussion proceeds as the seemingly mad, suspiciously astute double-man of Miguel Street embodies calypso, inscribes cricket into the landscape of his island with a stick—a miniature version of the phallic implements used by both stick fighters and cricketers—and eventually refuses to become the heroic saviour of his fellow men, and, Man.

In "Music, Literature and West Indian Cricket Values," Gordon Rohlehr establishes the aesthetic, cultural, political and economic intersections between cricket, calypso and the Caribbean literary imagination. Further, in "I Lawa: Masculinity in Trinidad and Tobago Calypso," Rohlehr examines the tradition of the warrior-hero of the stickfight, his evolution into the heroes of calypso and cricket (among others) and calypso's ability, ironic and humorous, to "elevate and deflate the ideal of phallocentric masculinity" (Reddock 345). Building on these insights, this paper considers the place and purpose of cricket and calypso in Errol John's yard play Moon on a Rainbow Shawl (1958) and V.S. Naipaul's collection of interwoven short stories Miguel Street (1959). By reviewing the cricketing narratives provided by the men in the yard and on the street, this paper suggests how and to what consequence John and Naipaul reflect upon and interrogate the models of masculinity and heroism laid before them as young Caribbean men in post-war Trinidad.

Moon and Miguel Street were both composed in London in 1955 and represent something of a literary re-crossing of the Atlantic as each author recalls and recreates the post-war Trinidad they left behind and fictionalises, if not rationalises, their own departure to England. Both pieces exhibit similarly cutting and unromanticised visions of poverty in Port of Spain and bear the marks of the 1930s barrack tradition of Alfred Mendes, C. L. R. James and others. In doing so, John and Naipaul rely heavily upon the sounds, styles and humour of calypso to localise, unify and animate their writing. Calypso also enables them to clear a cultural and psychic space for Caribbean identities, particularly working class male identities, in-between (though very much affected by) the competing economic and social influences of England and America during the transitional period before the Federation, and thereafter, Independence.

Calypso is a dominant feature of Moon's soundscape, it is the local sound and the sound of the locale inserted and asserted in between "Land of Hope and Glory" and Frank Sinatra, and is personified onstage by Ketch, the calypsonian forced to "chase the yankee dollar". Calypso is also the principle intertextual resource of Miguel Street as Naipaul uses at least fourteen calypso songs from the 1930s and 40s (Thieme 19). More importantly, Naipaul and his characters operate almost entirely within the ironic idiom of calypso and, as in Moon, the picong, machismo and gender-battle of calypso remain omnipresent. Against Lamming's condemnation of "castrated satire," Rohlehr argues that the employment of ironic and satirical strategies, as found in calypso, actually enables Naipaul to "examine the past without sentimental self-indulgence" ("The Ironic Approach"). The same can be said of John. Moreover, Thieme's rightly suggests that Naipaul imaginatively returns from England through calypso to express, perhaps for the only time, a "genuine concern for" and "degree of sympathy" for "the ordinary West Indian", specifically the black male (Thieme 19). In examining the past, and the men or examples of masculinity from their past, John and Naipaul employ calypso to probe the "Big man" complex—the problem of how "to be a man, among we men" (Miguel Street 14). They do this by presenting calypso and cricket as spaces in which men and male identities are at once established and undermined, performed and revealed as performance, remembered and exposed as false remembering.

In the yard and on the street, cricket exists as a boy's game and a manly topic of discussion that serves to distract from the reality of male boredom and, quite often, a physical sense of stasis or paralysis. For many Caribbean men, the sport appears to be a means of escape but it is portrayed by John and Naipaul as a Janus-faced illusion whose dreamlike promise of success and prosperity (obtained by an exceptional few) exists alongside defeat, exclusion, drinking and jail (for a wider majority) as experienced by Charlie and Hat. The works have, at their core, narratives of cricketing remembrance that illustrate the dialectic of cricket, its connection with calypso and the problems these fields of masculinity present for the leading male figures. In both texts, surrogate father-son relationships are created between the generationally separated male characters—Charlie and Ephraim in Moon and Hat and Naipaul's narrator in Miguel Street—which are clearly tied to their cricketing exchanges. In Moon, Charlie Adams shares the memory of his "broken" career as a fast bowler with Ephraim. In Miguel Street, Naipaul's anonymous boy narrator tells of his first trip to the Oval with Hat, relays the details of his uncle's cricket related wife beating and describes the above-cited example of Man-man.

In each case the act of memory functions to recall and remember (to imaginatively put back together) the older men and their previous masculine performances but also serves to expose the instability of those past performances and the disjuncture between them and their present emasculation; a disjuncture which pushes the younger men, Eph and the narrator (read John and Naipaul), to flee to the Mother Country. In addition, these stories of cricket, and cricket's relationship to masculinity, are read through calypso and calypso in fact influences the very style of cricket on display. Like numerous other commentators, Richard Burton has pointed out that the "street values" of calypso—reputation, aggression, bravado, etc.—inform or mould the type of cricket played in the Caribbean whether on the beach, on the street or in the international arena. Mobilising the works of Roger Abrahams and Peter Wilson, he believes that because of the two traditions found in West Indies cricket, those of Englishness and "Caribbeanness," the game must be read through the dialectic of inside/respectability/yard/women and outside/reputation/street/man that structures carnival. In this context, the following sections first address the men of John's yard and then move to consider those of Naipaul's street. While Burton's understanding of cricket, its two traditions and the values association with the yard and street is useful, this paper ultimately suggests that the battle to establish and maintain a coherent and stable masculine identity is one that takes place in both these sociocultural places/spaces because it is central to the pattern of gender relations that characterises the picaroon society portrayed.

First Written Work

The noble laureate V.S. Naipaul started his career as a freelance writer with his first written work of fiction Miguel Street in the year 1959. Miguel Street is a semi-autobiographical novel set in wartime Port of Spain, Trinidad and Tobago. Naipaul wrote this novel while he was employed in the BBC. Miguel Street won the 1961 Somerset Maugham Award. As Trinidad is V.S. Naipaul's childhood home, he minutely observed its tradition and culture. The readers are introduced to a galaxy of characters with different professions and features. They love to live in illusions and meet failures at every stage of their life.

Summary

Miguel Street is a collection of seventeen short stories told from the point of view of a nameless and seemingly fatherless boy narrator; all depict the residents of Naipaul's fictional Port of Spain street. Only one of the sketches, "The Maternal Instinct," concentrates on a woman, Laura, and Naipaul uses her to humiliate her partner Nathaniel whom she beats in a reversal of the calypso message of "Knock Dem Down". The other sketches present the men of the area and the narrator's examination of them where his role models and examples of masculinity are found outside the domestic sphere on the street. The young narrator and his friends, Errol and Boyee, learn from and attempt to imitate Eddoes, Bogart and Hat, the street's dominant males, the men who present "life lived ... on the pavement" (Walsh 11). The narrator tells of the performances of masculinity offered on the street but also explores the depths, problems and insecurities of these characters. Although the narrator journeys through his adolescence with varying heroes or male icons, he enjoys a special bond with Hat—the street's "smartman," a version of the hero of calypso. Hat is the man that boys and men aspire to be, who sets the street's standards of behaviour and the limits of laughter, who, more than anyone else, perceives "the pain beneath the pose" (Feder 165).

In the penultimate story, simply entitled "Hat," the narrator tells of his first encounter with Hat when Hat took him and eleven other children to the Oval for the last day of Trinidad versus Jamaica. This memory is placed alongside the narrator's outgrowing of Hat and the calypso culture of the street and Hat's fall from his previous, seemingly heroic, position. The last story is the narrator's own and tells of his parting with Hat and his departure to England.

Throughout *Miguel Street* cricket is played by the young boys and their games exhibit not only the make shift nature of street cricket from which so much of West Indies cricket is said to derive, but as their ball regularly gets wet "in the stinking gutter" (22) their game is quite literally tainted with the "stink" of the poverty in which they live. The men of the street discuss, bet on and observe cricket. It is a part of the supposed "leisure" of street life and a space in which they can invest their hopes, dreams and emotions whilst escaping the realities of their lives.

The trip to the Oval provides the event in which Hat's personality, his persona, is most clearly revealed. He takes twelve of the street's children to the game not as a kindness but as a joke, as a trick. His mock-fatherhood grants him attention, importance and respect among the crowd of interested eyes as the children appear to attest to his manliness, to his fertility, to his phallic credentials.

However, the validity of such an idea has already been undercut by the tale of Mr. Morgan, the Pyrotechnist, whose ten children did not prevent his public emasculation at the hands of his wife. Whilst watching the game, the two sides of Hat's persona are revealed. On one hand, Hat shouts, gesticulates, places "impossible bets" (156) and acts in accordance with the values of the street. His exuberance and excitement are very much part of the game's action and are examples of the close spectator-player relationship that characterises West Indies cricket. At the same time, he conveys cricket's traditions of gentility and honour to the narrator by teaching him about the beauty of the game, the cricketer's names, the scoreboard and that a batsman can be said to have "finished batting" (155) rather than just being "out." Here Hat embodies the two traditions of West Indies cricket that Burton categories as the white elite and its coloured imitators versus the black masses or the Anglo-creole "play up, play up, and play the game" versus the Afro-creole "play." Burton's position seems to accurately reflect Hat's behaviour when he explains that:

> West Indian men, it seems to me, watch and play cricket with minds, hearts, values and expectations shaped by the street culture of boyhood, adolescence and early manhood. Concerned as they are with the enhancing of individual and group reputation, those values are potentially—though rarely in fact—at odds with the values of respectability, seriousness, moderation and obedience associated with the home, the church and the ethos of the dominant white and coloured elites (*Liberation Cricket* 98)

Burton's point is made when Gerry Gomez reaches 150 runs and Hat cries out, without a hint of irony, "White people is God" (155). Whilst Hat's support for Trinidad's captain is entirely understandable in the context of an intercolonial game he does not praise Gomez individually but white people collectively. His shout proclaims the complexity of his own identity, of his identification with and alienation from both his own people and the "whites."

In this situation Gomez the "white," Cambridge blue, captain stands in for the traditions of England and Englishness that continue to dominate cricket and colonial hierarchies on and off the field: he is one of the "Savannah crowd." Hat's "crazy bets" also set Gomez against George Headley of Jamaica, who, in 1948, became the first black man to lead the West Indies team on the field and whose presence therefore gestures forward to a black regional collectivity and leadership within and beyond cricket. As the first black, working class batsman hero Headley was a hero to the entire region. He was a great batsman, if not the greatest that the West Indies ever produced and James writes about him as such in *Beyond A Boundary*. Headley carried the batting of the West Indies throughout the 1930s, and was largely responsible for the team's innings and, too often, the majority of their runs. Consequently, he earned the name "Atlas." He was also nicknamed the Black Bradman in reference to the most famous of Australian batsman—Sir Donald Bradman. As such, Headley is the cricketing counterpart to Black Wordsworth, *Miguel Street*'s struggling poet and calypsonian who claims that he and his brother, the White Wordsworth, are two halves of a single poetic whole.

In counterpoising Gomez and Headley, and, Headley and Wordsworth, Naipaul lays bare the two sides of Hat's identification with cricket and the pressure it exerts on his own sense of self. Hat's calypsonian persona of masculine bravado and self-assurance is unsustainable when faced with the supremacy of and his admiration for "white people."

Hence, it is in the same penultimate sketch that we learn of how, through marriage, domestic violence and jail, Hat becomes another aged calypsonian whose mask shatters under its own weight causing Naipaul's narrator to distance himself from his last and most significant masculine hero. Like Eph in *Moon*, the narrator continues to feel affection and sympathy for the older, now fallen man but he, again like Eph, fears for his own future and leaves in search of a bigger life outside of the calypso-island.

The act of wife beating that sends Hat to jail is a repeated feature of *Miguel Street* and Naipaul's works more generally. Both John and Naipaul situate their concern with men and masculine identities within male-female relationships and both show the cricket bat as a phallic weapon used in domestic violence where wife-beating is accepted as commonplace, performed in a kind of calypso comedy and supposedly undercut by the emasculating tongues of the women. In *Moon*, Prince takes up one of the bats Charlie mends and makes as if to strike Mavis, his new fiancee. When she rebukes him declaring that they "aren't married yet" he retreats to become "the patsy" again (55). In *Miguel Street*, Mr. Bhakcu, "The Mechanic" and narrator's uncle, beats his wife with a cricket bat and the narrator describes the situation:

> For a long time I think Bhakcu experimented with rods for beating his wife, and I wouldn't swear that it wasn't Hat who suggested a cricket bat. But whosoever suggested

> it, a second-hand cricket bat was bought from the Queen's Park Oval, and oiled, and used on Mrs. Bhakcu.

Hat said, "Is the only thing she really could feel, I think."

The strangest thing about this was that Mrs. Bhakcu kept the bat clean and well-oiled. Boyee tried many times to borrow the bat, but Mrs. Bhakcu never lent it.

[Bhacku] hated his wife, and he beat her regularly with the cricket bat. But she was beating him too, with her tongue, and I think Bhakcu was really the loser in these quarrels.

Whilst the humour of the scene is undeniable it only adds to the seriousness with which one views these ritualistic acts. These examples point, quite obviously, to the emasculating effects of the colonial system, microcosmically contained within cricket, being redirected into the physical domination of women. One can argue that the cricket bat is used to suppress, control and emasculate men of colour before they re-direct it against their women folk. In this sense, one should appreciate that when the traditional battle was between white batsman and black bowlers a coloured man taking up the bat is an attempt to offer some kind of anti-colonial stroke, a move to seize power from the grip of the white (bats)man. This is why black batsman like Headley, Sobers, Richards and Lara are crucial in offering a symbolic reversion of the traditional colonial order. However, Bhacku's situation disrupts this black/white dynamic and draws in Trinidad's wider racial picture. A probable descendent of indentured Indian labour, Bhakcu's seizure of the bat symbolises his struggle against white hegemonic masculinity and with its black opposition. His performance follows Reddock's explanation of Niels Sampath's depiction of:

> Indo-Caribbean masculinity as a difficult and sometimes confusing struggle against creolisation, on the one hand seeking acceptance within this paradigm, but at the same time seeking to maintain Indian domestic patriarchal power. This is a struggle, following Wilson (1969), between the values of honour (Indian) and reputation (Creole).

Still, even if the effeminised Prince and Indian Bhakcu are contesting hegemonic and black calypso-related masculinities, they reinforce the point that masculinities are typically united by their oppression, or attempted oppression, of women. Although Mrs. Bhakcu appears complicit in this oppression, the power of her tongue may recall the relatively strong position of Indian women during indentureship and male attempts to regain control over them post-indentureship. Importantly, in both instances the female tongue—standing in for the female voice and sexuality—defeats the men but does not improve their condition.

This only happens when the men decide to do something else, in Bhacku's case to become a pundit. Mavis and Mrs. Bhakcu are only able to "emasculate" their partners by destroying the mask of masculinity they wear because the men are afraid of losing this mask but are constantly doing so; a feature that may actually cause the violence. I suggest that in the same way that the objectifying gaze of the women in *Moon* may be a displacement of the white male gaze, one suspects that the verbal attacks of the women are really the verbalisation of the cricket bat's white hegemonic voice speaking back to the man of colour who uses it and that the women are on the receiving end of both.

The Plot

The whole novel is narrated by an unnamed fatherless boy who himself is a part of a group of kids on Miguel Street. He uses a humorous and satirist tone to describe the people who make up Miguel Street. The whole novel is divided into seventeen episodes and each episode describes the life and its situations targeting one character at a time. This approach of picking up one character at a time made this work easy to understand.

The novel contains a number of characters with great ambitions that never went anywhere and are only left to be recorded in books. The novel is written in the first person, with each character getting its own episode. The narrator's experiences are also woven in between where the protagonist is the narrator himself.

In Trinidad every small issue turned out to be a big event for the people. The novel is also about the outside influences on the narrator which lead him to leave his home in order to make something of himself.

Bogart

The novel opens with an episode of Bogart, named after the name of the protagonist in the story. Bogart lived in Port of Spain and pretended to be a tailor, who never stitched a single suit. Bogart was looked upon as the most bored man in the street, but still he managed to make friends. According to the narrator, he was the most popular figure in the street. He lived a peaceful life till he suddenly vanished one day. For the street people, he had always been a man of mystery.

After a long interval he returned to the street and to the amazement of Miguel Street, he seemed to be completely transformed. He had started drinking and talking a lot, which he never used to do before. He got a job on a ship and had gone to British Guiana, where he started smuggling things. He was going on well with his illegal business, when the police arrested him. Thereafter he returned to the street and became the most feared and awful man. Bogart disappeared the third time and finally when he appeared, he got arrested by Sergent Charles, in charge of bigamy. Thus Bogart's great ambitions ruined his life.

Popo

Another episode describes the character of Popo in The Thing Without a Name, Popo called himself a carpenter and is always working on a thing without a name. As per his image in the street he never finishes making anything despite of keeping himself busy in his work all the time. Popo was a married, contented man then, till his wife left him. Thereafter Popo left the street in search of his wife. When he returned he was not the same man. A negative change could be seen in him, just like Bogart in the previous episode. His wife Emelda returned after a span of time and their life became normal once again, till one day a newspaper headlines said" Calypso Carpenter Jailed". He was imprisoned for stealing new furniture. When he returned from the jail, he was a better man. From then he had started working seriously. Thus he set himself free from all the illusions of life and rather than wasting time in great ambitions which have no direction, he started earning his life seriously.

Man-Man

The narrator introduces the character of Man-Man, as a mad-man. The whole Miguel Street believed that Man-Man was mad and so they left him alone. Though he didn't look mad and went up for election of city council or legislative council every time. At every election he just received three votes. His only friend in Miguel Street was a little Mongrel dog. Man-Man was very attached to his dog and his death caused him turn good. He began talking to himself and clasping hands. He started walking about in his white robe, begging for food. Ultimately he declared himself a new Messiah and decided to be crucified. He insisted people to throw stones on him and when the people followed his command, he started shouting at them to stop. Finally he was disillusioned and was taken away by the police for good.

B. Wordsworth

In another important episode B. Wordsworth calls himself a poet. He declared to the narrator that he was in the process of writing the world's greatest poem, but never wrote past the first line. The narrator spent a great time with B. Wordsworth, without letting his mother know about his regular visits to the poet's house. When B.Wordsworth got sick he disclosed to the narrator that he was not writing any great poem. At last it was disclosed that he lived in illusion but on the death bed he set himself free from all the illusions.

Big Foot

Big Foot, the protagonist of the episode The Coward looked dangerous and everyone in Miguel Street was afraid of him. He was always ready to start a fight with anyone. He followed no particular profession. At one time he made three wardrobes as a carpenter and another time he became a mason. An Englishman boxer came to Trinidad and the next day the newspaper headlines said "Who will fight this man?" Big Foot's great ambitions led him to fight with the Englishman boxer. Big Foot lost the fight in points. At last big foot left Miguel Street.

Songs, Cricket and Courage

Vivid characters with tenuous means of support populate the place. They sing the latest Calypso songs and interest themselves in cricket matches and collect junk and talk about migrating across the narrow sea to Venezuela. If their attitude towards morals is informal it is shown openly, not covertly. Their standards of courage are high. They speculate endlessly on the tremendous trifles and mysteries that have troubled man's thinking throughout his tenure on our strange planet.

A room with a view of a mango tree may contain a boisterously quarrelsome family or a recluse devoted to carpentry or scholarship.

The popular beverage is rum, though the gay blades who enjoy it most turn to the ostentatious patronage of a milk bar during an interval when joy through strength becomes fashionable.

Talk is swift and vigorous. A Lardnerian precision in idioms animates it. The following scene concerns one Mrs. Morgan, who has the temerity to doubt the general prowess Mrs. Bhakcu ascribes to her lord and master, Mr. Bhakcu, a man of many devices.

Mrs. Morgan speaks first:

> "I hear your husband talking in his sleep last night, loud, loud."
>
> "He wasn't talking, he was singing."
>
> "Singing? Hahahahaaah! You know something, Mrs. Bhakcu?"
>
> "What, Mrs. Morgan?"
>
> "If your husband sing for his supper, both of all of you starve like hell."
>
> "He know a damn lot more than any of the ignorant man it have in this street, you hear. He could read and write, you know. English and Hindi. How you so ignorant you don't know that the Ramayana is a holy book? If you could understand all the good thing he is singing, you wouldn't be talking all this nonsense you talking now, you hear."

Love Everywhere

The pangs of love raise welts on Miguel Street. There is a lady living in sin with a man who seemed rather charming to her before her elopement and hating every minute of it. There is a girl who had eight children by seven fathers and grew suddenly and perplexingly prim when her daughter showed signs of carrying on the tradition. There are husbands losing wives and wives losing husbands all over the place.

Although World War II begins, continues and ends in the course of Mr. Naipaul's book, it seldom dominates the scene. The arrival of American armed forces to implement the bases-for-destroyers exchange between Britain and the United States brings measures of disquiet and measures of prosperity. But Miguel Street takes all that in its stride.

Trinidad has known many invaders, friendly and unfriendly, in its history. What winter- cruise addicts may miss here is the comparative absence of tourists. Those invaders were not often in season during these years. Or perhaps Miguel Street couldn't be bothered with them, particularly. It had so many other interests, anyway. Matters of rivalry, schemes for enterprises of passing great moment, dreams of escape and yielding to resignation in this island vanity fair.

Autobiographical Episodes

The last two episodes of the novel Hat and How I Left Miguel Street are autobiographical. Naipaul used some of his personal experiences in bringing these episodes together. Hat, the main character, loved to make mystery of small things. He was among the common people who make up Miguel Street. He enjoyed whatever he did. Hat was a man of settled habits. He became a responsible man when he brought home a woman named Dolly. After some time Dolly ran away and Hat chased her and found her with another man. They had a great quarrel and Hat took it out on Dolly. Thereafter Hat surrendered himself to the police. Hat was sentenced to four years. When he returned everything was changed and so was Hat.

Great Ambitions: Setting Oneself Free

These were some of the characters from the episodes of Miguel Street, which depict the life of different characters full of failure and illusions. But by the end of each episode they managed to set themselves free from all mistaken beliefs. There are many more idiosyncratic characters including Boyee, Errol, Eddoes, Titus Hoyt, and George who lived a life of failures. Most of the episodes are left open and the reader has to imagine the end. As a whole the novel is about great ambitions that never went anywhere. The narrator was also a part of Miguel Street and at last he was the only one who manages to escape from Miguel Street, in order to achieve something in life.

Narrator and His Stories

The reader never loses his perception of the narrator's satiric/ ironic vision throughout the novel. Thus the presence of the narrator is crucial to the meaning, for it is he who draws the protagonist into the centre of human affairs. The failures and disillusionments of his protagonists are presented as a necessary existential despair, which may become a turning point, a cause for change in a world that lives life as comedy of manners.

The element of personal realisation is also touched upon by V.S. Naipaul. This work depicts the realistic view of certain situations as the people in Miguel Street are easily amused by small events, which make up their life. Release from such localised and circumscribed life may be one of the important points this work tries to bring out. This has been the view of several commentators, but it should also be noted that the work itself does not explicitly state that good life and success are possible only when we exit from such locales.

Failures and disillusionment are easily identified even in other situations in other materially developed nations, which offer wider space and wider possibilities for individuals to prosper. While it is true that individuals wish to leave such contexts as they begin to receive higher education, they do reveal a longing to go back and see and experience that kind of life once more, at least once more. Some novels of V.S. Naipaul weave their stories in that direction.

Conclusion

The examples of Charlie, Hat and Bhakcu are united by the Queen's Park Oval that is, as James puts it, the "boss of the island's cricket relations" (49). The Oval is the sociopolitical force that Charlie describes as "pushing yer out of the stream—and on to the bank—So that yer rot in the sun" (63). As a bastion of white power and prejudice, the Oval embodies the corrupting pressures white hegemonic masculinity places on the other male identities seen in *Moon* and *Miguel Street,* particularly those based on the street values of calypso and its popular expression within cricket. Eph and Naipaul's narrator blame Trinidad itself for the situation they see before them and bemoan that "It ent much different" (*Moon* 62) for them than it was their elder counterparts and their point is supported by the two decades that pass between Charlie's cricketing career and the trip to the Oval.

Consequently, these young men run away from Trinidad and the men they think they will become if they remain. Unfortunately, they are running towards the very epicentre of the colonial imagination which will not provide them with any easy solutions, as the Windrush generation discovered. In contrast, Charlie and Sophia believe that Trinidad is changing and that it has and will continue to improve for men like Charlie and Eph. In cricketing terms, black men have risen since Frank Worrell and a black man has lead the West Indies cricket team from 1960 onwards. West Indies cricket has become a vehicle for the history and future of the Caribbean region. Over the course of the twentieth century it has increasingly become a means of the Caribbean expressing itself and its desires to the world. Yet, the continuing dominance of white hegemonic masculinity remains. Situated within the Oval and white cricket playing nations like England and Australia its residual influence means that West Indies cricket still exists within a system of white, predominantly colonial, masculine and cricketing signification.

For the men and nation of Trinidad, the historically situated performances of masculinity demonstrated by Charlie, Hat and Bhakcu, operating as they do within the traditions of cricket, calypso and calypso-cricket, seem to only entrench their identities within typical and accepted masculine domains of achievement via control and defeat over other men and gender identities. One suspects that they must engage with, learn from and ultimately unite with the very gender identities they seek to dominate or exclude. Finally, the disintegration of the heroes of calypso and cricket seen in *Moon* and *Miguel Street* seems to steer us away from an investment in the individual male as hero and towards a common collective based on something other than phallic power.

5 A House for Mr. Biswas

A House for Mr. Biswas is a 1961 novel by V. S. Naipaul, significant as Naipaul's first work to achieve acclaim worldwide. It is the story of Mr. Mohun Biswas, an Indo-Trinidadian who continually strives for success and mostly fails, who marries into the Tulsi family only to find himself dominated by it, and who finally sets the goal of owning his own house. Drawing some elements from the life of Naipaul's father, the work is primarily a sharply-drawn look at life that uses post-colonial perspectives to view a vanished colonial world.

In 1998, the Modern Library ranked *A House for Mr. Biswas* #72 on its list of the 100 best English-language novels of the 20th century. Time magazine included the novel in its "TIME 100 Best English-language Novels from 1923 to 2005"

The Background

Trinidad

Today East Indians (a term that distinguishes them from two other types of Indians in the Caribbean islands – the American Indians, and the West Indians) comprise just over one-third of the total population of Trinidad. They are of Hindu or Moslem belief. India was the main overseas source of cheap labour after the abolition of negro slavery in 1834. No negro would work on the sugar plantations, the scenes of their slavery, and there was a steady flow of labour into the West Indies between about 1845 and 1917. Almost half the remainder of the population is composed of people of African descent, and the other half is of mixed races. The first European to arrive in the island was Christopher Columbus, who discovered it in 1498. The first Spanish settlement was established in 1532, and the island was used mainly as a base for expeditions to the mainland in search of the fabled land of El Dorado, the subject of Naipaul's eighth novel. There was a large influx of Frenchmen in the late eighteenth century, who introduced the sugarcane. After war broke out between Spain and England in 1797, the island was captured and ceded to England in 1802. In 1962 it achieved independence within the British Commonwealth, and became a republic in 1976.

The period covered in the novel is approximately the forty-six years of Mr. Biswas's life between about 1905 and 1951. The main changes which are recorded are the decline of the Hindu culture and rituals as they undergo the process of 'creolisation', and the accompanying changes in attitude. Mr. Biswas himself is caught between the old culture from India and the emerging cross-fertilizations, which are shown in many ways, culminating in the departure of Mr. Biswas's own children, Anand and Savi, on scholarships to study abroad. Naipaul's own views on this process, as reflected by Mr. Biswas in the novel, appear to be ambivalent. He clearly regrets the passing of some of the old traditions, and satirises the new emphasis on materialism and self-advancement.

In his essay on Trinidad in The Middle Passage, which is of great relevance to the novel, he describes Trinidad as a 'materialist immigrant society' which lacks a culture and history of its own and emphasises 'modernity' at all costs, a modernity which involves ignoring local products and using those advertised in American magazines. It is a society which admires the picaroon (from a sixteenth-century Spanish term), or rogue, illustrated in the novel by the story of Billy who cheats people of their houses. Naipaul summarises his view in his image of Trinidad as: 'A peasant-minded, money-minded community, spiritually static because cut off from its roots, its religion reduced to rites without philosophy, set in a materialist colonial society ...' Although this essay was written in 1962, the views he expresses in it are relevant to, and reflected in, A House for Mr. Biswas. Naipaul is concerned primarily to describe what he sees, rather than to hanker after the past in a nostalgic way, or to offer panaceas for the future. The reader of the novel is made to sense the inevitability of progress, and this is shown as having some positive aspects.

The flow of American dollars into the island, with the growing American presence there during the Second World War, brings prosperity, as well as a growing spirit of competition. It enables parents to send their children abroad to be educated. Mr. Biswas fears for his son's future if the boy does not get some kind of education, but his fears are transformed into hope and optimism when his son goes abroad on a scholarship. The education system itself is viewed in an ambivalent way. It is both a progressive force and responsible for the decay of Hindu tradition. It is Mr. Biswas's education which makes him think differently from his illiterate brothers and question the family structure in which he finds himself, just as it is Owad's educational superiority that automatically secures his recognition as head of the Tulsi clan. The system of education, however, with its emphasis on European topics, is shown as remote from Trinidad. Mr. Biswas is taught about oases and igloos on his entry to the 'new world' at school in Pagotes, topics as removed from his experience as the comic irrelevance of the assignments he is sent by the English school of journalism.

Similarly, Anand comes to see the sacred thread ceremony merely as a convenient excuse for absenting himself from school, for he and his father know that he could not present a shaved head in school without inviting ridicule from the other children and teachers. He is encouraged by Mr. Biswas to spend his retreat learning school notes, and his performance of the *puja* at Shorthills is a mockery – he diverts himself by sticking flower stems under the god's chin, and cannot treat the rituals seriously. This is the world which Owad and his brother Shekhar had entered 'where education was the only protection.'

These cultural changes are reflected also in language; Hindi is seen as the language of the society into which Mr. Biswas is born, but English begins to be used on public occasions, as, for instance, when Tara addresses the photographer at Raghu's funeral, and Hindi becomes the language of intimacy. Mr. Biswas and Shama begin their marriage speaking in English, 'for there was as yet little friendship between them'. In the city it can be a 'secret' language, as used by the widows when they visit Mrs. Tulsi's house, and the 'readers and learners' understand Hindi, but cannot speak it. Mr. Biswas himself uses English at Hanuman House 'even when the other person spoke Hindi' as a gesture of rebellion and independence; and by the end of the novel it is Trinidadian Creole English which holds sway.

Although Naipaul has protested against the idea that the novel is 'documentary', stating that: 'What I would do was to write according to my imagination, and then consult people on little items of inconsequential information to lend vividness and verisimilitude to the story', the novel does record social change in a concrete and convincing way. L. White summarises it neatly:

> By the end of the novel a whole history has passed before our eyes.... [Naipaul] chronicles the stages in the loss of India, the shift from country to town, from Hindi to English, from a preoccupation with Fate to a preoccupation with ambition, so that as we move from the world of Raghu to the world of Anand, we are dealing not only with the life of a man but also with the history of a culture.

Hinduism

The religion of Hinduism originated among the Aryan tribes in India. Hinduism is based chiefly on the caste system rather than on a system of beliefs or doctrines. There are five main castes; the highest of which is the Brahmin or priestly caste, to which Mr. Biswas belongs. Members of this caste are treated with respect, and to be a Brahmin is a sign of great status. This is seen in the novel where Mr. Biswas goes as a boy to Tara's house and is 'respected as a Brahmin and pampered'. He is dressed in a clean dhoti, and given a gift of money and cloth. Again, at Pundit Jairam's place he travels with him to perform the mechanical side of his offices, and, 'invested with the sacred thread and all the other badges of caste' is everywhere 'the object of regard'. The duties of a Brahmin include the performance of puja, or worship, which for the orthodox Hindu is centred in the home. It takes place in a room set aside for this purpose and containing a shrine, with an image of the family's chosen deity, together with other symbols of the sacred and vessels and instruments of worship such as bowls and lamps. Household worship makes use of fire for purification (a symbol of the sun); water, also for purification; food-offerings; incense; flowers; and coloured powders for ornamentation. It is carried out at certain fixed times: sunrise, midday and sunset. When worshipping, the orthodox Hindu will be dressed in the traditional way, wearing the sacred thread, and caste or sect marks on the forehead and sometimes the arms and other parts of the body.

Certain sacraments also take place, and are usually four in number:

> birth, initiation, marriage, and death. The ceremony of initiation plays some part in the novel when Anand, despite his distaste for religious ritual, becomes attracted by this ceremony which most of his male cousins have experienced. It involves being invested with the sacred thread and going into retreat to study and learn secret verses. Its main attraction for Anand is the shaving of the head. He asks for a print of the goddess Lakshmi to be hung on the wall of his room to whom he says his prayers, but this worship soon ends when his main motive for undergoing the ceremony – to miss school – is thwarted when Mr. Biswas arranges for it to take place during the long summer holiday. The sacrament of death should take place on the bank of a sacred river, and following the death, the corpse should be carried to a sacred spot to be cremated. In the case of Mr. Biswas, the cremation takes place on the banks of a muddy stream.

Hinduism also figures largely in the novel as forming part of Mr. Biswas's campaign against the Tulsis when he joins a breakaway movement of protestant Hindu missionaries who had come from India and adopted the ancient name of 'Aryans'. They preach that caste is unimportant, that Hinduism should accept converts, that idols should be abolished, and that women should be educated, thus 'preaching against all the doctrines the orthodox Tulsis held dear'. Mr. Biswas is impressed by the speeches of the leader, Pankaj Rai, and finds himself agreeing with the ideas that idols were an insult to the human intelligence and to God, and that a man's caste should be determined only by his actions, a point which seems to be proved by his brother-in-law Ramchand whose clean and comfortable hut 'indicated lowness in no way'. Pankaj Rai is soon discredited and his place taken by Shivlochan, BA., and the movement seems to disintegrate amidst arguments about the relative virtues of peaceful persuasion or militant conversion. However, Mr. Biswas continues to be influenced by his Hindu background, as we see when, for example, he recites the words 'Rama Rama' as protection during the storm at Green Vale, and Hinduism is a vital and integral part of the novel.

Plot

Mohun Biswas (Mr. Biswas) is born in rural Trinidad to parents of Indian origin. His birth is considered inauspicious as he is born "in the wrong way" and with an extra finger. A pundit prophesies that the newly born Mr. Biswas "will be a lecher and a spendthrift. Possibly a liar as well", and that he will "eat up his mother and father." The pundit further advises that the boy be kept "away from trees and water. Particularly water". A few years later, Mohun leads a neighbour's calf, which he is tending, to a stream. The boy, who has never seen water "in its natural form", becomes distracted watching the fish and allows the calf to wander off. Mohun hides in fear of punishment. His father, believing his son to be in the water, drowns in an attempt to save him, thus in part fulfilling the pundit's prophecy. This leads to the dissolution of Mr. Biswas's family. His sister is sent to live with a wealthy aunt and uncle, Tara and Ajodha, while Mr. Biswas, his mother, and two older brothers go to live with other relatives.

Mr. Biswas is withdrawn prematurely from school and apprenticed to a pundit, but is cast out on bad terms. Ajodha then puts him in the care of his alcoholic and abusive brother Bhandat which also comes to a bad result. Finally, Mr. Biswas now becoming a young man decides to set out to make his own fortune. He encounters a friend from his days of attending school who helps him get into the business of sign-writing. While on the job, Mr. Biswas attempts to romance a client's daughter and his advances are misinterpreted as a wedding proposal. He is drawn into a marriage which he does not have the nerve to stop and becomes a member of the Tulsi household.

With the Tulsis, Mr. Biswas becomes very unhappy with his wife Shama and her overbearing family, which bears a slight resemblance to the Capildeo family into which Naipaul's father married. He is usually at odds with the Tulsis and his struggle for economic independence from the oppressive household drives the plot. The Tulsi family (and the big decaying house they live in) represents the traditional communal world, the way life is lived, not only among the Hindu immigrants of Trinidad but throughout Africa and Asia as well. Mr. Biswas is offered a place in it, a subordinate place to be sure, but a place that's guaranteed and from which advancement is possible. But Mr. Biswas rejects that. He is, without realising it or thinking it through but through deep and indelible instinct, a modern man. He wants to BE, to exist as something in his own right, to build something he can call his own. That is something the Tulsis cannot deal with, and that is why their world—though that traditional world, like the old Tulsi house which is its synecdoche, is collapsing—conspires to drag him down. Nevertheless, despite his poor education, Mr. Biswas becomes a journalist, has four children with Shama, and attempts (more than once, with varying levels of success) to build a house that he can call his own. He becomes obsessed with the notion of owning his own house and it becomes a symbol of his independence and merit.

Significance

This novel is generally regarded as Naipaul's most significant work and is credited with launching him into international fame and renown. The prose is often cited as some of the best writing in contemporary English studies and cemented Naipaul's reputation as one of the finest writers in the language.. *Time* magazine included the novel in its "Time 100 Best English-language Novels from 1923 to 2005".

Adaptations

The novel was later adapted as a stage musical, with compositions by Monty Norman. One of the songs written for the play, "Good Sign, Bad Sign", was later rewritten as "The James Bond Theme", according to the documentary *Inside Dr. No.* A two-part radio dramatisation, featuring Rudolph Walker, Nitin Ganatra, Nina Wadia, and Angela Wynter ran on BBC Radio Four on March 26 and April 2, 2006.

Summary

Mohun Biswas is a Trinidadian Indian who dies at the age of forty-six in a house in Port of Spain where he has been living with his wife and four children. He was born in a country village, surrounded by ill omens. His family is scattered after his father's death and he moves with his mother to Pagotes. At school he discovers a talent for lettering, and later becomes a sign-writer. Initially, however, he is sent by his aunt Tara to the household of a pundit to learn to be a Hindu priest; but he leaves in disgrace after eight months and works in a rum shop run by Tara's drunken brother-in-law.

After being wrongfully accused of stealing he joins a former schoolfriend in the sign-writing business, in the course of which he goes to Hanuman House, the home of the Tulsis. He is then trapped into promising to marry Shama, the sixteen-year-old daughter of Mrs Tulsi, as he is of the right Hindu caste. No dowry is offered and he is expected to join the family workforce by working on the land with the other husbands. He immediately rebels, but without any money or position of his own he finds himself dependent on the Tulsi household from then until shortly before his death.

After successfully disrupting the smooth running of the house, Mr. Biswas is sent to a small rural village, The Chase, to act as manager of a Tulsi food shop. During the six years he spends there with his growing family, the shop continually loses money, and his family spend an increasing amount of time at Hanuman House. Finally he joins them there, and is then sent to Green Vale to act as overseer for Mrs Tulsi's powerful brother-in-law. He is wholly unsuited to such work and feels persecuted by the labourers under him.

He suffers a mental breakdown and has to return to Hanuman House to convalesce after a storm destroys the ramshackle house he has built. Forced to earn his living again, he leaves the Tulsis and goes to stay with his sister and her husband in Port of Spain. He finds work as a journalist on the Sentinel newspaper, and this leads to a reconciliation with the Tulsis. He goes to live with his family at Mrs Tulsi's house in the city which she shares with her younger son, Owad, until he is sent abroad to study medicine.

Mr. Biswas takes a growing interest in the education of his son Anand and a close relationship develops between them. Meanwhile the Tulsis move to an estate at Shorthills and Mr. Biswas is persuaded to join them. The Tulsi family begins to disintegrate under new social and economic pressures, and Mr. Biswas leaves after the house he builds there is destroyed by a fire. He returns to Mrs Tulsi's crowded house in the city and remains there until he moves to his own house in Sikkim Street after a fierce quarrel with Mrs Tulsi and Owad. His job at the Sentinel has changed to that of social investigator of

'Deserving Destitutes' which leads to a new lease of life when he is given a government post in a Social Welfare Department. His hopes, however, increasingly centre on Anand, who wins an exhibition to the prestigious Queen's College in the city. The house in Sikkim Street leads Mr. Biswas into heavy debt, especially as it is overpriced and in need of major repairs, but he is overjoyed at possessing his own house and land.

After the government department is disbanded, he returns to the Sentinel until put on half-pay when he develops heart-trouble and is eventually dismissed. Anand is now studying at university in England and does not return during his father's illness, but his daughter, Savi, returns and gets a well-paid job. Mr. Biswas then dies suddenly and receives a traditional Hindu cremation, after which his wife and children return to the empty house.

Prologue

Mr. Biswas is dismissed from his job at the Sentinel ten weeks before his death. Neither he nor his wife have any money to pay the mortgage on the house, but he is comforted by his wife's efforts to help him instead of returning to her family and by the wonder and triumph of having acquired his own house where he can wander freely and feel secure. The house was bought from a corrupt solicitor's clerk who had concealed its shoddiness and makeshift design from the eager Mr. Biswas. As soon as he and his wife Shama (who had shown hostility to the idea and had refused to look at the house) move in, they discover all the defects in its structure and layout; but they adapt to these quickly, and it seems to Mr. Biswas – on his first return from hospital – a welcoming and ready-made world.

Commentary

This introduction reports the death of the novel's main character, Mr. Biswas; thus we know that the main body of the novel will trace his life up to this point, and while the element of surprise is taken away by knowing of the death, Naipaul is free to use a variety of stylistic devices such as flashback scenes depicting events prior to the narrative and prediction of future events, which involve us closely in Mr. Biswas's life. We are also informed of how much the house matters to Mr. Biswas as a symbol of his freedom and independence.

Part 1

Chapter 1: Pastoral: Mr. Biswas was born away from his father's village in the hut belonging to his grandmother Bissoondaye. He is born the wrong way round, at midnight, and with six fingers, all of which are seen as portents of ill-luck and disaster. The pundit also predicts that the boy will be a lecher and a spendthrift because of his widely spaced teeth, and that he should be kept away from trees and water. He will also have an unlucky sneeze, as happens on the occasion of his father's drowning in the pond.

After his father's death the family have to leave, and thus Mr. Biswas escapes the expected course of events. This would have meant his remaining illiterate and working as a grass-cutter in the fields, perhaps saving enough money to rent or buy a few acres of land where he could plant his own sugarcanes. This is a path which his brother Pratap follows; he even becomes prosperous, with a house of his own. Tara, his mother's sister, comes to organise his father's funeral, and takes his sister, Dehuti, to live with her. His mother, Bipti, leaves her village after her garden is ransacked by some neighbours who mistakenly believe that her husband, who was thought to be the richest man in the village, had buried bags of money there. She takes Mr. Biswas with her to the town of Pagotes, where they live as dependent relations of Tara in a back street. The two brothers are sent to Felicity to work on the sugar estates and Mr. Biswas, who finds himself increasingly distant from his mother, feels isolated and alone.

Commentary: The first words spoken in this chapter, which refer to Fate and how people cannot fight it, summarise neatly the attitude of the older generation of Indian Hindus from which Mr. Biswas descends. He differs radically from them, however, in that he attempts to determine the course of his life himself in an active way, despite all the ill omens and pessimism expressed at his birth. The value of homes and houses is also emphasised in the final paragraph, since we are told that Mr. Biswas is now leaving 'the only house to which he had some right' and will be a 'wanderer' for the next thirty-five years without a house of his own, and his only family will be the Tulsis with their 'engulfing world.'

Chapter 2: Before the Tulsis: No traces remain of Mr. Biswas's birthplace, although the land his mother once owned later yields oil, and the swamp region becomes a garden city. Even his birth certificate has to be invented and drawn up by a Muslim solicitor, F. Z. Ghany. At the mission school he is taught by Lal, a converted Hindu, and learns many useless facts. He befriends Alec, who shocks the school by taking Dodd's Kidney Pills and passing blue urine. They keep their home lives secret, partly because Mr. Biswas is not happy there and still views it as a temporary arrangement. He feels detached from his brothers, now grown men, and only sees his sister when taking part in a religious ceremony at his aunt's house, where he is respected as a Brahmin and treated with honour. He also goes there to read to his uncle Ajodha from 'That Body of Yours'. After six years Mr. Biswas is taken away from school, and goes to live with pundit Jairam where he learns religious ceremonies, including the morning prayer ceremony, or *puja*. Two episodes discredit him – one when he steals two bananas, and the other when he defiles the sacred oleander tree with his soiled handkerchief. He returns to his mother in Pagotes, an incident he later romanticises in a poem; but he is soon sent to the sordid rum shop where he rebels against uncle Bhandat's mean and suspicious nature by spitting in the rum when he bottles it. He leaves (after a violent scene where he is accused of stealing money) determined to establish his independence and get his own job and house. During his hunt for a job he visits Dehuti and her husband Ramchand, Tara's disgraced yard boy; although he feels very separate from his sister, he is impressed that their hut is clean and comfortable with no signs of Ramchand's lower caste. A meeting with Alec then leads to his job as sign-writer. He escapes into novels in search of romance, and identifies with the heroes of Samuel Smiles. Finally his search takes him to Hanuman House in Arwacas.

Chapter 3: The Tulsis: Hanuman House, and the reputation of the Tulsis among Hindus, are described in detail. They are respected, though little is known about them. Mr. Biswas passes a note to Shama and is called to an interview with her mother and uncle Seth. He is found to be a suitable husband and surprises himself by agreeing to marry Shama. After the ceremony he begins to think of escape; he is appalled at the hierarchical organisation of the house where the daughters' husbands' names are forgotten and they are expected to become simply Tulsis. He rebels and returns to Pagotes. Here, however, he finds that he has achieved new status with his relations and starts to accept his role, and soon returns to the Tulsi house to find that he is seen there now as troublesome, disloyal and untrustworthy. His invective against the Tulsis, particularly the 'little gods', develops into a campaign against them. He becomes involved with a breakaway Hindu movement and satirises the Tulsis for being false Hindus by sending their sons to a Roman Catholic college. The confrontation comes to a head when Mr. Biswas refuses the offering at the *puja* and then spills a plateful of food on Shama's brother Owad. He is attacked by her brother-in-law Govind, and then ordered by Seth to leave.

Chapter 4: The Chase: Mr. Biswas moves to this isolated village to manage a small food shop, a venture which is destined to fail from the beginning as there is a large number of such shops. To Mr. Biswas his stay there seems always 'temporary and not quite real', a preparation for real life elsewhere. The shop is Tulsi property; the house is blessed by brother-in-law Hari at Shama's insistence. Even his daughter, Savi, is named by Seth and Hari, and is seen as a Tulsi. The decline of the business is furthered by Mr. Biswas's attempt through the corrupt lawyer, Seebaran, to regain lost credit. He himself gets into debt as a result. He finds he has aged during these six years of boredom and futility, but he remains optimistic that 'some nobler purpose awaited him', and consoles himself with religion and philosophy, painting foreign landscapes and indulging in eccentric habits. A son is born and his family spend more time away at Hanuman House. He wins acceptance there as a person skilled in wit and argument and views it as a sanctuary from the impersonal outer world. At the same time he resents its hold over his family, and when Shama declares she wants to return there for good, they quarrel frequently until he hits her. He does not see her until their third child is born, when he too leaves The Chase and joins her at Hanuman House, staying there until he is given work on the estate at Green Vale.

Commentary: This chapter highlights Mr. Biswas's growing fear of the future as a blankness and an empty space, a void into which he is falling, which develops into the breakdown at Green Vale. The fear is also linked with the recurring image of the boy standing outside a lonely country hut at evening which he had seen years earlier. In spite of this feeling of emptiness, however, the period at The Chase is also a time of acquiring possessions and leaving marks of habitation.

Chapter 5: Green Vale: Mr. Biswas moves into a small room in the barracks in the damp and shadowed vale. Being largely ignorant of sugarcane and estate work, he is scorned by the labourers who fear only Seth. He wishes to move into his own house, but Seth's promises to build him one are never carried out. His frustration at the sordid surroundings and fear of the workers are expressed at first in abuse of the Tulsis to Shama, who again retreats to Hanuman House, and then in solitary periods in his room. Shortly after Christmas he visits his children, taking a large doll's house to Savi, which is subsequently destroyed by Shama because of the disruption and jealousy it arouses.

He takes Savi to live with him for a week to 'claim' her; his wife returns briefly but becomes pregnant again, and he is left essentially alone. In an attempt 'to arrest his descent into the void' Mr. Biswas employs an incompetent carpenter to build a house, despite having little money to finance it. He becomes increasingly disturbed and restless and finds the objects in his room threatening, as well as the people he encounters. During a visit by his family he again hits Shama, who is pregnant, saying that she and the Tulsis are trying to kill him. She leaves, but his son, Anand, asks to stay. They move to the one finished room of the house, where the killing of Mr. Biswas's dog is followed by a fierce storm and the climax of Mr. Biswas's fears that 'they' are coming to destroy him. The house itself is struck by lightning.

Chapter 6: A Departure: Mr. Biswas and Anand are taken back to Hanuman House. Mr. Biswas gradually recovers and is able to piece together the past with its memories of horror. He is relieved to hear that the house has been burnt down completely by the labourers, thus freeing him from the past memories. He reviews his situation, reflecting that his position is still that of someone without a vocation or reliable means of supporting his family and that he would not be missed. He determines to establish his independence and feels that 'real' life with its 'especial sweetness' is still waiting for him to discover it.

Part 2

Chapter 1: 'Amazing Scenes': Mr. Biswas takes a bus to Port of Spain where he stays for a time with his sister and her husband. He feels stimulated and excited by the city, but wearies of his freedom, and the spasms of fear return. After an abortive visit to a medical specialist he recognises that he has to accept the past as a vital part of himself, and this restores the 'wholeness' of his mind. He also recognises that the spasms of fear on seeing people were caused by regret, envy, and despair, rather than fear. He acts decisively and gains a job writing on the Sentinel newspaper under Mr. Burnett where his talent for fantasy and facetious, humorous writing gains expression. As a shipping reporter he feels in contact with different parts of the world. He is reunited with his family and sees his fourth child, and as the climax of his current good luck, is given rooms in Mrs Tulsi's house in Port of Spain. His friendship with Owad develops and he establishes a closer and more disciplined relationship with his children, involving himself also in their education. He takes a short-lived writing course from London on journalism, and invents stories with a fantasy heroine entitled 'Escape'. He plants rose-bushes in the garden and begins to think of the house as his own. This order is disturbed by news of Owad being sent to England to study medicine, and Anand's near-drowning at the docks.

The first, macabre stories Mr. Biswas writes for the Sentinel reflect his guilt and anxiety about leaving his family, and also his feelings of insecurity and anxiety are given expression in the report of the Scarlet Pimpernel (his assumed name as he tours the island) spending the night in a tree.

Chapter 2: The New Regime: The house feels empty, as if awaiting change. Disaffections spread at Hanuman House as Mrs Tulsi ceases to control it effectively, and internal quarrels develop. The Sentinel's tone of frivolity becomes inappropriate with the approach of war and Mr. Burnett is sacked. The new editorial policy demands a strict adherence to fact, which Mr. Biswas finds sterile and unrewarding. He fears for his job also, sensing that his work is mediocre. Prices rise with the impact of the war and the quality of food declines. The quarrels with Shama, and his sense of being trapped, intensify, and the sense of expectation he had of the city and his life there disappears. Anand's life of study in the exhibition class is also taxing. The destruction of the rose garden by Seth to provide space for his lorries provokes a violent scene in which Mr. Biswas damages some of the furniture in the house.

Chapter 3: The Shorthills Adventure: The Tulsis leave Arwacas for a new estate in the mountains northeast of Port of Spain. Hanuman House is full of talk of the glories of the estate with its lush landscape and Shama wants to be part of the adventure. Mr. Biswas consents to move there after he visits it with Mrs Tulsi and is attracted by the idea of building his own house there and living cheaply. Shorthills represents for him an adventure, an interlude, and he remains detached from its declining fortunes, since his job gives him independence and he is able to plunder the land and exploit the philosophy of 'every man for himself'. For the children it means a nightmare existence with the problems of travel to school, and shortages of food.

The death of Hari is followed by that of Padma, and it seems that family has lost its cohesive power of virtue. Mr. Biswas decides to build his own house and withdraw, despite the isolation of the site. He invites his mother for a visit and she helps to clear the ground for the firing. It is this event which leads to the destruction of Mr. Biswas's third house by fire. His rivalry with another brother-in-law, an ambitious extrepreneur, begins at Shorthills. Mr. Biswas calls him 'W. C. Tuttle', this being the name of the author of his large collection of books, labelled by Mr. Biswas as 'trash'. Their rooms are opposite to each other.

Chapter 4: Among the Readers and Learners: Transport becomes impossible and Mr. Biswas moves back to two rooms in Mrs Tulsi's house in Port of Spain, along with the Tuttles, Govind and Chinta, and the widow, Basdai. A comic rivalry ensues over possessions, and the crowds and noise, increased by Basdai's schoolchildren boarders from Shorthills, drive Mr. Biswas to walk in the streets and to see his office as a haven. He feels he is excluded from the growing prosperity in the island and fears for Anand's future job prospects as involving only 'intrigue, humiliation and dependence'. He is appointed investigator for the Deserving Destitutes Fund, and is exposed constantly to failure and misery, as well as requests for help from the widows and Bhandat. He continues to visit Ajodha and becomes friendly with Jagdat, Bhandat's son; but there is much hostility between Ajodha and his two nephews. The internal rivalries in the house preoccupy him, including that between Anand and Vidiadhar, who are both in the exhibition class. Anand's schooling and personality are described fully with the build-up to the vital examination, which he passes with great success. Mr. Biswas's mother dies, and he commemorates her in an embarrassingly emotional prose poem which he writes for the literary group he has joined. He also writes a long letter to the doctor who delayed in signing her death certificate, and is rewarded by his letter being sent back and so acknowledged.

Mr. Biswas destroys his fantasy 'Escape' stories with their barren heroines when confronted with the sordid realities of Bhandat's lodging where he vilifies his Chinese mistress as an 'awkward barren cow'. This can be seen as part of Mr. Biswas's acceptance of the life around him and his past, though it could be seen also as a gesture of defeat and pessimism.

Chapter 5: The Void: Mr. Biswas involves himself closely in Anand's work at the college, and looks to his son increasingly as embodying his hopes for the future. He even loses his vision of possessing his own house again and feels much despair. A new job in a government social welfare department, however, gives him a fresh interest and sense of security. He earns extra money and has the luxury of a holiday in North Trinidad, as well as new clothes and a new car which he enjoys showing off. He feels his luck is too good to last as the department comes increasingly under attack. The Tuttles leave for their own house and the ailing Mrs Tulsi returns and exerts her tyrannies until revived by preparations for the return of Owad. Mr. Biswas has to move temporarily to a tenement, and revisits Hanuman House. The family then return to one room in Mrs Tulsi's house.

Chapter 6: The Revolution: Owad returns to a full house, 'like an old Hanuman House festival'. He is recognised as the new head of the family. His exploits are recounted endlessly, together with his glorification of Russia and anticipation of the socialist revolution in Trinidad. A strong antagonism develops, however, between Anand and Owad after a quarrel, and Mr. Biswas 'gives notice' after a breach with Mrs Tulsi. His meeting with the solicitor's clerk in a cafe leads to a visit to the house in Sikkim Street which at first seems inaccessible, though most desirable. The sale of the house at Shorthills makes the price of five thousand dollars less prohibitive and he goes ahead with the purchase, in spite of Shama's disapproval, after borrowing four thousand dollars from Ajodha. Owad spends more time away from home at his brother Shekhar's house – Shekhar has married a Presbyterian, Dorothy, who upsets the Tulsis – and with medical colleagues. Talk of the revolution now ceases.

Chapter 7: The House: The deficiencies of the new house are soon revealed, as well as the financial commitments it involves, and Mr. Biswas abuses the clerk as a crook and jerry-builder, a description which is confirmed by his elderly neighbour. The Tuttles visit, however, and are easily deceived and impressed by the house, and its inconveniences are rapidly forgotten. The yard is expanded and a garden planted.

Commentary: This chapter repeats and expands several points which were made in the prologue, but here the emphasis is on the importance of the house to the children, especially Anand, as providing a stable focus for their lives and a fixed point around which their memories of childhood can be organised. Owad marries Dorothy's Presbyterian cousin and establishes a private practice in San Fernando. The Community Welfare Department is abolished with the new urge to self-improvement brought about by the war and the American influence. Mr. Biswas returns to the Sentinel, but finds the work tedious and feels increasingly burdened by his debts. Savi and Anand go abroad on scholarships, and Mr. Biswas receives unhappy and worrying letters from his son which he responds to with long humorous letters of his own. His sense of waiting for events to happen (in this case the return of his children) intensifies. He suddenly suffers a heart attack and spends a month in hospital, after which he is put on half-pay by the paper. He grows lethargic and irritable, and is sacked after spending more time in hospital. The return of Savi compensates in part for Anand's absence, and things seem to grow bright.

The tone of his last letter to Anand is one of joy and thanksgiving. His death is then reported flatly in the paper, and Shama's sisters visit for the cremation ceremony on the banks of a muddy stream, followed by the return of Shama and the children to the empty house.

Some points and details given in the Prologue are repeated here and expanded. The technique of reporting Mr. Biswas's death in an impersonal form, as an item in a newspaper, adds to the pathos of his death and prevents any note of melodrama or sentimentality. The elegiac mood is also continued in the constraint and control of the final paragraph with its closing image of the empty house. This image also emphasises the significance of the house as a symbol in the novel.

Character of Mr. Biswas

Mohun Biswas (who is referred to as Mr. Biswas even when still a small baby) is a person who is subject to misfortune, as the ill omens present at his birth suggest. He is marked, however, by his continual resilience and optimism. Despite his feeling of being trapped by the Tulsis, he fights to maintain his independence and feels confident that life will eventually yield to him its sweetness and romance. A sense of despair and disillusionment troubles him later in life, but he fights against that too, and retains faith in the future both through his children and through achieving the status of a house-owner. At Hanuman House he conducts his campaign against the Tulsis with humour and inventiveness which show his wit and sense of absurdity. He invents a catalogue of animal names for the family, such as 'the old hen' for Mrs Tulsi, and mocks them for their strong and exclusive family loyalties and mixed religious affinities. At times his actions can seem petty and spiteful, and yet Naipaul succeeds in retaining our respect and liking for him as a character.

It is worth thinking about how Naipaul achieves this difficult balance. Part of the answer is that Mr. Biswas is able to make fun of himself as well as of other people, and so avoids becoming too superior and smug. He acts the role of clown or buffoon frequently, and even mocks his own appearance. In a scene at The Chase, he reflects how he does not feel like a small man, and yet the clothes hanging up were unmistakably those of 'a small man, comic, make-believe clothes.' A sense of insecurity also remains with him, so that he never feels periods of good fortune can be permanent, or believes in them fully. The effort to achieve the ownership of his house, reflected in the very title of the novel, thus becomes a need to establish a firm reality and independence of his own. The creativity shown in his painting and writing reflects this need further, as does his reading of fiction and philosophy. He needs to believe in the possibility of romance, and much of his frustration in the novel stems from the feeling that romance is always eluding him, especially after he becomes involved with the Tulsis.

This involvement reveals another major theme of the novel: that of the complex relationship between freedom and commitment. Freedom is shown as something which is desired, but feared at the same time, as it can cause feelings of emptiness and of not belonging or being necessary to another person or to society as a whole. These feelings are frequently at war in Mr. Biswas, and this conflict is shown in his changing attitudes to Hanuman House. Although he quickly rebels against its attempt to destroy his individuality by making him conform to the established rules and codes of behaviour, he also welcomes the feeling of security and orderliness which it offers. Here he is no longer simply a nonentity, but has a recognised role, even if it often seems a negative one. He himself feels on occasions that his campaign is pointless and degrading, and that his presence in the household is basically irrelevant since if he left, the family rituals would continue as before. It is at this point, at the end of Part 1, that he recognises that rebellion – to be constructive– must be accompanied by the positive act of constructing a better alternative, and he leaves for the city with this intention.

The process of building a separate identity and accepting the results of one's past actions and involvements is shown to be a painful and difficult process. It involves the shedding of fantasies and illusions we all possess, symbolised for Mr. Biswas in his 'Escape' stories which he eventually destroys, and accepting the reality and commitments which have (like Mr. Biswas's possessions) gradually accumulated almost without his being aware of it. The novel is thus partly about growing up, and attaining maturity and a sense of responsibility.

A similar ambivalence is shown in Mr. Biswas's religious views. Although he claims to reject any traditional Hindu attitudes, such as the rigid caste system (as is shown when he joins the Aryans), he enjoys his Brahmin status when at Tara's and Ramchand's homes, and possesses a certain fastidiousness about foods and smells – he refuses to stock salt beef and lard in his shop at The Chase, and in moments of fear and stress he chants Hindu phrases. He also receives a traditional Hindu cremation. Naipaul is showing us here the complex relationship that exists between the forces that shape an individual and his attempts to form his own personality and beliefs.

Mr. Biswas displays also a certain naivety or innocence in the judgements he forms of other people. It seems that he can be easily misled by people who can take advantage of his fears and ambitions. This deception happens with Moti and the lawyer Seebaran at The Chase; with the carpenter, Maclean, at Green Vale; and with the solicitor's clerk. At Hanuman House also he is deceived into thinking that he is marrying into a wealthy family and will receive a large dowry, but this hope proves hollow. A further concept that Naipaul is illustrating in the novel is the difference that can exist between appearance and reality, and this contrast is often a source of humour. The walls of Hanuman House appear to be concrete, but are in fact, as Mrs Tulsi proudly tells him, made of clay bricks. This disparity is shown most clearly in the house in Sikkim Street which again looks deceptively solid and deceives Mr. Biswas, and then, comically, the Tuttles.

Mr. Biswas himself is not all that he appears to be. As he says sadly to Shama: 'That is the whole blasted trouble. I don't look like anything at all. Shopkeeper, lawyer, doctor, labourer, overseer – I don't look like any of them.' As one of the Tulsi sons-in-law and as a journalist he can achieve a kind of status, but has always to return to his 'crowded, shabby room'. During his job as investigator of Deserving Destitutes, he reflects that the conditions he is living in are as bad as the people about whom he is writing. This element of vulnerability and lack of certainty help to make Mr. Biswas into a human and sympathetic person, as well as a kind of Everyman with whom we can identify. This also explains his words to his son during his breakdown at Green Vale when Anand asks him in a bewildered way 'Who are you?' Mr. Biswas replies: 'I am just somebody. Nobody at all. I am just a man you know'. Thus he resents, as we all do, the attempts of other people to categorise him and so reduce his individuality. He even alters his daughter's birth certificate where he is described by Seth as a labourer, and signs himself 'proprietor'.

His attempts at self-definition, then, constitute the main body of the novel. By finally owning his own house away from the Tulsis, who are described at the end of the prologue as 'that large, disintegrating and indifferent family', he has succeeded in laying claim to his portion of the earth and escaped the fate of having 'lived and died as one had been born, unnecessary and unaccommodated'.

Other Main Characters

To understand and appreciate Mr. Biswas fully, it is necessary to examine his relationship with three characters who are of particular importance to him: his son, his mother and his wife. His relationship with his son is close and often tense as they recognise in each other a common weakness and vulnerability. Each feels responsible for the other, and one senses that Anand, in particular, sometimes resents this emotional tie. This point may explain why, at the end of the novel, he decides not to return home when his father is dying. It is also significant that it was during this period, after Mr. Biswas was sacked from the Sentinel, that he most needed 'his son's interest and anger' since 'in all the world there was no one else to whom he could complain'. Mr. Biswas seems much closer to his son than he is to his wife Shama, as they share many characteristics and Anand models himself on his father. When Mr. Biswas first starts to take an interest in his son, after initially regarding him as a disappointment, he is struck by the fragility of his appearance. Their first real contact occurs when Anand chooses to remain with his father at Green Vale because, as he shyly admits, 'they was going to leave you alone'. Another link between them is established here – that of education, as Mr. Biswas teaches his son about Copernicus, and later introduces him to Dickens and other novelists. He is anxious that his son should not be like him; he wants him to succeed in a worthwhile career, and his hopes for the future increasingly focus on his son. He pays for private lessons and the esteemed diet of milk and prunes, and even helps with the writing of his essays. Despite Anand's claim that he does not want to be like his father when he is older, the boy is strongly influenced by him, and also in a sense learns from his mistakes and difficulties.

Thus we are told that, among the children at Shorthills, Anand is considered strong, though he is kept apart because of his 'satirical sense'. This began at first as 'only a pose, and imitation of his father' but then developed into an attitude of contempt which led to 'inadequacies ... self-awareness and a lasting loneliness' and also made him 'unassailable'. Though Mr. Biswas uses his gifts of caricature and humour to protect himself, particularly at Hanuman House, we still feel his essential vulnerability and suffering, partly because of his strong need and desire to belong and feel at home in society. Unlike his son, he can never sustain an attitude of detachment and aloofness for any length of time.

The relationship between Mr. Biswas and his mother, though it is not dealt with at any length, is felt as a strong force in the novel, and is treated by Naipaul with great delicacy and sensitivity. The relationship is expressed largely in negative terms in its effect on Mr. Biswas. After the death of his father, Mr. Biswas looks to his mother for greater support and comfort. After he returns from the rum shop, he asks his mother sadly why she keeps sending him to live with other people, and complains that: 'I have no father to look after me and people can treat me how they want'. When they live together at the back trace in Pagotes, she fills him with anger and depression as she constantly bewails her fate, and is shy of showing him affection in a house of strangers. He turns to Tara for motherly support – it is to her that he recounts the humiliating tale of the bananas, in the hope of being comforted.

There is, however, a shift in Mr. Biswas's view of his mother in the novel. He realises that she is a woman who is still energetic and capable when he visits her at Pagotes during his period at The Chase, and again when he sees her at Pratap's home during his travels as the Scarlet Pimpernel. She comes to stay with him at Shorthills for a fortnight and again surprises Mr. Biswas and wins his respect by her efficiency, and by the calmness and acceptance with which she views their relationship. He still, however, feels very guilty about his mother, knowing that he has neglected her in the past and has felt ashamed of her poverty. He feels after her death that he has never known her or loved her, and his poetic tribute to her – as well as his lengthy letter to the doctor – are attempts to express his grief and guilt, and so come to terms with them and be 'whole' again. This guilt also influences Mr. Biswas's purchase of the house in Sikkim Street when the solicitor's clerk uses the pretext of needing to provide his own ageing mother with greater comfort as the reason for a quick sale. Naipaul succeeds in presenting this flawed relationship, linked as it is with a sense of loss and of 'something missed', without any traces of sentimentality or idealisation. This is one of his great strengths as a novelist: in his treatment of Mr. Biswas and other characters, he is able to blend a certain detachment and objectivity with human warmth and compassion.

The same comment can be made about the relationship between Mr. Biswas and his wife. This, too, is flawed in that neither husband nor wife really understands each other. Shama, with her mixed allegiances to the Tulsis and to her husband, remains largely a puzzle to her husband. Though she occasionally rebels against her husband for his disruptive behaviour, usually by leaving him, she is staunchly loyal and accepts what fate has given her. She is able to share his jokes about her family, though reminding him of his dependence on them. She fears any severing of her ties with the Tulsis since, as Mr. Biswas recognises with an element of bitterness, ambition for her consists largely of 'a series of negatives: not to be unmarried, not to be childless, not to be an undutiful daughter, sister, wife, mother, widow'. Unlike her husband, she is happy to conform, and cannot understand the necessity for his rebellion. Nonetheless Mr. Biswas is glad of her presence and company. At The Chase, for example, she banishes the silence and loneliness, and his breakdown at Green Vale is partly caused by her long absences with the children and his subsequent isolation. He comes increasingly to rely on her powers of judgement, even though he still acts independently, as over the purchase of his last house. He is sometimes embarrassed by her lack of education, as in the scene with Miss Logie, where Shama talks garrulously to her during the drive to Sans-Souci. This scene also shows that Mr. Biswas is unaware of certain aspects of his wife's character, just as he was surprised to find her childhood mementoes, signs of her contact with the outside world, in the drawer of the dressing-table during their move to Green Vale. In spite of its inadequacies, the marriage tie is shown as strong and enduring, providing a point around which both characters can build and define their lives.

Minor Characters

Mrs Tulsi: Mrs Tulsi is the centre of the Tulsi family around which the other characters revolve. She is the widow of Pundit Tulsi, a respected figure both in his native India and in Trinidad, and the whole family gain prestige from his reputation. Mrs Tulsi (or 'Mai', meaning mother, as she is frequently called) maintains a matriarchal tyranny over the household and its various members. It is significant that in Hanuman House, the usual Hindu tradition by which daughters go to live with their husbands and become almost servants of their mothers-in-law is reversed, in that the husbands stay in the daughters' household and become subservient to their mother-in-law, Mrs Tulsi. This is part of the humiliation which Mr. Biswas feels so strongly and tries to reject. The manipulation which Mrs Tulsi directs towards those around her is cleverly concealed (though not from Mr. Biswas) under an appearance of martyrdom and suffering. If someone steps out of line, she faints and retires to the Rose Room where she is endlessly massaged by the faithful Sushila and other daughters, and remains there until the offending son-in-law, who encounters silence and hostility on all sides, is forced to capitulate and apologise to her.

Mr. Biswas is on many occasions subject to the whims and emotional blackmail of the 'old fox'. She is able to control her moods according to the occasion, to become maudlin and sentimental to disarm her opponent. This is shown when she tries to win Mr. Biswas back to family allegiance after the birth of Savi, whom he wishes to name Lakshmi. She makes a number of simple statements which strike Mr. Biswas as possessing a 'puzzling profundity', and he finds himself listening against his will and being 'trapped' by her mood. She is proud of her authority and her 'oldfashionedness', and the floggings she has administered to her daughters have become legendary. She will also resort to a biting sarcasm when necessary and Mr. Biswas, on first meeting her, is struck by her command of English. When Mr. Biswas offends against the Tulsi demand for the suppression of individuality by buying the large doll's house for Savi, Mrs Tulsi declares that she is poor and gives to all but cannot 'compete with Santa Claus' and she asks Shama to give her notice before moving to 'her mansion'. Like her brother-in-law Seth, who rules with her, she is capable of surprising crudity in her language as when she tells Mr. Biswas to 'go to hell' during their final quarrel.

The novel shows the decline of the Tulsi family which is caused by internal wrangles and the disruptive effects of a different culture. Mrs Tulsi is anxious for her sons to succeed and sends them to a Roman Catholic college, thus compromising her Hindu beliefs – as Mr. Biswas is quick to point out with his image of her as 'the orthodox Roman Catholic Hindu' who has salmon only on Good Friday. Mrs Tulsi moves to Port of Spain when she feels that the 'younger god' Owad should be looked after during his schooling following his brother's marriage. It is at this point that the power structure in Hanuman House begins to be threatened, since Seth, though he can maintain control, fails to impose harmony. The family feud with Seth furthers the decline of the household, and when Owad is sent abroad to study to become a doctor, Mrs Tulsi appears to lose interest in the family and ceases to direct it until she is revived by the move to Shorthills. Here again, however, her interest soon languishes, though she issues some directives about food and possible economies.

We are told that, after the death of Mrs Tulsi's sister, Padma, the 'virtue' of the family dissolves, and Mrs Tulsi assumes more and more the role of an invalid. She is still able to exert control over her daughters, and on her move to the city from Shorthills, succeeds in making their lives a misery as she develops her command 'of invective and obscenity'. She is revived by the return of Owad, and exerts herself to please him while her health improves 'spectacularly' under his treatment, thus betraying her obvious hypochondria. After Owad is alienated by the quarrel with Anand and his increasing association with his own friends and Dorothy's cousin, she tries in vain to win him back by talking about his boyhood and Pundit Tulsi and her own sufferings; but it is now too late. She is a character for whom the reader feels little sympathy, but she is a source of much humour and satire in the novel, as well as showing the decline of traditions through her failure to maintain them. We also see, through her involvement with Roman Catholicism, the dilution of Hindu culture and religious ritual.

Seth: Seth, the husband of Padma, is presented as a powerful figure in the novel who intimidates Mr. Biswas with his bullying manner and the self-assured way in which he flourishes his ivory cigarette holder though dressed in muddy boots and a stained khaki topee. He shows contempt for those who are not prepared to work on the land and dirty their hands, and is nicknamed the 'big thug' by Mr. Biswas. He is a staunch supporter of family loyalty in the first half of the novel and conducts the family tribunals, where the misdemeanours of Mr. Biswas are criticised and ridiculed. It is Seth who names him 'the paddler' and who refers to the house being turned into a republic with a 'serpent' in its midst. Seth is still shown as possessing some good points; at times he shows a brusque kindness to Mr. Biswas – addressing him as Mohun, joking with him over the birth of his first child, and rescuing him from trouble with the police when cycling without a light, though this is partly to protect the family name. There is a note of amused irony in some of his comments to Mr. Biswas which suggests that he is both puzzled and amused by his persistent rebellion. Thus he questions him about his 'dear friend', Pankaj Rai, and jokes that he will now have 'Creole converts' as brothers. In contrast to the rather naive Mr. Biswas, Seth appears a worldly figure with his plans to 'insuranburn' and his later business ventures, and he seems to adopt an avuncular attitude to the former at times. After his breakdown at Green Vale, Seth says 'I suppose we have to bring the paddler home'. It is Seth's disaffection, which begins obscurely with an internal family quarrel involving Shekhar, that marks the break-up of the close family network. Seth begins to be seen as an outsider, and his character is adversely affected.

We see this when he comes to uproot the rose bushes in Mrs Tulsi's garden to make room for his lorries. He tells Mr. Biswas's children that everyone seems to be defying him, and rather cruelly tells them that their father was 'picked up' by him when 'catchingflies.' He is excluded from the move to Shorthills as the disagreement becomes open war, and starts to claim Tulsi property as his own, even attempting to establish a rival store. The feud then dwindles after he gets involved in legal charges against him, and becomes 'quiescent.' Our last view of him is of a rather sad and pathetic figure, dressed incongruously in a cheap suit, trying in vain to effect a reconciliation with the family through Owad on the latter's return. Like Mr. Biswas, we feel sympathy for Seth here, with the contrast between his present position and the one he occupied previously at Hanuman House.

Owad: Owad, the younger of the two 'little gods,' is noted for his terrible temper as a boy, and he confronts Mr. Biswas directly and wants him to apologise to his mother for calling her names. He accuses Mr. Biswas of being a Christian after he rejects the offering at the morning *puja*. He is also the victim of the contents of the plateful of food which Mr. Biswas throws from the balcony, and urges Govind to kill Mr. Biswas during their tussle. This conflict is later forgotten when Owad and Mr. Biswas form a friendship while living at the house in Port of Spain, based on a mutual respect for each other's intellectual pursuits, and Mr. Biswas is upset and envious when Owad goes abroad. On the latter's return, there is a distance between them, and Owad becomes largely a comic figure whom Naipaul satirises for boasting about his contacts and importance abroad and for his superficial and short-lived adherence to the Russian Revolution. Being viewed as the new head of the family, he is listened to and consulted as an absolute authority. We learn that because of Owad's objections to the behaviour and habits of Indians from India, who were 'a disgrace' to Trinidad Indians, in one afternoon 'the family reverence for India had been shattered.' He emphasises physical strength and manual skills, and entertains the family by recounting his adventures. His allegiances soon shift to his own friends, the 'new caste' of educated professional men, and his friendship with Dorothy, the renegade Presbyterian sister-in-law, leads to his eventual marriage to Dorothy's Presbyterian cousin, an Indian girl from South Trinidad. In this way, he reflects the changes that have taken place in the society at this period.

Shekhar: Shekhar is the other 'little god.' He figures little in the earlier part of the novel, and, after initial rebelliousness, marries a

Presbyterian girl whose family have successful commercial concerns. He leaves Hanuman House and goes to live with his wife's family, thus going against the Hindu custom and the family tradition of bringing the bride home. He prospers as a businessman, though reputedly envying his brother his travel abroad, having himself wanted to go to Cambridge. Like Owad, he becomes distant from the Tulsis and their traditions as he acquires more sophistication, shown by his parting gifts to his brother: a bottle of wine, American magazines, and an English history book. He also runs cinemas as part of his business, and offends the widows by offering them work there, an insult which they regard as the influence of his wife, Dorothy. She displays Western influences: she wears short skirts, calls herself Dorothy, and 'flaunts' her education. She also speaks Spanish to her five daughters and her husband in the presence of her sisters-in-law. Both she and Shekhar are friendly with Mr. Biswas, and later with Owad, though Mr. Biswas comes to resent the role of buffoon to which they expect him to conform, and feels nervous and vulnerable when the party of Southern businessmen with whom Shekhar is involved issue veiled threats about the viability of the Community Welfare Department. But Shekhar's party is defeated in the colony's first general election, and Shekhar withdraws from public life to concentrate on his cinemas. Thus, like Owad, he reflects the decline of Hindu influences and the emphasis in the 'new' world on education and self-advancement.

Govind: Govind, whose wife Chinta is Shama's closest sister, is used as a contrast to Mr. Biswas, particularly as regards their status and attitudes at Hanuman House. Mr. Biswas is struck by the way Govind conforms to the Tulsi tyranny and is degraded in the process. In the presence of Seth, he becomes obsequious and weak in his anxiety to please. Mr. Biswas is pained by the capitulation of this tall and handsome man and tries to spur him to rebellion. However, his abuse of the family is reported by Govind who is intent on protecting the family, as he shows again when he fights Mr. Biswas for having insulted Owad. Their next contact is when Govind carries Mr. Biswas into Hanuman House after he is brought from Green Vale, so putting himself 'on the side of authority'. He clearly finds security in Hanuman House which raises him from his former position as an illiterate coconut-seller.

After leaving Hanuman House, Govind attempts to become more independent. At Shorthills he sells trees from the estate, and becomes increasingly surly and bad-tempered. He buys a second-hand car and runs it as a taxi in Port of Spain. On the move to the city, he expands his business and acquires several suits which become part of the battle of possessions in the household. His rivalry with Mr. Biswas is continued through their sons, Vidiadhar and Anand, who both study for the exhibition to the college. Govind then becomes increasingly violent and behaves in an odd and unpredictable manner, and is regarded as 'the terror of the house' until he takes to beating his wife and confines his aggression to that outlet.

Hari: Hari is another brother-in-law whose position at Hanuman House contrasts with that of Mr. Biswas. He has won for himself a definite place of respect in the Tulsi hierarchy and is even excused from labouring work because of his reputation as a holy man and pundit, as well as his illnesses. He is a colourless man who '... offended no one and amused no one', though Mr. Biswas makes fun of him as the 'constipated holy man.' He takes no part in disputes and his apparent goodness is attributed largely to 'a negativeness that amounts to charity.' After his death, which evokes some pathos when we learn through Anand that he had known he was going to die for some time, he is found to have been indispensable. He is indirectly responsible for Mrs Tulsi's growing conversion to Roman Catholicism since she cannot find an adequate replacement for Hari at the *puja*. Like Govind, he suggests the price of conformity through the drabness of his character, and though Mr. Biswas occasionally envies him his position in the Tulsi household, he knows that he himself could not live the life of a 'sick scholar.'

W. C. Tuttle: W. C. Tuttle functions mainly as a comic figure in the novel. He is named by Mr. Biswas when he first meets him at Shorthills and they develop a rivalry over possessions, referring to each other's books as 'trash.' He is a man with a variety of interests and allegiances. He is a strict Hindu, proud of his Brahminical status, but is as interested in the material as the spiritual life. At Shorthills he engages in a number of business ventures, which include starting a furniture factory and a quarry. On the move to the city, he takes over most of Mrs Tulsi's house, and dominates the house with popular Western songs on his gramophone. He is 'all for modernity' and shocks the household by acquiring a statue of a naked woman. He regards himself as blending the Brahmin culture with the 'finer products' of Western civilization, and views the Tulsis as barbarians, adopting towards most people an attitude of silent contempt which he conveys by a quivering of his nostrils. He appears to win decisively the battle of possessions when he acquires his own house, a move to which Mr. Biswas reacts 'badly', but the latter is compensated when the Tuttles come to visit him at his own house in Sikkim Street and are clearly impressed by the house, even being somewhat jealous of its apparent size and comfort.

Ajodha: Ajodha is the husband of Tara, and uncle to Mr. Biswas. He is a man of wealth who has freed himself from the land, and was one of the first men in Trinidad to buy a car. The chief fascination he has for Mr. Biswas during the latter's childhood is when he asks Mr. Biswas to read him the newspaper column entitled 'That Body of Yours', a job which is later taken over by Anand. He functions later as a model of contentment for Mr. Biswas, since he possesses his own house and has an attentive wife. To the Tulsis, however, he is a renegade who has deserted the Hindu faith and aligned himself with wealth, comfort and modernity. He becomes increasingly preoccupied with his quarrels with his two nephews, Jagdat and Rabidat, who live with him after being deserted by their own father. He feels bound to his nephews since, like Mrs Tulsi, he fears being alone in his old age, and distrusts strangers too much to allow them to help in his business. The model of family contentment thus becomes an illusion on Mr. Biswas's part, as he recognises himself. It is significant that he goes to Ajodha to borrow the money for his house and thus reinforces his ties to his own family, rather than depending on the Tulsis as before.

Tara: Tara is Bipti's more powerful sister. She is regarded as a person of standing through her marriage to the wealthy Ajodha. When Raghu dies, she takes over the funeral arrangements in an energetic and capable manner, and is scornful of her sister's ignorance of her husband's financial affairs. She adopts a motherly role towards Mr. Biswas and she decides to have him trained as a pundit. It is she to whom he returns later with his children on a series of regular visits, from which his wife excludes herself because of the old antagonism between the two families. Tara also has strong moral standards; she refuses to allow Dehuti to be mentioned after she elopes with Tara's yard boy, Ramchand, thus depriving her of two family servants, and her brother-in-law Bhandat receives the same treatment because of his drunkenness and Chinese mistress.

Bhandat: Bhandat, the brother of Ajodha, is a symbol of failure and destitution. He is a small man with a whining voice and irritable manner. He drinks and cheats by altering the accounts in the rum shop which he runs for his brother, helped briefly by Mr. Biswas. He reappears later as a destitute in the city, and writes to Mr. Biswas for help. When the latter visits him, he adopts a sentimental and self-pitying manner, as well as playing the schoolboy prank of pulling Mr. Biswas's hair. He is clearly frustrated and tormented and abuses his Chinese mistress in Hindi. He himself is deaf, and is a figure for whom we feel a mixture of contempt and pity in his futile attempts to compose slogans for a competition, and the squalor in which he lives.

Style and Structure

The novel is divided into two parts, enclosed by a Prologue and an Epilogue. The plot structure is part of a long British novelistic tradition as represented by Charles Dickens (1812–70) with its concentration on the life history of a single protagonist, and the tracing of his fortunes from birth to death, with the accompanying search for self-fulfilment and recognition. The novel also traces the rise and fall of the Tulsi family, and the changes in society over a period of fifty years. It is difficult to date the events in the novel precisely, but it seems to cover the period between 1905 and 1951, so including the two major world wars – the second of which does impinge on the novel with its economic effects and the growing American influence. Naipaul, however, does not wholly conform to the model defined above. The hero's death, for instance, is reported in the Prologue, and throughout the novel there is a subtle series of cross-references and recurring images.

A minor example of the latter is the description of the legs of Pratap and Prasad on returning from the muddy buffalo pond which had turned white 'so that they looked like the trees in fire-stations and police-stations which are washed with white lime up to the middle of their trunks,' an image which Mr. Biswas recalls when he leaves Hanuman House and Arwacas after his period of convalescence and sees the palm trees in the drive to the police-station. A more notable example is the catalogue of Mr. Biswas's possessions which is used to represent different phases of his life and to act as a concrete reference to his past experiences. At each move to another house, the growing list is detailed. After the time at Shorthills, for example, Mr. Biswas has gained 'only two pieces of furniture: the Slumberking bed and Théophile's bookcase'. For the reader, also, each item of furniture becomes overlaid with particular associations, and so helps to bind the novel together and give it unity. A feeling of pathos is also evoked by the list of these 'gatherings of a lifetime' when they are exposed for the last time on the move to Sikkim Street and seem 'unfamiliar and shabby and shameful'.

Perhaps the most striking characteristic of Naipaul's style is his power of observation. He shows precision and clarity, as well as a close attention to detail and an ability to create mood and atmosphere in a realistic and evocative way. He comments in An Area of Darkness that landscapes are not truly real until they have been given the quality of myth; but there is always a solidity and concreteness about his descriptions. The barracks at Green Vale, for example, are described at one point as 'a place that was nowhere, a dot on the map of the island, which was a dot on the map of the world'.

This abstract comment is then followed by the observation that '... dead trees ringed the barracks, a wall of flawless black'. Naipaul does not flinch from describing unpleasant sights, such as the scabs formed by the sores which Mr. Biswas has as a child, but the language used is never sensational or exaggerated.

This sense of control comes partly from the distance that Naipaul maintains from the material he is handling, which enables him to avoid falsely romanticising his subject and makes the material seem realistic and credible. An example of this is the careful detailing of Mr. Biswas's breakdown at Green Vale. By reporting this process in an unemotional tone, usually in the form of statements, he gives the writing great power and dramatic effect.

When Mr. Biswas moves into his incomplete house, he becomes obsessed with the asphalt on the roof which melts and looks like a number of snakes. They even begin to appear in his dreams, and 'He began to regard them as living, and wondered what it would be like to have one fall and curl on his skin'. When this horror occurs, it is reported in a matter-of-fact way which serves to intensify the horror far more than a more melodramatic description could have done. 'A snake had fallen on him. Very thin, and not long. When they looked up they saw the parent snake, waiting to release some more'.

This restraint in the writing is a difficult achievement for any writer, and is one of Naipaul's great strengths. We experience the sufferings of Mr. Biswas more intensely because of this careful and delicate contrast between the awfulness of a particular event and the contained way in which it is described. A further example is the destruction of the doll's house which Mr. Biswas has given his daughter, one of the most traumatic experiences which he has in the novel. Once again, however, the event is described in a simple style which allows the reader to imagine the emotions involved vividly. Mr. Biswas discovers the doll's house thrown against a fence in the yard at Hanuman House: 'A broken door, a ruined window, a staved-in wall or even roof – he had expected that. But not this. The doll's house did not exist. He saw only a bundle of firewood. None of its parts was whole. Its delicate joints were exposed and useless.'

Symbolism and Imagery

The example of the doll's house also shows the powerful use of symbolism in the novel. Here the doll's house, and its destruction, are identified with Mr. Biswas himself. The house appears to have a human body, with the references to 'delicate joints' and later to 'torn skin.' There are many uses of symbolism in the novel: symbols can be linked with places and with people, or with both. Thus the description of Hanuman House as an 'alien white fortress' suggests the foreign nature of the Tulsis and their Hindu religion in Trinidad, and the way in which the house will be a prison to Mr. Biswas against which he must rebel with his own weapons. This could be termed a 'multiple' symbol since it evokes more than one image, and there are several other symbols which operate in this way. There is the recurrent image of the boy standing outside a house at dusk which Mr. Biswas first observes when acting as a conductor on one of Ajodha's buses. It becomes associated for him with a feeling of desolation and loneliness, and is linked symbolically with his need for stability and a home to give a sense of certainty and security.

Naipaul also uses descriptions of nature and landscape to echo the themes of the novel and to act as symbols. When associated with the Tulsis, the landscape often takes the form of an uncontrolled and decaying jungle. The shop at The Chase is surrounded by abandoned land which fosters nettles and weeds, and around Green Vale there are half dead leaves, and it is 'damp and shadowed and close'. At Shorthills the fertile and productive land is largely uncultivated and becomes a wilderness. In Mr. Biswas's house in Sikkim Street, however, nature is seen as something beautiful and even lyrical, with the coolness of the laburnum and the scent of the lily which comfort Mr Biswas during his final illness. When he plants a garden at Mrs Tulsi's house in Port of Spain the rose trees flourish; but as his despair and disillusionment deepen, the roses, untended, grow 'straggly and hard' and are damaged by a blight. The symbolism in the novel is rarely obtrusive or heavy-handed, and, like the central symbol of the house itself, the symbols gradually accumulate additional force and meaning in the course of the novel.

One isolated symbol which deserves comment is the image of the winged ants which Anand watches during the storm at Green Vale. In this episode we see the destruction of one type of ant by another more fitted to survive. Anand tries to kill the black, biting ants but abandons this as futile when he is suddenly terrified by their anger and vindictiveness. This episode can be seen as illustrating the compassion that Anand feels for the victim, but also his frustration and anger when he recognises the futility of the weak trying to help the weak. These feelings are echoed in his relationship with his father, particularly at this moment when Mr. Biswas is huddled on the bed reciting Hindu words, and imagining that 'they' have come to get him.

Humour and Satire

These two elements are central in the novel and are often linked, since satire uses ridicule, irony, and sarcasm to criticise its object. Irony is the dominant technique for creating humour, particularly in the descriptions of the feuds between Mr. Biswas and the Tulsis. Mr. Biswas comments to Shama at one point, when she is threatening to return to Hanuman House after a quarrel, that she will be given 'some medal at the monkey house'; and he invents animal names for the main members of the family, as well as referring to Mrs Tulsi's two sons as the 'little gods'. These descriptions, though absurd and farcical, also contain some truth and so gain our sympathy and we laugh with Mr. Biswas at the pretensions and petty tyrannies of the Tulsis. Particular incidents at the Tulsi establishment are also humorous and even border on slapstick, such as the spilling of a plate of food on Owad's head.

The humour is also directed at times against Mr. Biswas himself; this adds to the complexity and richness of the novel since it avoids a simplified response in the reader, and also contributes to the picture we have of Mr. Biswas's character.

Thus, when he refers to Hanuman House as being like a 'blasted zoo', Shama comments that he has the role of a barking puppy dog, a description which, again, contains an element of truth. Mr. Biswas is frequently satirised in the novel, and his weaknesses exposed. The use of the third person – Mr. Biswas – creates in itself a distancing effect for the reader, and we see Mr. Biswas as essentially a complex and rounded character. There is humour in his battle for possessions with W. C. Tuttle at the house in Port of Spain, a battle in which he is fully engaged and which continues until he finally buys his own house. A similar rivalry is shown with Govind over clothes. There is a humorous scene when Mr. Biswas dresses up in his expensive new suit and goes to a cricket match to show it off, only to find that the match is almost over.

6 In a Free State

In a Free State is a novel by V.S. Naipaul published in 1971, consisting of a framing narrative and three short stories, the last one also titled *In a Free State.* It won the Booker Prize for 1971.

The work is symphonic with different movements working towards an overriding theme. What that theme is, is not too clearly spelled out, but there is an important aspect relating to the price of freedom with analogies between the three situations. The narrator is initially on a ferry to Egypt, and concludes many years later as a tourist in Egypt again.

Summary

"In a Free State," winner of England's Booker prize ($12,000), takes the story one step further. How does the expatriate fare after he leaves the island? Is he better off in a bed-sitter than in a wooden house off a dusty road on a tropical island? The author doesn't quite put it that way.

He lifts the argument above and beyond geographical circumstances, beyond material success and social position. These new stories focus on the failure of heart, on the animallike cruelty man exhibits to other men and on the avarice that, as Chaucer's Pardoner told, is the root of all evil. Are we in a free state really? Or are organisms driven by the violent compulsions within us?

In England, a brother takes advantage of a brother, patrons of a shopkeeper, one group of workers of another group. On a ship to Alexandria, two Lebanese, with the help of a German who in other circumstances would not have soiled his hands with them, turn on a poor ratty tramp. In Egypt, an Egyptian flunky lays his whip to the backs of children scrounging for uneaten sandwiches thrown on the sand by Italian tourists. What the author is saying is that neither customs nor colour nor culture seems able to quiet that impulse to destruction, that murderous wantonness that is so much part of our makeup.

The longest story in the book, the title story, is set in an African colony, once British, now given its freedom. Two tribes, long enemies are struggling to rule the freed state. The head of one is the King; the head of the other is the President. With the help of the Army, the President wins out. The point is that in spite of modern trappings (President vs. monarch) the contest is the continuation of age-old rivalries by other means. Each tribe is happy to exterminate the other.

At a time when the crisis is coming to a head, two white English civilians, a civil servant and his woman passenger, are returning to the safety of their compound along a road that is far from safe. That road becomes another Mississippi in "Huck Finn," another wine- dark sea of the Odyssey. For the adventures on that highway reveal the new state to the occupants of the car and themselves to each other. An old English colonel, a leftover from the past, who runs a cheap hotel, humiliates his cook before his guests—an act that is sure to bring reprisals. The young driver, sympathetic to the aim of the new state, exhibits the usual white man's arrogance as soon as his vehicle suffers minor damage. The servants of the independent regime, having stored up their wrath, show the same savagery to the travellers as was once shown them. All the reactions are senseless. They are responses to fear, to previous hurts, to the absence of charity. It is ironic that the couple in the car hasten to the compound for safety, though in a fundamental sense there can be no safety there either. Mr. Naipaul draws no overt moral, but it is present on every page.

First Tale

The first tale concerns an Indian servant from Bombay who, having no real alternative at home, accompanies his master on a diplomatic mission to Washington, D.C.. The two Indians suffer abominably from the poor value of Indian currency. The servant lives in almost a cupboard and inadvertently blows several weeks salary just buying a snack. However he gets to meet a restaurant proprietor who offers him an apparent fortune as a salary, so he absconds and works for him. Once he has his affairs in reasonable order, however, he starts to live in fear that his master will find him and order him back. He also learns that he is working illegally and liable to deportation. The only way of resolving the situation is to marry a woman who had seduced him but whom he had avoided ever since out of shame for his behaviour.

Second Tale

The second story has an unreliable narrator. It concerns a rural West Indian family, a set of cousins, one of whom being in a better situation manages to humiliate the narrator. The richer family has a son who goes to Canada and is destined to do well, while the others can expect nothing. The younger brother of the second family then sets out for England to study engineering, while his elder brother does all he can to support him. Eventually the elder brother follows him to England with the aim of helping him further. He works all hours in demeaning jobs to keep him, but eventually makes enough money to set up his own business. However he discovers that the brother, despite appearances is doing no studying at all, while his restaurant is frequented by yobs. The narrator, in a fit of rage, murders one of these yobs, who is in fact a friend of his brother. The story ends when he attends his brother's wedding, with a prison guard for company.

Main Tale

The story is set in an East African state that has recently acquired independence. The King, although liked by the Colonials, is weak, and is on the run while the President is poised to take absolute power. The level of violence in urban centres of the country is rising and there are rumours of violence in the countryside. There is mention of the Asian community being "deported". Bobby is an official who has been attending a conference in the capital city. He now heads back to the governmental Compound where he lives, and he has offered a lift to Linda, another colleague's wife. We learn early on that Bobby is homosexual. He is rebuffed by a young Zulu when he tries to pick him up at the Hotel bar. He soon discovers that Linda has plans of her own as they embark on the journey.

The relationship between the two is complex from the outset; it seems Bobby is intent on aggravating the initially calm Linda. His previous history of mental illness is explored. Things go from bad to worse when they put up at a Hotel, run by an old Colonel who can not adapt to the new conditions in the country. There, they have dinner, and they witness a scene between the Colonel and Peter, his servant, who he accuses of planning his murder. Furthermore Bobby discovers that Linda was planning some extra marital activity with a friend along the way, and he becomes furious and hostile.

The two reach their destination, but not before witnessing the site where the old King was recently murdered, a philosophical Muslim planning to move to Egypt and the beginnings of a genocidal wave of violence. Bobby is beaten by the army at a check point, where he and Linda experience first hand the growing violence. The story follows the conventions of a road trip with the reader becoming aware, as do Bobby and Linda, of the situation and how serious it has become.

7 The Enigma of Arrival

The Enigma of Arrival: A Novel in Five Sections is a 1987 novel by Nobel laureate V. S. Naipaul.

Mostly an autobiography, the book is composed of four sections which reflect the growing familiarity and changing perceptions of Naipaul upon his arrival in various countries after leaving his native Trinidad and Tobago.

Most of the action of the novel takes place in England where Naipaul has rented a cottage in the countryside. On first arriving, he sees the area surrounding his cottage as a frozen piece of history, unchanged for hundreds of years. However, as his stay at the cottage where he is working on another book becomes extended, he begins to see the area for what it is: a constantly changing place with ordinary people simply living lives away from the rest of the world. This causes Naipaul to reflect upon the nature of our perceptions of our surroundings and how much these perceptions are affected by our own pre-conceptions of a place.

He re-examines his own emigration from Trinidad to New York, and his subsequent removal to England and Oxford. Naipaul's narration illustrates the growing understanding of his place in this new environment and the intricate relations of the people and the land around them.

His landlord is modelled on his real-life landlord Stephen Tennant (1906–1987) a 1920s socialite and a *Bright Young Thing* who is also the model for the Hon. Miles Malpractice in novels by Evelyn Waugh and Cedric Hampton in Love in a Cold Climate by Nancy Mitford.

Introduction

To represent Naipaul's use of doubling in his writings is the main aim of this paper. For this, his famous novel 'The Enigma of Arrival' (1987) is referred here. Naipaul used variety of techniques to explore his own former status as colony, as margin to the centre of the dominant imperial powers. Naipaul uses doubling as a process of setting up a pair of showy opposites. He uses doubling to explore the process of cultural mixture. His works show that how a certain characteristics becomes a dividing line of a given category and further it becomes a shared similarity. His 'The Enigma of Arrival' is best example of it. Naipaul uses several binarisms to describe his life in England but, he never uses his own name.

The Enigma of Arrival has had critics and reviewers wondering whether V. S. Naipaul had been pulling the old "lucus a non-lucendo" trick on his audience: "I'll call it a novel because it's not; it's an autobiography." Though most of the book does indeed present a chronological account of the writer's days in Wiltshire, it is only by overlooking what Naipaul is insistently foregrounding that we can classify it primarily as a memoir. I am primarily concerned here, however, not with the issue of genre but with the strategies of how the novel's apparently objective descriptions of landscapes and events are used to create moral tension and how direct expression is substituted by more indirect ways of generating meaning.

Abasie device is the repetition of an incident which releases its moral meaning only upon its second or third occurrence. I will here concentrate on the first chapter since the main structural device in the novel as a whole is the setting up of that chapter as an archetype whose patterns are repeated in the following three sections, while the fifth, brief chapter functions as an epilogue.

The quest for vision is an equally important structuring device, constituting a unifying theme. The moral character that is always attached to this kind of search is here strengthened by the intimate relationship between vision and action, in fact by the need to let vision work with, rather than hinder, action. In a ciuciai part of the novel, this is exemplified by dwelling as an activity (that is, actually "building" a dwelling place) as opposed to a passive state, offering us the key to the the matisation of landscapes and places.

More generally, we detect a kind of spiralling progress, which is in itself a way of affirming the circularitv of existence not as hopeless return to the same but as the concession of a second chance, the certainty that every death will be followed by are birth. This latter point manages, without ever being explicitly stated, to answer the all-important question formulated in the last chapter: "Death was the motif; it had perhaps been the motif all along. Death and the way of handling it—that was the motif of the story of Jack". This is perhaps the most striking example of the way in which form and moral content work together in a novel/autobiography whose main concern is, at various levels, the bringing together of man and writer.

The centrality of writing itself is punningly hinted at in this novel by a very simple and, as Bruce King reminds us, characteristically Naipaulian device. King identifies the sentencc "With me, everything started from writing..." as the centre of the book. This device applies also to the first chapter, entitled "Jack's Garden." At a central point in the chapter (both in terms of pages and of the number of sub-sections) Naipaul describes Jack's last visit to the pub just before his death. In fact, this episode is also "central" in relation to the moral convictions expressed by the novel, particularly in the formal movement of discovery that brings about the achievement of vision.

The importance of the episode is signalled by the narrator—in a characteristically offhand way—when he finds it necessary to comment on the lark of emphasis with which it was related to him: "She spoke quite casually, giving me this news, now more than a year old. She was just making conversation". As a matter of fact, it is only in a similarly indirect way that the narrator can bring himself, towards the end of the novel, to make that statement which it is difficult not to take as the moral of this work: "This melancholy penetrated my mind while I slept; and then, when I awakened in response to its prompting, I was so poisoned by it, made so much not a doer (as men must be, every day of their lives), that it took the best part of the day to shake it off (emphasis added).

However, the episode of Jack's driving to the pub at the point of death (and on Christmas eve, which is also the pagan festivity of the rebirth of the sun) makes the same statement:

To be with his friends; to enjoy the last drink; to have the final sweetness of life as he knew it. What an effort it would have taken! To have those blocks of ice for lungs; to be in capable of getting warm; to be fatigued and faint; to want nothing more than to lied own and close one's eyes and sail away into the fantasies that were claiming one.

This is the narrator's epiphanic achievement of a moral vision. But Jack is also associated with vision — in a more literal, more gradual way. It is, in fact, through Jack's observation that the narrator finally overcomes his difficulty in "seeing," which he describes most compellingly in relation to two specific imagery:

> the seasons and the landscape. The opening, emblematic sentence reads: "For the first four days it rained. I could hardly see where I was." Four paragraphs later, we are introduced to the narrator's inability to distinguish among the seasons (establishing his tropical origins). This is connected to the vision motif by the use of the term "blur":

the year — so far as vegetation and even temperature went — was a blur to me. It was hard for me to distinguish one section or season from the other; I didn't associate flowers or the foliage of trees with any particular month. (11 Jack, on the other hand, who "celebrated the seasons" as in "a version of a Book of Hours" (2 0), 1 seems to possess as much a right of abode with the changing times of the year as within the landscape—another respect in which the narrator sees Jack at first as blessedly free from his own inadequacies:

I felt unanchored and strange. Every thing I saw in those early days, as I took my surroundings in, every thing I saw . . . made that feeling more acute. I felt that my presence in that old valley was part of something like an upheaval, a change in the course of the history of the country.

> Jack himself, however, I considered to be part of the view. I saw his life as genuine, rooted, fitting: man fitting the landscape. There is yet another way—an exquisitely formal way—by which Jack is the focus of the narrator's progress towards the achievement of vision. The encounter with

> Jack is, in fact, delayed and substituted at first with the appearance of persons or things which are in synecdochical relation to him. First, throughout the first sub-section Jack mentioned obstinately not directly but in relation to his cottage: there are seven occurrences of the phrase "Jack's cottage", there are also two more complex syntagms: "the still living row of agricultural cottages, one of which Jack lived in" and "the cottage-row in which Jack lived".

The one exception to this occurs at the beginning of page 15, and is as important as the rule:

> The first afternoon, when I reached the farm buildings, walking down the steep way, beside the wind break, I had to ask the way to Stonehenge.... The reappeared to be many paths, some leading off the wide valley way, I was confused. Such a simple enquiry, though, in the emptiness; and I never forgot that on the first day I had asked someone the way. Was it Jack? I didn't take the person in; I was more concerned with the strangeness of the walk, my own strangeness, and the absurdity of my enquiry. (emphasis added)

Here is one of the patterns which is repeated at crucial points in the following chapters: the missed or delayed encounter. It knits together the various parts of the novel, but more significantly it keeps reminding us of the problems of vision. In fact, the repetition of the pattern is that as the novel progresses the vision becomes more fleeting and less illuminating. In the first chapter, it is given prominence by a series of textual devices whose main function may well be that of pointers that establish the presence of a "mystery." In the second chapter, there is the explicit mention of a "vision" in relation to the writer's career. In the third, the pattern is repeated in connection with two meetings with his landlord; but, as the writer realises afterwards, the first glimpse, however "confused," was to remain his "only true glimpse". Finally, in the fourth and most disenchanted chapter, all we have is a story, at first interrupted by the arrival of the rooks, which tells us of a death and a burial ceremony, affording us aver)' brief glimpse of green, which momentarily covers up the stark chalky whiteness of death.

Naipaul has not written a consolatory novel in the ordinary sense. Learning to cope with the bare fact of change and death is the main part of its concern, but whatever action is taken, and whatever progress is made, has to be accepted as a value in itself, not because of where it leads. At most, it is a progress to vision that is similar, in its employment of formal devices as well as in its outcome, to the overall process of the "discovery" of Jack.

Jack's deferred entrance, the master pattern through which vision is problematised in the novel, is demonstrated in various ways. The narrator says, "It was not Jack whom I first noticed on my walks. It was Jack's father-in-law". This "Wordsworthian figure" in fact recalls an even more icastic literary character: he is Jack's life instinct stripped to its most basic and primitive aspect, the instinct of survival (he creates "safe padded places" to cross the barbed wire; he crucifies the crows or rooks, symbols of death); he is "The Fuel-Gatherer" and in fact fits the old stereotype of the native ("He was fantastically, absurdly bent, as though his back had been created for the carrying of loads"). He is, in short, Caliban.

The narrator continues to defer Jack's entrance: "But before I got to know Jack I got to know the farm manager". The characteristic that the encounter with the farm manager invites us to assign to Jack is independence:

> I suppose (because Jack lived in one of the agricultural cottages attached to the farm) that the farm manager was Jack's boss. I never thought of them in that relationship, though. I thought of them as separate people.

This sub-section ends with a vision of Jack working in his garden "as a free man". This aspect, which is not developed any further with regard to Jack, becomes important in contrast with the dependency that affects like an original sin several other characters in the novel.

The process of discover)' through metonymy and synecdoche first appears in this account:

> The old man first [Jack's father-in-law], then. And, after him, the garden, the garden in the midst of superseded things. It was Jack's garden that made me notice Jack.. .. But it took some time to see the garden....It took some

> time before, with the beginning of my new awareness of the seasons, I noticed the garden I noticed his hedge first of all.

Jack's garden and hedge now become the objectivisation of the man-must-be-a-doer imperative, bearing witness at one and the same time to the futility and the necessity of the gesture:

> The hedge hid nothing.... And beside Jack's garden, Jack's hedge: a little wall of mud-spattered green, in the openness of the drovewav, like a vestige, a memory of another kind of house and garden and street, a token of something more complete, more ideal.

Later, the garden itself succumbs to the perpetuity of change and decay of which the narrator has become so painfully aware in the course of the chapter. He is now able to take a step further, however, as he assures himself that the object of Jack's undaunted activity will enter a new cycle at some later point:

> So at last, just as the house was cleansed of Jack's life and death, so the ground he had tended finally disappeared. But surely below all that concrete over his garden some seed, some root, would survive; and one day perhaps, when the concrete was taken up (as surely one day it would hi-taken up, since lewd dwelling places are eternal), one day perhaps some memory of Jack, preserved in some similie or (lower or vine, would come to life again.

This is again an offhand way of making essential statements:

> It is an important qualification to the narrator's adherence to the doctrine of karma.

His rejection of fatalism leading to spiritual paralysis is left to emerge slowly and to drift into the reader's consciousness as the repetition of a pattern blossoms into meaning:

> the survival of Jack's garden under the concrete: the path cut by Pitton through the enclosure, which "awaited only this cut to reveal the old order and beauty and many seasons' tending that lay beneath"; the manor greenhouse, so solidly built that it would have been "the work of less than a week . . . to replace its wilderness with order"—

> these all testify lo the same idea that whatever is well made (and the moral sense is here as strong as the technical one) will survive and provide its own justification for existence.

Jack's garden is also an essential element in the process of discovery through the seasons ("His garden taught me about the seasons, and I got to know in a new way things I must have seen many times before") and, above all, through the explosion of the myth of the landscape. The ruin of Jack's garden after his death finally cures the narrator of his faulty vision and, consequently, of his sense of his own irremediable out-of-placeness. At first, the narrator says that "Jack and his garden and his geese and cottage and his father-in-law" seemed to be "emanations" of "literature and antiquity. After Jack's death, so much that had looked traditional, natural, emanations of the landscape, things that country people did . . . now turned out not to have been traditional or instinctive after all, but to have been part of Jack's way. When he wasn't there to do these things, they weren't done; there was only a ruin.

The whole of this chapter may be read as a Bildungsroman whose outcome is not the achievement of some sense of perfection but, on the contrary, a therapeutic awareness of the fact that perfection does not exist and never has existed. The narrator being an excolonial, this realisation has a more specific value for him than the implication that, therefore, "decay" does not really exist either. What has seemed "perfect" to him on his arrival in Wiltshire would really have been at its apex during the days of the British Empire: "But in that perfection... there would have been no room for me".

An especially interesting example of the way in which Naipaul uses repetition to suggest moral fact is his allusion to the myth of the Fall. Ironically, it is thought the universalising (anti-dogmatic, anti-essentialist) stance of this novel that this—the principal—myth of Western civilization is used here to highlight a problem that Naipaul has elsewhere depicted in relation to developing countries: the immobilism induced by a more or less explicit system of caste (as the sense of what is owed to oneself).

The first chapter of The Enigma of Arrival contains two more locations, in addition to Jack's garden, which the author can exploit as settings for a first paradigmatic representation of the myth of the Fall: the valley as a whole, and the manor garden.

These three lines of representation are all introduced in the sixth section of the first chapter. This section introduces Jack's illness and the ruin in his garden. It contains also the first mention of the "bigger changes" in the valley, later exemplified by the common fate of the three successive stores of hay and eventually described as a "withdrawal at the centre"—a term with metaphoric post-colonial significance. And finally, it introduces Les and Brenda (though we do not know their names yet), who perform the roles of Adam and Eve in our virtual Eden.

We first see Brenda sunbathing in the "ruined garden" of the pink cottage into which she has moved with her husband. She is, the narrator tells us, "seemingly careless of showing her breasts." But it is in relation to the manor garden that her behaviour most clearly shows a metaphorical dimension: she moves in it, as we might say, careless of her nudity and unaware of the seasons (her bare midriff "not quite suitable at that time of year"), and "like someone who had been granted the freedom of the grounds and was at that moment beginning to taste the new freedom'. Meanwhile, her husband has been picking fruit in the manor garden, tentatively at first ("like a man nervous of being observed"), but then as if encouraged by the presence of his wife. To the narrator, as he had told us earlier, those "were not fruit to eat". Later on, referring to the "classical gesture" with which Les had offered him a basket of vegetables, the narrator comments: "I had seen him at one of his best moments", during a golden age, which was to come to an end with the exclusion of the couple from the manor. But the pattern becomes perfectly clear only with the shock we experience when the presence of evil finally manifests itself. It is motiveless, frightfully effortless evil: all the two other women do to cause Brenda's ruin is nothing: they do not relate the message that would have defused the tragedy. Brenda's fatal mistake, therefore, is not her elopement with another man, not her attempt to live (as is said later in connection with her sister) a "life of choice and passion"; on the contrary, it is that in a crucial moment she had put her life into the hands of others.

As we learn from the narrator's conversation with Brenda's sister, this was no accident but rather part of her way of being, her original sin. As the narrator reflects on her life story, he understands Brenda to have been the victim of a doctrine of karma which transcends all boundaries of time and place: "It is as if we all carry in our make-up the effects of accidents that have befallen our ancestors, as if we are in many ways programmed before we are born, our lives half outlined for us". From very early in her life Brenda had lived with a sense that something was owed to her. This had made her dependent. And the echoes of her attitude in that of the inhabitants of the valley (whose "sense of history, the assurance of continuity" is synonymous with their "sense of something owed to oneself) show how positions of apparent strength and assurance may be beset by this kind of fallacy as easily as those of more obvious subjection:

> History, glory, religion as a wish to do the right thing by one self — these ideas were still with some people in the valleys round about, though there had been some diminution in personal glory, and the new houses and gardens were like the small change of the great estates of the last century and the beginning of this century. These people — though they had come, many of them, from other places — still had the idea of being successors and inheritors. It was because of this idea of historic a inheritance and succession that many new people in our valley went to the restored church. The church had been restored for people like them; it met their needs.

However, in spite of this pervasiveness, there is a way out, and it is paradoxically provided by the Fall itself. Though Brenda had been unable to live through the failure of her idea of herself and had eventually let "fate" destroy her, when the pattern is repeated in the following chapters the story has a different ending. Both Pitton (after he loses his job as gardener in the manor) and Mrs Phillips (after the death of her husband) eventually get a new life. There is no glamour, no sense of triumph, in this. But their time of dependence, of servitude and mimicry, is definitely over. They have survived the enigma or, as Naipaul calls it in Finding the Centre, "the blankness and anxiety of arrival". Later on, illness drives the narrator himself from his valley, from the cottage in which he had spent eleven years, experiencing a "second childhood of seeing and learning". As a response to this, he builds his own house out of two old cottages a few miles away. The reflections that are generated by this gesture and by its consequences (when a former dweller in one of the old cottages sees herself deprived of her past) sum up what the narrator has learnt about the right attitude to history, change, and appropriation of the land through his stay in Wiltshire. What we are made to recognise as the correct attitude is defined mostly by the rejection of a series of alternatives.

In opposition to the inhabitants of the valley, the "successors and inheritors," the narrator realises "how tenuous really the hold of all of these people has been on the land they worked or lived in," since their world, like Jack's—like anybody's—"was too precious not to be used by others". This justifies his own appropriation of part of that world. This, however, does not exonerate one from adopting what is later described as a "reverential" attitude.

The opposite to such attitude is again exemplified through a repetition pattern, in three paradigmatic episodes: the badly gelded pony which probably bleeds to death in the first chapter, the rose that Mrs Phillips cuts "right back" in "Ivy", and the incompetently run shop which ends up as "an expression of the owner's wish to abandon the project, run away" in "Rooks". In these episodes, the metaphorical impact and the polemical tone are more direct than usual. Taken together, these examples provide unusually "explicit" criticism of a criminally inept kind of intervention. They also confirm the impression of Naipaul's continuing engagement in his "country idyll" with the issues of his more controversial writings: here too Naipaul's "eye is always focused on the human costs of ill-conceived and wilful attempts at the management of human affairs". But this is very much an exception rather than the rule, the only instance of total condemnation in a novel which is otherwise pervaded with the awareness of relativity—as in the beautiful petering sentence that concludes the second sub-section of "Rooks":

> The wet river banks, the downs: everyone saw different things. Old Mr. Phillips, with his memories of chalk and moss; my landlord, loving ivy; the builders of the manor garden; Alan; Jack; me. This awareness of relativity, which means coming to terms with the workings of history, finally gives its results in the consciously reverential attitude adopted by the narrator in building his own cottage. Observing Jack, learning to see him as a "doer"

> rather than as an "inheritor" has done much to help him find his own way, but now he must go beyond Jack. Jack "had disregarded the tenuousness of his hold on the land"; a great part of his achievement had been due to his "not seeing what others saw." Though the narrator celebrates Jack's ability to act "as if in the face of universal confusion, we are told that his treating his garden like a front garden, whereas in the cottages around it is no longer possible to distinguish front from back, and his careful tending of his hedge in spite of its being "meaningless" both derive from the same "instinct". In the last analysis, his action is largely a result of lack of comprehension,—as seen in his greeting to the narrator, "which came over less as defined words than as a deliberate making of noise in the silence".

What the narrator adds to Jack's attitude therefore is awareness and the need and ability to testify consciously for what Jack had merely "sensed": "that life and man were the true mysteries", the "true religion of men". Jack "had created his own life, his own world, almost his own continent." He had not, for all we know, built his own house.

The most powerful incentive towards building our own house is, of course, if we were not given one. In this important respect the narrator's relationship with Jack is paradigmatic with another oppositional pair, developed especially at the beginning of the fourth chapter—that between the narrator and Alan, the self-destructive English writer, a frightful example of what the narrator himself might have become if he had not been constantly forced to face his own uprootedness. The disjunction of man and writer is explicitly one of the problems that The Enigma of Arrival tries to address. This issue is developed most clearly in the second chapter, "The Journey." But even this chapter—which more than any other section of the book seems to be autobiographical—participates in the game of paradigmatic relationships, helping set up the chapter about "Jack's Garden" as an archetype by repeating in a more discernible way the patterns of the first.

"The Journey" begins with the narrator's arrival in Wiltshire. Chronologically, however, this chapter contains the story of the young writer's difficulty or "literariness" of vision and the account of his missed encounter with what ought to have been the writer's subject, his Trinidadian background, as he comes to realise years later: "Nearly five years before vision was granted me, quite suddenly one day, when I was desperate for such an illumination, of what my material as a writer might be". Again, however, the vision is lost as soon as it is achieved because in the meantime "the world had not stood still" and the writer realises that the centre is neither in England nor in Trinidad, that there can be no centre only a perpetual encounter with the enigma of arrival. A few sentences after the centre of the book, Naipaul repeats the opening of the novel: "For the first four days it rained and was misty; I could hardly see where I was". But some pages later we are warned that we are not simply back at the beginning:

> The man who went walking pastjack's cottage saw things as if for the first time. Literary allusions came naturally to him, but he had grown to see with his own eyes. He could not have seen like that, so clearly, twenty years before. And having seen, he might not have found the words or the tone. The simplicity and directness had taken a long time to get to him; it was necessary for him to have gone through a lot. (emphasis added)

This observation (given at the end of "The Journey") is obviously not the condition of the narrator at the beginning of the first chapter, to whom everything seems to be emanation of literature and antiquity and who only relates to the landscape through the works of painters and poets or through a purely linguistic kind of knowledge: "So much of this I saw with the literary eye, or with the aid of literature". This latter condition, in fact, is in paradigmatic relation with that of the young writer leaving his island and arriving in England towards the beginning of the second chapter. The two similar sentences therefore identify a more complex movement than circularity, that of being on two points on the same axis but on different coils of a spiral. This parallel treatment of the human and the literary experiences provides one way of validating on a formal level what we are actually told in "The Journey": the moment in which the writer finally had his "vision" was also the start of the process through which "man and writer came together again". In an even more intriguing way, we find the same concept not affirmed but rather enacted in the first, archetypal chapter: there the achievement of vision for the man corresponds to the onset of narration. Near the end of the ninth sub-section, we are reminded one last time that the narrator "had arrived at [his] feeling for the seasons by looking at Jack's garden". He then surprises us with a demonstration of his newly acquired understanding in the form of a detailed description of the manor gardener's seasonal activities. From now on, the narration loses its vague timeless quality and becomes truly narrative, with a chronological setting also provided by references to the seasons: "It was a good thing that the autumn was well advanced"; "some weeks later, before the winter turned to spring"; "One autumn afternoon".

The use of proper names provides more specific evidence of the fact that "narration" begins with this particular section (the tenth sub-section, beginning with "Friendship has its odd ways . . ."). Up to this point, all we have had are innumerable mentions of the almost mythical "Jack," a handful of "Bray" and one "Peter" (in direct speech); so that the introduction of "Mr. and Mrs. Phillips" at the beginning of this sub-section strongly contributes to our impression that the tone has suddenly changed. In the following pages, "Pitton" (or "Mr. Pitton"), "Les" and "Brenda" are also given their proper names for the first time, and even a "Michael Allen" makes his appearance. This transferer of the benefits of vision into narration prefigures the end of The Enigma of Arrival, in which the writer, having lived through his wealth of experiences, transforms everything into the act of writing the very book we have just finished reading. And it is fascinating to see, as a final example of the book's strategies, how something similar happens with what is probably the most sensitive issue in the novel, its exposure of that kind of organised religion which panders to the human tendency towards dependence, while in fact being unable to provide the answer everybody (including the narrator/protagonist) is looking for. This theme surfaces several times, most strongly in the corruption of Bray, set beside Jack as an example of free man. But it is as an indictment against a faulty narrative that it finally achieves its most arresting form:

> He began to tell a story. I couldn't understand the story. An important man in the community had asked him one day: "What do you think is the best Hindu scripture?" He, the pundit, had replied, "The Gita." The man had then said to some body else present, "He says the Gita is the best Hindu scripture." There should have been more to the story. But there was no more.

"Implicit statements" of the kind I have tried to underline in the course of this essay, even when they are not as strong and potentially controversial as this last one quoted, inevitably raise the issue of responsibility. By making his higher meaning arise as of necessity from his expressive means—his textual strategies and his rhetoric of repetition — the author is inviting his readers to share the responsibility for his statements; in fact, his readers are required to work them out for themselves. This is perfectly in line with the mood of "return and reconciliation," which has often been detected in Naipaul's more recent work; however, I would not wish to suggest that it may be a defensive strategy on the writer's part.

Naipaul is here above all affirming not simply the identity of the man's vision with the writer's vision but rather the priority of the latter over the former. It is a manifestation of what I would call Naipaul's humanism: the use of literary form to express a strong concern with the human condition, in such a way as to resist all kinds of dogmatic and essentialist attitudes. As we have seen, partiality, difficulty, and relativity of vision, and retrospective realisation run throughout the novel as leitmotifs; they also, more important, provide its structure, a winding path towards awareness in which the moral and the literary are stubbornly intertwined."

Summary and Analysis

The anonymous narrator of V.S Naipaul's *The Enigma of Arrival* has set himself upon a voyage of discovery in time. The walks about the hills and fields around his secluded rural cottage are not conducted towards awareness of space but rather as movements in time through layers of remembrance and imagination. The visual field he is met with in these walks is a multi-stratum expanse of history, not of linear progression and dates but individual experiences and interactions. Outside the main location of the novel, the farm in Wiltshire, the episodes around the London boarding house and the trips to and from Trinidad and Africa are as well exercises in historical manifestation where emotion and memory are exposed in a prose monologue on the nature of selfhood in time. We propose that this is the 'enigma of arrival,' in that arrival does not happen so much in the spatial sense of actual coming to a place, but rather it occurs in time, with the gradual realisation that one has become a feature of that place and it has become part of the individual's imaginative and emotional awareness.

In reading *The Enigma of Arrival* as periplus the narrator is identified as an explorer and the creator of the map. This performs a shift in the colonial experience in one sense as the narrator has come from Trinidad, a Crown Colony, to the heart of the fading British Empire. In Trinidad he was a member of an Indian family that had been brought to the island as workers by the English. He has been educated by the system administered by the English and has a highly developed context of English history and literature. Despite this familiarity his time in England is portrayed as one of discovery and this is the how the periplus is expressed, not necessarily as a navigational device for others to follow but rather as a report or testimony of one man's experiences in discovery. This unfolding of a landscape or location in a temporal sequence occurs throughout the narrative of the novel but to take just one example I choose the narrators approaching one of the major symbolic structures of England, Stonehenge:

> The grassy way, the old river bed (as I thought) sloped up, so that the eye was led to the middle sky; and on either side were the slopes of the downs, widening out and up against the sky. On the one side there were cattle; on the other side, beyond a pasture, a wide empty area, there were young pines, a little forest. The setting felt ancient, the impression was of space, unoccupied land, the beginning of things. There were no houses to be seen, only the wide grassy way, the sky above it, and the wide slopes on either side. *(Naipaul 1987)*

By making reference to the path of the eye it is as if the narrator is the exterior observer looking at a painting rather than standing in a rural landscape. The vision is acknowledged as a subjective one, "as I thought", and the principles and judgements of that speaking subject shape a central part of the narrative, in such words as "ancient" and "empty" the emotional values of the place are suggested. These carry connotations of mystery, origins, and insignificance on the part of the narrator in comparison with the grand space he is occupying at the time of the relating. The significance of the narrated space is registered in the encompassing temporal terms of "ancient" and "beginning". The grammatical tempus of the passage is one of continuous past tense, the experience is related as a recorded event spoken of in hindsight as a journey now completed. It is this construction of the temporal in the negotiation of space that connects the subjective narration of the text to the periplus reading.

In the *Enigma of Arrival* the temporal manifestation of space is also represented by narrative descriptions of seeing time preserved in a landscape. In passages reminiscent of Hardy's *Return of the Native* the earth is given a historical memory which can be read by the aware witness,

> ...my feeling for the age of the earth and the oldness of man's possession of it was always with me. A vast sacred burial ground, bounded by the sky – of what activity those barrows and tumuli spoke, what numbers, what organisation, what busyness in these now virtually empty downs! (Naipaul 1987).

It is not a covered over (cement) or exploited (technology) earth but an earth that is permeable and breeched, with openings such as graves which provide a texture which can be entered into with understanding. In the more contemporary army training school at Larkhill there is also an effort to imbue the earth with a narrative based in history but it is not of openings and underground. Here on the surface the trees are planted to represent the positions of the ships at the Battle of Trafalgar "or was it Waterloo" (Naipaul 1987:24). The unreliable narrator shifts the emphasis of this example from the old to the newer and doing so builds a stronger connection to the 'natural' manifestations of geographic narrative as opposed to those made during recorded history. Some features of place are more "purer" in their connection with the place and therefore their manifestations of their narratives are as well. In the Wiltshire episodes the most profound connection to the landscape is expressed as the synthesis "Of literature and antiquity and the landscape [of which] Jack and his garden and his geese and cottage and his father-in-law seemed emanations." (Naipaul 1987:25). It is by degrees that all are held by the place and must act out their time accordingly, including the narrator of the *The Enigma of Arrival.* However the sense of this narrative matrix being under threat is also included in the progression of time which the spatial landscape contains and nurtures.

The beginning of change in the lives of the characters is manifest in conjunction with changes in the landscape;

> "I looked for cracks and flaws in it and hoped that the little abrasions and water erosions I noticed would spread and make it impossible – fantasy taking over from logic – for the machines to lay down a new asphalt mixture."
>
> *(Naipaul 1987)*

In this passage there is the naive wish (fantasy) that if the physical space can be maintained then the temporal state will be so as well. The nature of this change is compared to that of Columbus bringing unevenness into "the evenness of history on the other side" (Naipaul 1987:44) with his voyages to the Americas. In this change from perfectly even time and proper form there is a particular conceptualisation of nature which is important. Once again nature is the pre-arrival untouched state, a purity which is constructed as before the history of those using machines and covering over the earth. The sterility of the imposed concrete skin is taken up in several places in *The Enigma of Arrival* such as the appeal over Jack's garden demands "But surely below all that concrete over his garden some seed, some root would survive, and one day perhaps..." (Naipaul 1987:86). It is as if the anonymous narrator needs to see the land in order to be able to read it and map it, and not being able to read it means that it has been included into the uneven time of those that use the machines. The gardener is also such a character who can read the space of nature being a "magician, herbalist, in touch with the mystery of seed and root and graft. (Naipaul 1987). This mythologising of the garden and the gardener provides for a strong modernist flavour to the work and is also consistent with *The Enigma of Arrival* being a periplus map developed around the subjective emotions and memories of the narrator. In the same way that author of an ancient periplus was both story teller and guide. Like the returning traveller here we have a man telling us the landscape as he saw it through all the subjectivity and we may follow his narrative map in order to reach a similar, but perhaps not the same destination.

The periplus reading of the text which constructs the map as being provided for the reader by the omniscient narrator is a non-diegetic textual characteristic. In it not overtly stated in *The Enigma of Arrival* that the narrator is mapping the Wiltshire Downs or the journey from Trinidad to London via New York. In many sections of the text the mapping is not a physical description of the topography or physical features encountered by the travelling narrator, rather it is about the emotional or connotative reactions he experiences in these places. There is until the very end of the novel an unfolding of new ground in the sense of the periplus due to an emotional map merging with the descriptive map being constructed by the narrator. This psycho-geographic mapping can be broken down into well defined segments in the non-diegetic landscape: *Jack's Garden* and Wiltshire being allegoric with memories of childhood and birth, *The Journey* section being connected to Africa and growth and education, *The Ivy* being based on people, and depicting the adult stage and society.

Finally *The Rooks* is heavily laden with themes around community and old age and death. To move through each of these stages is to map a life, both as it progresses and in retrospect. The final chapter *The Ceremony of Farewell* is the funeral and the departure from the great map planet earth that is; "Our sacred world – the sanctities that had been handed down to us as children by our families, the sacred places of our childhood, sacred because we see them as children and had filled them with wonder, places doubly and trebly sacred to me because far away in England I had lived in them imaginatively over many books and had in my fantasy set in those places the very beginning of things, had constructed out of them a fantasy home..." (Naipaul 1987)

Here the alignment between place, emotion and the subjective experience based on imagination and fantasy is synthesised. The being in a place is not just about physical presence but psychic presence whereby one can "live in them imaginatively" while being "far away", as we all construct maps in our heads, subjective versions of place.

Central to every one of these subjective places is time as once we have captured the image of a place in out minds it does not progress outside the time we experienced it. The narrative associated with a particular place becomes that place in our imaginative recollection of it. In the case of the narrator of *The Enigma of Arrival* he had been given a pre-constructed "official" version of England as a subject of the British Empire, going to school in Trinidad and gaining a scholarship to attend Oxford University as a young Indian West Indian Commonwealth citizen. With his physical arrival at the places he had learnt and imagined about from reading books he begins his own synthesis of knowledge, fantasy and the experiences undergone in the place itself.

Just as a place becomes a feature of living memory and imagination, the periplus is also a living narrative for those who follow it as a map. The descriptive narrative provided by Naipaul in *The Enigma of Arrival* is his periplus but this in turn goes on to feed the imagination of others. Of those who read the text perhaps some even become wanting to experience in the physical the image they have from it of the Wiltshire Downs. Just as the narrator and the author as well had a desire at early stages of their lives to travel to the heart of the British Commonwealth and experience it directly. Naipaul does employ stereotypes and the literary sources he sites in the text show his canon of literature is clearly conservative in many ways, but the quality of the prose and the craft of his language is evident. Of the book the author says "It's about England, a kind of country life, but not as others write about it. It sets ideas about country life on their head." (*The Guardian* Saturday September 8, 20013).

This again is a subjective appraisal, even coming from the author, but a periplus map is acknowledged as subjective (they all bear the tile of their author) and perhaps for this reason it was abandoned in navigation in favour of the visualised map projections we use today. The periplus instead could be seen as the ancestor of the travel book, for which Naipaul is also well known.

8

A Way in the World

A Way in the World is a 1994 book by Nobel laureate V. S. Naipaul. Although it was marketed as a novel in America, *A Way in the World* is arguably something different.

Introduction

A Way In The World note as a matter of course that Naipaul models the figure of Lebrun on the historical figure C.L.R. James, a fellow Trinidadian who, as Naipaul has done, achieved international renown as a thinker and writer during his lifetime. Naipaul includes several such characters, based on thinly disguised public figures, in his novel. Foster Morris, for example, the minor British writer whom the young narrator at first envies because he seems debonair and once wrote a "serious" book about Trinidad politics called Shadowed Livery, is based on the English novelist, Arthur Calder-Marshall, whose documentary, Glory Dead (1939), provides a detailed account of the political background to the 1930s oilfield riots in Trinidad.

Naipaul's method depends on readers "in the know" being able to pick up on these factual details, enhancing our sense that what we are reading is fact. However, Naipaul does not change the names of all of his loosely historical character: Sir Walter Raleigh and the Spanish adventurer Miranda remain Raleigh and Miranda. Henry Swanzy, the producer of Caribbean Voices Programme and an associate of Calder-Marshall, remains Henry Swanzy. On the whole it seems that only the characters whose lives he must manipulate in order to produce the effects he needs are given new names.

It is difficult, though, to decide what we are to make of Lebrun, as the few facts of Naipaul's acquaintance with C.L.R. James seem identical with his representation of the relationship between his narrator and Lebrun. Moreover, such deviations as there are between his description of Lebrun's career and the received record of James's life can be documented easily by reference to the numerous volumes by and about James that have become available since his death in 1989. James is such a well-known public figure in Leftist and Caribbean circles that altering his name seems to be as futile a gesture as it would have been for Naipaul to alter Raleigh's name in his chapter on the explorer.

Naipaul's insistence on distinguishing Lebrun from James, therefore, seems to be his way of signalling his interest in imagining the private life of a public figure; to recreate through fiction the most intimate motivations of someone like James (or like himself), rather than to put on record an accurate historical estimate of the political contribution of C.L.R. James, the man. Thus, Naipaul can use Lebrun, the writer and intellectual, as a foil and mirror for himself, in ways he could not have done with the specific historical figure of C.L.R. James, even as he draws on the public record of the life of his fellow countryman to create the illusion of fact.

James is one of the few Caribbean intellectuals, certainly the only other Trinidadian, to have attained an international reputation equal to Naipaul's as a consequence of his writing. In spite of significant political differences between them, Naipaul clearly respects this distinguished graduate of his alma mater, Queen's Royal College, and his precursor on the British and American intellectual scenes. James had also anticipated many of Naipaul's themes in his own publications as he and Naipaul share an interest in the history of the Caribbean and Latin America and in Trinidad's role within that history (131). Indeed, Naipaul's awareness of James's achievement probably goes further back than he discusses in this novel. James was the co-founder of the early Trinidad literary magazine, The Beacon, with whose extended circle of literati, Naipaul tells us elsewhere, his father, Seepersad Naipaul, interacted. Naipaul himself was probably directly influenced by the stories of the Beacon group. He refers in the essay "Jasmine" to a handful of local short stories he encountered as a child through which he "began to appreciate the distorting, distilling power of the writer's art. Where I had seen a drab haphazardness they found order; where I would have attempted to romanticise, to render my subject equal with what I had read, they accepted. They provided a starting-point for further observation; they did not trigger off fantasy" (27). Seen through these connections to Naipaul's father, Naipaul's school, Naipaul's intellectual interests, and the international literary scene, the historical James was probably an early role model for Naipaul, as the younger writer acknowledges in a review of James's Beyond a Boundary:

> To me, who thirty years later followed in his path almost step by step—but I only watched cricket, and I won the scholarship—Mr. James's career is of particular interest. Our backgrounds were dissimilar. His was Negro, Puritan, fearful of lower-class contamination; mine was Hindu, restricted, enclosed. But we have ended speaking the same language; and though England is not perhaps the country we thought it was, we have both charmed ourselves away from Trinidad. 'For the inner self,' as Mr. James writes, 'the die was cast.'

James had to struggle with the limitations of a colonial society not that much different from Naipaul's, if anything it was, as Naipaul notes, a world much harsher than his own in its racial divisions. Yet James had made a way for himself in the world. He had become known through his writing, in all the ways that Naipaul as a literary novice in the 1950s, must have aspired to be known.

Perhaps the most important aspect of Naipaul's relationship to James is his unfeigned respect for James as a fellow craftsman of words. This is one of the qualities Naipaul gives to his fictional Lebrun, who publishes a review article about the narrator's work in "one of the Russian 'thick magazines'"—not unlike the early review of Biswas that James wrote:

The article seemed to me a miraculous piece of writing. It stuck closely to what I had actually written, but was about so much more. Reading the article, I thought I understood why as a child I felt that history had been burnt away in the place where I was born. I found myself constantly thinking, "Yes, yes. That's true. It was like that." (114)

The words "seemed," in the first sentence quoted, and "I thought I understood," later on, prepare the reader for the painstaking deconstruction of Lebrun's reading that follows this passage. Yet the tone of the narrator's response communicates an intuitive recognition of a fellow mind—a fellow something—which the figure of Lebrun represents for Naipaul at this moment in the story.

Lebrun's essay evinces the attention to surfaces capable of excavating the writer's hidden meanings, that Naipaul tells us elsewhere in A Way in The World is the essence of good close reading. Indeed, the intensity of Lebrun's critical engagement with the narrator's novel returns to the author a satisfying assurance of having been seen and heard. Naipaul even displaces onto Lebrun's reading insights that originate in his own writing.

Most of Naipaul's critics are familiar with his pronouncement in The Middle Passage that "history is built around achievement and creation; and nothing was created in the West Indies" (29). In this rendering of his ideal reader, however, it is Lebrun who provides the narrator with the language through which to articulate a half understood childhood notion that "history had been burnt away in the place where I was born" (114). By converting his written dismissal of Caribbean history into a thought that comes unbidden to his narrator as a child, and which the respected public oracle, Lebrun, is able to divine, Naipaul anticipates the absolution he hopes history will give his political pronouncements. He displaces his harshest judgements onto his reader via Lebrun, but in a form benign enough to suggest insight and acceptance, rather than what some have seen as the defensiveness of Naipaul's original formulation or, of the critical responses to it. "Look," he seems to say, "Lebrun can see what I mean. He has a wonderfully expansive intellect that is not afraid of the truth. He has borne witness to what many others can see but are afraid to acknowledge in their readings of my work. He has anticipated what the world may only come to understand about my aesthetic vision in retrospect many decades from now."

When the narrator finally meets Lebrun, he characterises his conversation as being,

> Like Ruskin's on the printed page, in its fluency and elaborateness, the words wonderfully chosen, often unexpected, bubbling up from some ever-running spring of sensibility. The thought-connections—as with Ruskin—were not always clear; but you assumed they were there. As with the poetry of Blake (or, within a smaller compass, Auden), you held on, believing there was a worked-out argument.

Never mind the tongue in cheek, the Naipaulesque insinuation, too mischievous to let pass, that there may indeed have been no worked-out argument beneath the elegantly formulated rhetoric. Naipaul is comparing Lebrun here with the literary models that dominated his colonial education and subsequent literary initiation at Oxford. His association of Lebrun with the mercurial genius of Blake, the perfect poise of Ruskin, and the contemporaneous glamour of Auden, whose plays and poetry were much in vogue at Oxford in the 1950s, allows Naipaul to mark the narrator's enthusiasm as an initiate's naive response to a specific notion of literary greatness that he has been taught to admire. At the same time, however, Naipaul makes the point that in terms of what at that moment it was possible to imagine oneself as a colonial striving to attain through language, Lebrun had achieved it all.

Naipaul's representation of the relationship between his semi-autobiographical narrator and the public oracle, Lebrun, as opposed to a simple account of the relationship between V.S. Naipaul and C.L.R. James, allows him to foreground a number of similarities between himself and a historical figure who many consider his nemesis. For contemporary Caribbean aficionados, James epitomises a tradition of committed black intellectual thought associated with such figures as George Padmore, Frantz Fanon, and Eric Williams, to name a few.

It is a tradition from which Naipaul often has been accused of distancing himself. This perspective on the opposition between Naipaul and James sits well on both sides of the literary and ideological divide, where Naipaul is ostracised, by one camp, as a betrayer of the Third World and lionised, by the other, as the consummate aesthete and man of conscience—embodying all the essential purities Kripalsingh projects onto his Aryan ancestors in The Mimic Men. For both kinds of readers, the essential Naipaul is a man divorced from his Caribbean roots: the purist made nauseous by filth and flesh, or the racist who has "forgotten" his own family's sojourn in the cane fields of the New World.

Naipaul signifies on both the purist and racist readings of his work in his description of two meals, one of coo-coo, with Lebrun and other West Indians in London, with Lebrun's influential American friends in Manhattan. The meal with Lebrun takes place in a Maida Vale flat in London, filled with overstuffed furniture. Naipaul describes those present with the kind of meticulous attention to racial nuance we West Indians invoke as a matter of course when describing ourselves.

Thus, the host is described as Lebanese Trinidadian, his wife as a Creole who could pass for white but is from one of the smaller islands. Lebrun himself, though fairly dark in complexion, has a dash of Amerindian that gives his skin a reddish tinge. Only Lebrun's woman friend, described as a Polish or Czech woman, is given no ethnic specificity at this point. Their meal, which Naipaul, somewhat anachronistically, calls coo-coo, is described in even greater detail:

> A heavy glistening mound was placed on my own plate. I probed it: boiled yams and green bananas and possibly other tubers mashed together with peppers, the whole mixture slimy from the yams and—the Lebanese touch—olive oil. Below the pepper it had almost no taste, except one of a tart rawness (from the green bananas), and I thought it awful, the texture, the slipperiness. I didn't think I would be able to keep it down. I let it be on my plate. No one noticed.

While Lebrun ate, and his dutiful woman friend ate, and the smell of meat and oil became high in the squashed sitting room with the old upholstered chairs, and people asked the Lebanese where they had got the yams and green bananas from, I (feeling that I was betraying them all, and separating myself from the good mood of the evening) remembered my aunt twenty years before, fanning her coal pot on the concrete back steps of our house in Port of Spain, and talking about Grenadians boiling their "pitch-oil tin" of ground provisions once a week. (120)

Naipaul sets up this moment of excruciating embarrassment and gross satire very carefully. The cosmopolitan mix of the company around the table is set off by the crude peasant meal of coo-coo they make a point of eating; their stuffed mouths and the high smell of the food in the cramped room, against the elevated intellectual conversation Lebrun proceeds to initiate. Furthermore Naipaul draws into this moment, through the reference to his narrator's aunt, the ramifications attached to this meal for him in its original Caribbean setting.

Naipaul associates the ingredients of the meal with the Grenadian and Vincentian labourers he describes earlier in the chapter, who flocked to the Trinidad of his colonial childhood in search of work. In the course of this earlier description, the narrator first introduces the satirical portrait of his aunt—now "an alert, generous, elegant woman" (80), resident in Canada but then a somewhat garrulous character, fanning a coal pot on the back steps of the Port of Spain house, filled with recently relocated migrants from the countryside.

Her derogatory reference to small islanders and their pitch oil tins of ground provisions indicates some of the consequences for the status of Indo-Trinidadians that this "small island" invasion produced. Before the influx of immigrants, the Indo-Trinidadian peasant population of Trinidad was considered by many to occupy one of the lowest rungs on the very complex ladder of Trinidad social status.

Further down in colour hierarchy than the other indentured labourers of Chinese and Portuguese origin, less urbane and cosmopolitan than the black and mixed race Creoles of the city, Indo-Trinidadians who began to make the transition from country to town in the interwar years, may well have seized the opportunity to revise the public image of their community as backward and foreign when a new group, with even less prestige, arrived in the island after World War II.

Thus, the narrator's aunt does not need to acknowledge the squalor of her coal pot on the back steps if the living and cooking arrangements of the small islanders can be represented as even more primitive. At the same time, any provincial unease with the cosmopolitan foods and customs of Port of Spain she may have felt can be transformed into disgust, when redirected at the foods and customs of the new immigrants she most dreads being lumped with at the bottom of the social ladder.

All the words through which Naipaul makes the coo-coo seem revolting can be associated with the ramifications Naipaul brings to its description from other moments in the novel, especially from his earlier presentation of small island squalor and East Indian social angst. The way the elements of the meal are mashed together recalls the overcrowded Port of Spain house both the narrator and his aunt have since fled, even as it explains the need to enhance their social standing that dictated the distance Indo-Trinidadians struggled to maintain between themselves and the bodies of the unassimilated small islanders. The emphasis on the meal's indiscriminate mixing of African, Indian, even Lebanese ingredients, which the narrator's probing fork uncovers, also signifies on the racial mixture—not to say sexual promiscuity—associated with Trinidad Creole culture that the narrator, like a reader of pornography, approaches with a mixture of curiosity and revulsion.

The narrator's characterisation of the taste and texture of the meal, as that of "tart rawness" overlaying blandness and of "slipperiness," has obvious sexual overtones, as do the visual images associated with tubers and green bananas. These are further codified for the Caribbean reader through the popular association in Trinidad calypso between dried saltfish—the side dish usually served with coo-coo—and the female genitalia. Finally, the meal's sexual connotations are reinforced by the narrator's mildly envious allusions to Lebrun's reputation as a successful womaniser, repeated throughout the chapter, but conveyed in the passage quoted here through the narrator's uncomfortable awareness of the devotional attitude of the Polish or Czech woman friend at Lebrun's side, dutifully consuming the slimy meal.

Naipaul's emphasis on the racial and sexual connotations associated with coo-coo highlights the cultural distinctions that still persist in the Trinidad popular imagination between the island's Indo-Trinidadian population, with its supposedly homogenous social contours, and the much vaunted cultural hybridity of the wider Creole society. One of the reasons why the narrator cannot quite bring himself to eat this "mushed-up" meal with the gusto and aplomb of the other middle class West Indians at the dinner party—for some of whom it also is an exotic dish—is that his relationship to cultural mixture, to culinary slumming if you like, is complicated by the conservative notions of cultural separateness that others assume he associates with various aspects of Indo-Trinidadian culture. Thus, when the narrator notes parenthetically, in the passage quoted, that he feels as if he is betraying them all, he is expressing both an ironic distance from what he perceives as their staged indulgence in the culture of a class of people to which no one at the dinner party (including Lebrun) belongs—poor, uneducated, black, small island labourers—and a genuine sense of the limits placed on his Creole identity. His feelings of isolation are exacerbated by the way in which his Indianness in this self-consciously Creole context is never quite fully assimilated, even (especially!) when it is overlooked.

Critics in the "Naipaul as purist" cultural camp will be quick to celebrate the narrator's squeamishness as evidence of Brahmin sensibility, which Naipaul codes here through his references to the high smell of meat (actually another anachronism, since if the meal had been coo-coo it would have been served with would have been salt fish or flying fish). On the other hand, critics of the "Naipaul as cultural betrayer" camp will want to claim his over refined expressions of disgust as one more piece of evidence for his distaste of all things associated with black West Indians.

But Naipaul's position at this stage in his narrative is a lot more complex. Earlier in the chapter on Lebrun, Naipaul makes a point of noting the influence of George Lamming's first novel on his literary development. Lamming's successful use of comedy in In The Castle of My Skin affirmed for Naipaul something he had been unable to acknowledge until then in his attempts to write; that "comedy, the preserver we in Trinidad had always known, was close to me, a double inheritance, from my storytelling Hindu family, and from the creole street life of Port of Spain".

Naipaul thus uses his connection to a Black Caribbean writer to underwrite his literary sensibility as deriving from both Creole and Hindu cultural influences. Similarly, Lebrun's Creole urbanity is one of the features Naipaul allows his narrator to admire in his fictional rewriting of James, whose 1936 "barrack yard" novel, Minty Alley, is one of the clearest precursors of Naipaul's urbane satirical style in Trinidadian fiction. Within Creole culture, no racial or ethnic trait exists beyond co-optation. A Lebanese Trinidadian may integrate coo-coo into her cuisine with the same matter of factness that an Indo-Trinidadian writer can emulate the satirical conventions of the calypsos he hears on the streets of his neighbourhood, or of the folk tales he absorbs via Caribbean writers of African and Indian descent.

The problem with Creole appropriation, however, is that it inevitably involves a loss of ethnic specificity. All Trinidadians constantly negotiate the tension between their specific ethnic and racial origins and their sense of belonging to a multiracial Creole culture. In fact, it is the elegance with which these contradictions are finessed that constitutes the hallmark of Creole cultural hybridity.

But once this hybridity is perceived in terms of loss, rather than opportunity, it is possible to read the Creolisation process as a denial of difference, a form of cultural erasure. This is the defensive sentiment that fuelled in part the Black Power reassertion of African roots in the Caribbean during the 1960s and 1970s. It is also the fear that constrains Naipaul's narrator: the minority sensibility that rewrites the inclusive gestures of Lebrun's dinner party as a denial of the specificity of his Indo-Caribbean background, including his embarrassing private insecurities about consuming or being consumed by small island food.

The limits of the Creole identity the narrator at one level seems so anxious to claim, are indicated obliquely by Naipaul's naming of coo-coo as the meal his narrator cannot consume. Naipaul's choice of the word coo-coo as the name of the meal he describes enables a second intertextual reference to Lamming's In the Castle of My Skin. The closing chapter of Lamming's first novel contains a famous passage describing how G-'s mother prepares a final meal of coo-coo for him before he leaves Barbados for Trinidad.

In his essay, "Cuckoo [sic] and Culture," the critic Edward Baugh reads this passage as marking the moment at which the boy G- affirms and accepts the African/peasant roots of his culture, "so that every movement of his mother's hands, every ingredient that is added to the meal, becomes a kind of last sacrament and celebration of a culture which the boy G-, until this moment, has experienced with deep ambivalence" (22-23). Paradoxically, this insight comes at a point in the novel when the narration shifts from the third person, in which the boy is signified by the anonymous "G-," to a first person, "I," narrator, through whose agency the boy finally becomes an independent speaking subject. Separated from his mother and insulated from her culture, he can now reify each, as madonna and sacrament.

The meal of coo-coo in Lamming's text is thus both a gesture of embrace and a sign of the process of individuation that disrupts the connection between mother and son. The narrating, "I," who reifies the folk, is less enmeshed in the folk culture than the boy, "G-." By highlighting the difficulties his Indo-Caribbean narrator experiences when invited to participate in the same sacramental rite of consuming coo-coo, Naipaul helps us understand how Lamming's gesture could be read as an aggressive act of cultural appropriation, similar to the culinary slumming for which his narrator indicts the Caribbean intellectuals at Lebrun's dinner party.

He also may be making the point that the limits to cultural and literary convergence between himself and Lamming, or himself and James, are imposed ultimately by the different relationships to power reflected in their respective social histories. Lamming's narrator's ability to simultaneously claim and distance his mother's dish of coo-coo does not liberate Naipaul's narrator automatically from the complexly different sociocultural anxieties he brings to a similar meal.

Read in relation to the response of Lamming's "G-," however, Naipaul's narrator's refusal to eat may also signal a failure of the maturation process: an inability on the part of this narrating "I" to free himself of primal anxieties around status and identity embedded in his unconscious. Thus, the flashback to his garrulous aunt and his recourse to her language of "ground provisions" and "pitch oil tins" may be a way of signalling his failure—and everyone else's struggle—to complete the process of separation from an infantile identification with an imaginary mother culture.

The impressionable child, who has never quite freed himself from the half articulated fears and dreams of his maternal community, resurfaces in the hysterical man, gagging inexplicably when faced with a meal that triggers the feelings of suffocation, vulnerability, and inarticulateness that also assault the boy, "G-," but which Lamming resolves in his novel by creating an independent speaking subject.

In Lamming's resolution, to be Creole is to be mature, that is, to be capable of choosing for oneself those aspects of one's own cultural heritage, as well as the cultures of others, which one wishes to celebrate or reject, to perform an identity one writes for oneself, rather than to live out an identity provided by others. This is the notion of identity that the Caribbean group at James's dinner party seems to celebrate when its ethnically diverse members self-consciously reclaim the humble small island meal of coo-coo as part of their shared culture. It is also a perspective on personal choice that Naipaul supports, or at least sees as an inevitable condition of modernity, in his emphasis on the personal rewritings of the self in all of the stories in this novel. Yet, in this story about Lebrun, Naipaul reminds us that the borrowed cultural practices in which these "new men" (and women) clothe themselves coexist at all times with more deeply held, primal patterns of belonging, from which none of us is ever fully liberated.

Moreover, these new identities may threaten or erase the subjectivity of others — the black small island labourers represented only by their coo-coo at Lebrun's cosmopolitan dinner; the Indo-Trinidadian whose induction into the Creole cultural circle around the table conceals a threat or promise far more fraught than that associated with the inclusion of Lebrun's completely foreign Polish or Czech woman friend.

Naipaul uses the fear of cultural appropriation his narrator's inability to participate in the ritual meal of coo-coo intimates to reflect on the threat of cultural appropriation implicit in Lebrun's consummate ability to read his work. "The man want to take you over", the chief minister says of Lebrun in the course of another significant meeting and meal. Trinidad historian and former Prime Minister Eric Williams, the model for this character, was one of the most famous of James's proteges to later part company with his mentor.

Through him, the narrator comes to realise that what at first seemed to be an ideal interpretation of his writerly intent in Lebrun's article may have concealed a gesture of political co-optation that relegates the narrator's specific vision to a niche within Lebrun's elegantly formulated materialist reading of global culture. From that perspective, there is something sinister about a globalising impulse that can cheerfully exoticise the narrator's racial difference, while at the same time insisting that the narrator demonstrate his successful assimilation by consuming Creole food. When Lebrun, between mouthfuls of coo-coo, launches into a consideration of the debate between "Lenin and the Indian delegate, Roy, at the Second Congress of the Comintern in 1920", the narrator feels even more like the token outsider among the guests at the meal. In the end, he concludes that the price he must pay for his inclusion in Lebrun's vision of international solidarity is simply too high. It demands that he trivialise his aunt's deep-seated fear of poverty and squalor, expressed in her casual jab at small island culture. It calls upon him to fit his complex understanding of himself as Indo-Trinidadian into the broad generalisations about "Indians" that structure the debate between Lenin and Roy. From Naipaul's perspective such generalisations merely exoticise his narrator's racial specificity, by reducing it to one more instance of local colour, divorced from its original setting like the now harmlessly fashionable meal of coo-coo served up in a Maida Vale flat.

But perhaps ultimately race, or cultural difference, is not the point. There is a real distinction—one might say, a disciplinary distinction—between Naipaul's narrator's position on co-optation and that of Lebrun that has everything and nothing to do with race. For him, a writer who approaches the representation of experience by formulating a theoretical position and then attempting to read the world around him in terms of that theoretical claim, is doing something quite different from a writer who works, as Naipaul does, empirically; that is, from a specific gesture, an observable trait, an emotional insight, towards a reading of his world.

That is not to say that both writers do not start off with certain—perhaps identical—framing assumptions about the worlds they inhabit, or that both writers are not ultimately dependent on the power of the specific images their words evoke for credibility and rhetorical force. And, indeed, the two approaches to reading the world can be viewed as complementing each other. This is why at a certain level James remains Naipaul's ideal reader. He can use his theoretically honed vision to excavate layers of meaning below the surface of Naipaul's text that the creative writer can only indicate through anecdote and elision. As a theoretician, James is not bound by the limits of the world he can see or reproduce imaginatively.

This freedom allows him to extrapolate layers of meaning from Naipaul's work so that he can explain the process by which the writer constructs the world in a certain fashion. But the theoretician's paradigms also can generate speculative universes, which operate according to the laws enumerated by his theories but which bear no relationship to reality as experienced by any human society. Divorced from their empirical grounding, such theories can abstract human experience to the point where they obscure rather than elucidate the truths they purport to apprehend. By manipulating logic and language, they can substitute concepts for each other that in the "real" world may have been diametrically opposed, thus achieving a theoretical or political resolution where a lived contradiction may remain.

Between Lebrun and Naipaul's narrator, these disciplinary differences acquire additional nuances when race and culture become part of their concern. For Naipaul, racial attitudes and cultural perceptions have their origins in a plethora of factors affecting his characters, which his fictions can never pretend to exhaust. For his stories to work, he cannot merely summarise his racial situation, as part of an Indo-Trinidadian minority in a culture shaped by the early confrontations and accommodations between Africans and Europeans, in the categorical terms I am using in this sentence.

We can read his garrulous aunt as expressing a racist stereotype when she dismisses small islanders and their pitch-oil tins of ground provisions but, in the context of a fiction, she merely may be articulating her desire to escape the heat of her own coalpot, or repeating a catchy phrase she has picked up from her Creole neighbour, or invoking a barely remembered culinary taboo from her own forgotten cultural antecedents. Or maybe she is just a cantankerous old curmudgeon. There is, after all, something quite splendid about her theatrical dismissiveness that compels our attention as readers of fiction, the more so as the narrator tempts us to fantasise about how these qualities are subsumed into the facade of her later incarnation as a sedate, conventionally generous dowager living in Canada.

The successful fiction must find a way to leave all of these possibilities open. It must move beyond literary cliche or theoretical paradigm even as it appropriates this one characteristic impression of the aunt to convey the multiple associations Naipaul imposes upon her words in the context of Lebrun's dinner party. And indeed, the writer of fiction is never quite in control of the how his readers will interpret his characters, as my earlier reading of this moment in conjunction with Lamming's novel as a hysterical failure of the narrator's voice demonstrates. Naipaul acknowledges this understanding of the disciplinary and stylistic boundaries that separate a writer like himself from a writer like James when his narrator says of Lebrun, "we both soon got to recognise—what I felt sure we always knew—that the relationship between us was forced. We shared a background and in all kinds of unspoken ways we could understand one another; but we were on different tracks".

The problem of appropriation, of what from Naipaul's perspective it means to be read through someone else's intellectual assumptions, whether it be through the transplanted Creole norms of Caribbean immigrant culture or the intellectual paradigms of Lebrun's essay, is crucial to an understanding of what is at stake in Naipaul's reading of the meal of gefilte fish that he shares in Manhattan with Lebrun's powerful friends. Through the second meal, the narrator comes to realise that Lebrun, too, has been the victim of co-optation; that what Lebrun describes as the "political resolution" through which he comes to terms with the humiliations of his racial history is in part a form of spiritual capitulation to the meanings others have assigned to his body and his writing. During the Maida Vale meal, Lebrun recounts his humiliation at realising that his great-uncle's stories of being treated like a guest in the kitchens of London Great Houses in the mid-nineteenth century were fantasies nurtured to deny the realities of colonialism and racism.

The narrator uses this story to anchor his imaginative insights into Lebrun's inner life. Lebrun claims that he is only released from the shame he connects with his own participation in his great-uncle's self delusion when he can tell this story in public to others. But he also maintains that, "every black man has a memory like that. Every educated black man is eaten away quietly by a memory like that". And, indeed, the narrator remains unconvinced that the shameful desire for approval, which fuels the great-uncle's fantasies of equality with white servants, is not still eating away at Lebrun. Thus, as Lebrun approaches senility, his compulsive need to repeat his great-uncle's story marks the persistence of the trauma caused by this early childhood memory, just as the narrator remains unable to move beyond the range of his aunt's invective when confronted with small-island food.

Naipaul invites us to read the second meal of gefilte fish from the perspective of the shame surrounding this painful legacy of gratitude to one's oppressors which Lebrun's great-uncle bequeaths his nephew. At first, the narrator is horrified to realise that the sophisticated Manhattan intellectuals into whose company he has been admitted by virtue of Lebrun's introduction can see him only through the paradigms offered by Lebrun's article in the "thick" Russian magazine. All their vaunted knowledge of the islands has been siphoned off second-hand from their readings of Lebrun and other Left wing theoreticians. They seem to him to have no feeling for the nuances of cruelty, betrayal, indifference, and joy that separate and connect different regimes and racial groups within the region with which they claim solidarity.

Where Lebrun offers the narrator coo-coo but is at least willing to overlook the fact that he cannot eat it, Lebrun's Manhattan friends appear to treat the narrator's refusal of their meal of gefilte fish as a kind of betrayal. Like the contrived global paradigms through which Caribbean societies often are read in metropolitan intellectual circles, the worked over, indeterminate mass of gefilte fish is offered to the narrator as a token of the automatic solidarity between oppressed Jewish and Caribbean peoples:

> The idea of something pounded to paste, then spiced or oiled, worked on by fingers, brought to mind thoughts of hand lotions and other things. I became fearful of smelling it. I couldn't eat it. With the coo-coo or the foo-foo in the Maida Vale flat I had been able to hide what I did to the things on my plate. That couldn't be done here: everyone knew that the gefilte fish had been specially prepared for Lebrun's friend from London.

Naipaul never names Lebrun's friends directly as left wing Jewish intellectuals, just as he never gets further than identifying Lebrun's woman friend as Polish or Czech. For his narrator, the ramifications of all their racial and ethnic histories remain opaque. He can see no organic link between the affluence and sophistication of his New York hosts and the social limitations of his Caribbean childhood, just as someone from the outside who did not know his aunt before she became a gracious Canadian lady would have had difficulty associating her with the shrieking harridan fanning a coal pot on the back steps of an overcrowded Port of Spain house.

Or, as someone who had not read the novel's earlier descriptions of Leonard Side, the Trinidadian descendant of Lucknow's Shia Muslim dancing transvestites, whose long perfumed fingers iced cakes and laid out dead bodies at Parry's Corner, might miss the necrophilic associations Naipaul brings to the description of the way his narrator imagines gefilte fish is prepared. The narrator concedes in his story of Leonard Side that "we go back all of us to the very beginning; in our blood and bone and brain we carry the memories of thousands of beings". But he sees that legacy as expressing only "a fragment of the truth" we understand about our racial inheritances. He distrusts his hosts' insistence that he equate their history of oppression with what they imagine is his own; that coo-coo is somehow equivalent to gefilte fish and that the consumption of such meals confer on their eaters a badge of authenticity as representatives of the oppressed. For him, the distinctions in social status between himself and his hosts of which he remains most acutely aware have less to do with the coincidences of oppression within their respective histories than with the ease with which they now assume they can read him. They take it for granted that they can co-opt and categorise his experience, even as they prescribe how they expect him to read their own.

As he struggles with the social ostracism to which he imagines his refusal of the meal of gefilte fish exposes him, Naipaul's fictional double begins to reflect on the difficult line someone like Lebrun must constantly walk among such powerful patrons; the extent to which his global paradigms can be read as an attempt to protect himself from the appropriative power of his mentors, even as they seduce him into simplifying the stubborn contradictions of his specific history. He speculates that Lebrun's consummate rhetoric and his air of having transcended the legacies of slavery and racial oppression may in fact conceal a sense of incompleteness, a desire to be accepted, like that of his nineteenth century great-uncle, that betrays him into the false securities of unequal alliances.

Naipaul's speculations about the private motivations behind Lebrun's "political resolutions" produces one of the novel's most direct autobiographical statements and one of the few moments in the text when he seems to distance his narrator completely from Lebrun. The narrator is able to refuse the form of solidarity he imagines he has been offered over the meal of gefilte fish because he values his personal integrity as a writer above his hosts' approval. By contrast, Naipaul reads Lebrun's consent to the appropriation of his ideas by people, who neither acknowledge the moral ambiguities nor understand the personal humiliations out of which his political resolutions arise, as evidence of Lebrun's feelings of incompleteness:

Few of us are without the feeling that we are incomplete. But my feelings of incompleteness were not like Lebrun's. In the things I felt myself incomplete Lebrun was—as I thought—abundantly served: physical attractiveness, love, and sexual fulfilment. But there were other yearnings that no shedding of skin could have assuaged: my own earned security, a wish for my writing gift to last and grow, a dream of working at yet unknown books, accumulations of fruitful days, achievement. These yearnings could be assuaged only in the self I knew.

There is a double subterfuge at work in this passage. In the first place, Naipaul structures his observation in such a way that Lebrun's gifts and insecurities are reduced to those that Naipaul's narrator can read through his own limitations. So, in a way, he is asking us to read Lebrun through his narrator's limited paradigms—in exactly the way he accuses the Manhattan crowd of reading his work exclusively through Lebrun's paradigms. And it is also difficult to avoid the impression that Naipaul is protesting too loudly.

His distancing of his narrator from a particular reading of Lebrun's capitulation masks a defence of Naipaul himself from similar charges of having "sold out" to the influential champions of his work within the literary mainstream. Naipaul uses the representation of his narrator as perversely difficult, as someone who refuses to make the kinds of compromises Lebrun has made and for whom the excellence and integrity of his work as a writer is paramount, to counteract the image of himself as the Third World writer who has made a fortune saying the derogatory things the First World wants to hear about his world. Thus, just as his writing seems most clear, most forthright, most free of elision, Naipaul conceals between the lines a passionate defence of himself from a criticism of his work that remains unformulated as such within his text.

Perhaps in the end this is the point of Naipaul's estimate of James and himself through the character of Lebrun. For Naipaul, Lebrun is always most interesting when his facade of consummate urbanity cracks; when his naked sexual envy in relation to the writer Foster Morris flashes out, just as Naipaul's narrator's literary vanity is piqued by this same man; when his bitterness about a personal dilemma betrays him in Africa, as it has at times betrayed Naipaul in other settings, into vicious or reckless political pronouncements which others then proceed to take seriously; when the old hurt and humiliation associated with his great-uncle's gratitude over being allowed to take tea with the servants in an English Great House betrays his pain at having to accept the way his ideas are co-opted by his powerful patrons—just as Naipaul's have been. Through Lebrun, Naipaul sees men like himself and James as "men on the run."

Both writers have relinquished membership in the communities of their birth in order to pursue fame through their writing, thus gambling with the possibility of their co-optation by more powerful communities on a global stage. Both have claimed for themselves the license, as Naipaul notes of Lebrun, to critique anything and anybody wherever they find themselves but neither has stayed long enough anywhere to have had to live with the consequences of their pronouncements.

The difference between them from Naipaul's perspective is that his narrator claims to be aware of the dangers and limitations inherent in his way of reading the world, whereas a public figure like Lebrun, whose work has been politically appropriated by others, is constantly shielded from the consequences of the "real world" limitations of his vision by those who lionise him. Thus, while Naipaul's narrator must constantly revise his reading of himself in the face of relentless criticism, Lebrun remains "oddly pure" because the ideals of revolution and African redemption that he espouses have become fashionable "progressive" cliches whose inherent contradictions no one cares to expose.

Naipaul's novel builds on the anecdotal. It incorporates into the character of Lebrun recognisable traits of C.L.R. James as well as observations Naipaul has made over time of other writers and colonial impresarios of James's generation. Naipaul offers us little concrete evidence that James ever evinced the fears or responses the narrator imputes to Lebrun. But Naipaul's autobiographical narrators have often evinced just such forms of personal angst. They know what it means, as the narrator says in his final estimate of Lebrun, to have one's "intellectual growth ... at every stage ... accompanied by a growing rawness of sensibility," to face the realisation that "[one's] political resolutions, expressing the wish not to go mad, [have] been in the nature of spiritual struggles, occurring in the depth of [one's] being".

Through the ambiguous gesture of generosity and co-optation contained in this epitaph, Naipaul imputes to James, via his construction of the character of Lebrun, all the real and imagined fears of appropriation he has experienced as a writer. He challenges readers who have seen him and James as representing diametrically opposed strands in Caribbean intellectual thought to acknowledge the anguish and insecurity, even the petty viciousness, that must of necessity have lain behind James's perfectly poised public persona.

Without an understanding of this angst, Naipaul contends, we cannot fully appreciate either the greatness of a man like James or the limits of his vision. At the same time, Naipaul presents himself, through his narrator's words, as having been able to refuse most of the accommodations someone like James in his opinion has had to accept. He claims he is able to do so, on account of the accidents of history that brought him into the literary world at a less brutal moment than James. These include the changes in the politics of racial patronage that separate a Caribbean intellectual impresario of the 1930s from a Caribbean Oxford graduate of the 1950s, as well as Naipaul's understanding of himself as a creative writer rather than a political theoretician.

Finally, Naipaul sees the double dispossessions of his Indo-Trinidadian racial heritage as making him less susceptible to the myths of racial affirmation that in his opinion have created the dissonance between the themes of global transcendence and cultural nationalism in James's political pronouncements.

Synopsis

A way in the world is a worthy capstone to a world-class career. It also is deeply flawed, as only a late-career book by V. S. Naipaul can be. Naipaul's relationship with his native Caribbean remains fraught and no doubt painful; this is obvious in his arguably offensive portrayal (as "Lebrun") of C. L. R. James, the Trinidadian Marxist who is considered the patriarch of Caribbean writers in this century. Why, for example, does Naipaul falsify the reputation of James's justly famous book The Black Jacobins (1938)? "His purpose in writing the book in the 1930s had been to prove his old point about the revolutionary nature of the islands; to give himself and his ideas a great past, to link the revolutionary stir of the 1930s to the stir caused in the region by the French Revolution. . . . All that labour, and I doubt whether a dozen people in Trinidad or Venezuela had read his book."

Naipaul's attitude and relation to James are important to readers who would understand his career as a whole. To Naipaul's credit he confronts James, however self-servingly, in a way in the world. As Naipaul himself once told an interviewer: "The good person, if he is dedicated, always makes his limitations into virtues."

Summary

"A way in the World, a collection of essays by V.S. Naipaul, published in 1994, travels around the Caribbean, dealing with the battles between the Spanish and British to colonise Trinidad and Venezuela. One particular episode describes the visit of a cruise ship to Trinidad in the thirties through a travel article, "The Shadowed Livery", 'Portraying subject people as a whole unto themselves", written by an Englishman, Foster Morris. Although the reputation of the writer diminishes," it was strange that a man so much in search of his own voice should have been the one to help me find mine," Naipaul wrote.

As an undergraduagte at Oxford University, Naipaul sent Morris a manuscript of his first novel. Morris wrote back right away,"..abandon it immediately." Naipaul followed this advice, and later, published his first novel. He kept up a relationship with Morris until the older author died, seeing Morris's star fall while Naipaul enjoyed increasing success.

Analysis

If today, the Caribbean men and women who began to publish their work in the 1950s are considered the first cohort of internationally recognised Caribbean writers, then those of us born in that decade can count ourselves among the first generation of Caribbean readers, that is, the first generation of Caribbean children to grow up taking the existence of Caribbean literature as a given.

By the time I entered secondary school in Trinidad in the 1960s, independence had washed over the "islands of the bluuuee Caribbean sea," as we sang of them in our new national anthem, and books by local authors were beginning to find their way into libraries, literary soirees, and middle class homes. Unlike our parents, we took it for granted that West Indians could give birth to books, although, since practically none of these writers still lived in the islands, we weren't quite sure where or how this literary conception happened.

The silence in our school curriculum on the subject of Caribbean writers raised additional doubts about the literary merit of such works as well as the moral standing of their authors, so we tended to talk about them, like the uncle who had fled to Venezuela to escape a little problem with the police, in the past tense, or the subjunctive.

To make matters worse, the snippets of Caribbean poems and stories we heard recited at special events at the Public library downtown or at the USIS Library children's hour, we considered embarrassingly folksy, not to say vulgar. Like students subjected to today's politically correct educational agendas, we quickly worked out that many of the adults around us considered such events an uncomfortable duty, not nearly as appealing as attendance at the latest British Council evening of operatic arias. Public readings of West Indian literature were a bit like sex education; an attempt to make something we all knew was perverted sound straightforward and unremarkable.

Deviance delivers its own pleasures, however. Lacking the official seal of approval of the Cambridge School Certificate examination board, Caribbean books were free to pervert us rather than to uplift. Samuel Selvon's Turn Again Tiger and Edgar Mittelholzer's Children of Kaywana were the first "dirty" books I remember having read. I found Selvon's tucked away in the back of a bookcase in my grandmother's house. My older sister bought the cheap paperback edition of Mittelholzer's Kaywana Trilogy with her own money and waved it inches away from my nose as a book that was "too old" for me. Of course I had to read it. It did not disappoint.

Even more than illicit sex these novels were about racial transgression. It was not just that they showed Caribbean people of different races in relationships of appalling intimacy with each other. Their stories presented non-white characters in ways that transgressed the conventions of the nineteenth century English and twentieth century American novels we usually read.

Indians did not just skulk around in exotic, Kiplingesque settings, charming snakes and sleeping on nails. Blacks did not merely cower and croon. Chinamen were not sages whose pigtails always hung behind them. They were teachers, bakers, shoemakers, schoolchildren, cane farmers, laundresses, insurance salesmen and saga boys. Some were enterprising, others lackadaisical, still others downright evil but, at least in Mittelholzer, in a savvy, complex fashion. And the whites were not all missionaries or Governors General doing time in the tropics either. Many were bored housewives or struggling clerks, who'd never been to the Mother Country, and who lived in backwaters like Berbice, British Guiana, or on sugar estates in Tacarigua, Trinidad, or in crumbling family villas along Old Hope Road in Jamaica.

We knew all these people. Some were our playmates, some, friends of our parents, others, relatives. Some were just people whose mango trees we lusted after. But until now they had not existed for us with the certainty with which we knew that Miss Havisham in Great Expectations existed. I devoured those books, furtively, defiantly, and obsessively. In return, they delivered up those pleasures that Freud assures us are part of the process by which shame becomes bound up with the erotic, and desire with art.

The Caribbean books we read may have been transgressive, but that did not mean that they were politically "progressive." Many of these early writers valued the colonial legacies they attacked. Today it has become fashionable to see early Caribbean writers who failed to abjure their relationship to the colonising power as somehow unliberated, or lacking in self-assurance.

Nonetheless their ambivalence bequeathed to my generation of readers something the writers themselves had never had: a vast new library of words and images—some borrowed, some cloyingly folksy, some illuminating, some downright embarrassing—with which to begin to name all our worlds; a language through which to express all our desires, however politically retrograde some of them may now appear. They allowed us to see our world clearly for the first through the prism of art, which afforded us the luxuries of self-deception—as well as the promise of self-fabrication.

And indeed, we laughed hardest where we most refused to recognise ourselves. Movies, dances and football games were off-limits for Mrs. Cobham's daughters, so most of our teenage suitors had to make do with the blue wicker couch on the front gallery. I no longer remember whose copy of Miguel Street we found wedged between the blue cushions, but I remember one suitor looking at the title and saying with an air of self importance; "That's Luis Street, you know," which was the street at the other end of Woodbrook where he lived. We read Naipaul's stories out loud to each other. I remember laughing till I cried at Man Man on the cross, urging the onlookers to "stone me, brethren, stone me!" and screaming with delight at the idea of his dog leaving symmetrical piles of droppings on the stools in the Cafe at the corner of Alberto Street where we regularly stopped for sweet drinks. And of course we were convinced that Man Man really must have been Mr. Assee, whose endless chalked sentences on the pavement of Damien Road we were careful to circumvent when we took the short cut from the Avenue to Roxy Roundabout.

It never occurred to us that we also might have been the subjects of Naipaul's satire: Mrs. Cobham's daughter, hedged in by all the elaborate protocols of black middle class respectability, but longing to play out a grand passion before the cinema audiences she could not be a part of. The suitor, somebody's well behaved boy child masquerading as a Black Panther under his Afro and knitted beret, reading short stories on the blue couch when he really wanted to do something else.

"The first sentence was true. The second was invention", Naipaul says in Finding the Centre of the famous opening exchange in Miguel Street: "Every morning when he got up Hat would sit on the bannister of his back verandah and shout across, 'What happening there, Bogart?' Bogart would turn in his bed and mumble softly, so that no one heard, `What happening there, Hat?'". That claim itself may be a writer's fiction but it captures something of our first response to Miguel Street.

We saw but did not see our world in the pages of Naipaul's novel. We imagined that our own lives were not that sordid or petty and yet we knew that we had heard all the words, seen all the sights Naipaul described a hundred times before.

The second sentence was always fiction; the first, already fact. Naipaul's his sleight of hand convinced us that our experience as readers of his text—of any text—was as authentic as that of any other reader. He allowed us to gaze at our lives without feeling ourselves to be merely the diminished object of that gaze. For Naipaul framed our lives with art and art is always distancing and oblique.

My essay examines the meaning of this achievement in the work of a writer whose accomplishments over the past fifty years have been sustained and celebrated. That achievement has allowed Naipaul in recent years to experiment with forms which, in the work of writers of lesser repute, might have been considered too eccentric for serious consideration.

It has given him a protected space to face up to issues that earlier he may have been too insecure or too inexperienced to confront, even as it leaves him open to the temptations of narcissism and isolation such license conceals. Naipaul knows that his work will outlive him, and in this later writing he is fighting for the right to influence the way in which that legacy will be read. The readings I offer here from Naipaul's A Way in the World demonstrate how the project of writing one's critical legacy can be understood as an overriding thematic concern as well as an important source of stylistic innovation.

In A Way in the World, Naipaul uses a character named Lebrun to talk about his fellow countryman, the political activist and intellectual, C.L.R. James. By basing Lebrun's character on James, Naipaul finds a way to examine the problems of co-optation that come with fame—problems with which both he and James have had to struggle. I will focus on his descriptions of two meals that Naipaul's semi-autobiographical narrator shares—the first with Lebrun, the second with Lebrun's Manhattan friends.

Naipaul challenges readers who have seen him and James as representing diametrically opposed positions in Caribbean intellectual thought to acknowledge the angst and insecurity, the refusals and accommodations that must of necessity have lain behind James's poised public persona. Without an understanding of this angst, he contends, we cannot fully appreciate either the greatness of a figure like James or the limits of his vision. At the same time, this reading of James through the fictional character Lebrun offers us strategies for understanding the fictional persona Naipaul has created for himself in his writing.

Novel or Sequence?

Naipaul reportedly agreed to call *A Way in the World* a novel at the request of his publisher, having himself suggested "sequence" as a sub-title: the word sequence has been adopted by some reviewers. Despite his achievements as a novelist, in later life Naipaul has described the novel as an outmoded form.

Relationship to the Loss of El Dorado

A Way in the World is more fictional than the Naipaul's earlier historical work *The Loss of El Dorado* (1969), which deals with some of the same material, for example the lives of Sir Walter Raleigh and Francisco de Miranda. Naipaul also includes autobiographical material, partly fictionalised, which was not in the first book.

9 India: A Million Mutinies Now

India: A Million Mutinies Now is a nonfiction book by V. S. Naipaul published in 1990. It is a travelogue written during the author's sojourn in his ancestral land — India. It was the third of Naipaul's acclaimed Indian trilogy which includes *An Area of Darkness* and *India: A Wounded Civilization*. True to his style, the narration is anecdotal, using examples and specificity in its descriptions.

Naipaul expresses serious misgivings about Indian attitudes and the Indian way of life. On the other hand Naipaul notes the economic growth and its associated emancipation of the various peoples of India. The title makes an analogy between the emancipation of millions and the Mutiny of 1857. The book is somewhat optimistic about the country and its peoples.

Introduction

This third part of the trilogy is considerably different from the first two volumes especially in Naipaul's attitude to India. This travelogue describes India of the late 1980s and the early 1990s. Since the time the author first visited this country India has gone through numerous transformations and reforms and still a great deal of changes is to come. Naipaul observes with the greatest pleasure that India drives itself in a right direction. Although, as I have already suggested, there are still many transformations to be done and the struggle for modern India is not over, it is clear that Indian people had finally woken up from long years of passivity and stagnation.

Naipaul comes to India at the time of extensive agricultural revolution and industrial development; the social and economical situation of the country improves. Indian people discovered the ineffectiveness in their caste system and traditional Hindu principals. They are less ignorant to the political situation of the country. India is finally facing straight to the future and starts to direct its way.

Naipaul sees India from a much more relaxed point of view. Perhaps the time that passed since his first sojourn in India and the changes that India underwent helped Naipaul to conquer the original feelings of disillusion. It is far more optimistic and it differs very much in style. Naipaul abandons his sophisticated, melancholic comments and reveals the true state of India to the reader through the vivid descriptions of actual people and their stories. He tries to cover the whole social and cultural spectrum of the society, nonetheless, most of the people Naipaul interviews are men and they are mostly "urban, middle aged, and middle class". The author comments on his decision to present India through the interviews with people:

> The idea of letting people talk in the book on the South was really quite new to me. And so in this book [India: A Million Mutinies Now] I thought it was better to let India be defined by the experience of the people, rather than writing one's personal reaction to one's feeling about being an Indian and going back – as in the first book [An Area of Darkness] – or trying to be analytical, as in the second book [India: A Wounded Civilization].

The tone is rather optimistic though in comparison with the two previous books Naipaul leaves much space to the reader to make his own judgements. He does not reveal his attitudes to such an extent. Nevertheless, it is clear that the overall tone of the book is positive.

In comparison with the first two volumes, India: A Million Mutinies Now may seem somewhat lower in topics covered, which can be ascribed to the fact that it is written in the form of dialogues, the author only rarely comments, expecting the reader to make his or her own conclusions.

Naipaul especially focuses on the improvement of Indian agricultural, economic and industrial development. He describes many projects intended for improving the living conditions and agricultural and industrial production. He still realises some of the inadequacies but, in general, he has very positive feelings about Indian future and no longer sees India as a stagnant, ruined country unable of any further development. He is more empathic in his attitudes to Indian people.

The visual aspect of the country improved as well. There are far less squatting beggars in the streets, not because there would not be any in India, but because, for the author, they are not as symbolic for India as they used to be. Poverty of people is not that shocking and the conditions of living ameliorate with every new day.

Naipaul is very much concerned with the changes in social structure. Caste system still exists in India, but the Indian people are aware of a necessity to release its bonds. Among the interviewed people there are those who do not care about their caste at all. Hinduism still has a very powerful role within the country, because Indians have always been deeply religious people, but even the Hindu traditions go through substantial changes to satisfy the needs of modern society.

People start to be focused on their individual needs and the spiritual world that used to be the core of their existence is replaced by the materialistic world. The achievement of self-awareness and individuality is seen as the predisposition for the development of the nation and creation of national identity. "India has entered a state of regenerative disintegration".

Indians, like people in other countries, strive hard to improve their standard of living. Education is very important for them and many young people go to finish their studies at the universities abroad. The position of women in the society gets better. Women are no longer seen as mothers, whose only target is bringing up their children. They start to build their own careers.

Naipaul uses the term "million mutinies" for the strife of individuals against long ago established social and cultural norms. The individuals in India feel the need to change their country and India is full of small riots on the basis of individuals and small groups of people.

A million mutinies, supported by twenty kinds of group excess, sectarian excess, religious excess, regional excess: the beginnings of self-awareness, [...] a central will, a central intellect, a national idea. The Indian Union was greater than the sum of its parts. (Million Mutinies)

Conditions of Living and Reforms

People had a little more money now. [...] Indian poverty was still visible, the middens, the broken-down aspect of houses and lanes. But the fields, of sugar-cane and cotton and other crops, looked rich and well-tended; the village houses were often neat, with plastered walls and red-tile roofs. There was nothing like the destitution I had seen 26 years before, when I had travelled through on a slow, stopping bus. There were none of the walking skeletons, with their deranged eyes.

The agricultural revolution was a reality here; the increased supply of food showed. Hundreds of thousands of people all over India, perhaps millions of people, had worked for this for four decades, in the best way: very few of them with an idea of drama or sacrifice or mission, nearly all of them simply doing jobs. (Million Mutinies 149)

As apparent from the extract above, the living conditions in India extensively improved. The situation is still not ideal, but in comparison with the situation described in the previous two books of the trilogy, the poverty manifests itself in a much more suppressed form and the living standard of people increased. This is due to the changes in people's thinking. The materialistic aspects of their lives gained considerable importance. With the introduction of new technologies the conduction of people's everyday affairs is much easier. What used to be seen as the craze of people of higher social status and the manifestation of power and wealth several years ago, slowly but surely becomes the necessity and commonplace for a larger scale of Indian social spectre.

Because of industrialisation, and the green revolution in the rural areas, a new class of nouveau-riche persons are emerging, and these people are being exposed for the first time to university education, comfortable urban life, stylish living, and western influences – materialistic comforts. During this transition period, we are slowly cutting from the moral ethos of our grandfathers, and at the same time we don't have the westerner's idea of discipline and social justice. Yet there remained certain contradictions in the author's pictures. He still sees the Indian poorness, but unlike in the previous two books his tone of narration is less accusing, sharp and bitter.

Level or fully made footpaths are not a general Indian need, and the Indian city road is often like a wavering, bumpy, much mended asphalt path between drifts of dust and dirt and the things that get dumped on Indian city roads and then stay there, things like sand, gravel, wet rubbish, dry rubbish: nothing ever looking finished, no kerbstone, no wall, everything in a half-and-half way, half-way to being or ceasing to be.

Moreover, Naipaul also comments on even darker aspects of Indian life; crime and murders being part of everyday life, lingering bureaucracy and corruption, "prostitution and despair in the back streets" (Million Mutinies).

Naipaul broadly writes about many reforms running through the country in agriculture, industry and living standard. He describes the electrification in villages, irrigation system in agriculture and sanitary improvements of the slums. The Indian scientific growth and development is no less important.

India is slowly recovering from its failures. The intellectual capacity of the country is increasing and the new technological centres are established like space research and aircraft industry in Bangalore. "Every kind of scientific institution was in Bangalore" (Million Mutinies). There is a significant reform in women's position within the society.

Women care about their education and careers. A relevant step afore for the strengthening of their position within the society is the publication of women's magazines and newspapers such as Woman's Era, Eve's Weekly or Femina. There were no Indian women's magazines before independence. Middle-class Indian women read the two popular British magazines, Woman's Weekly and Woman's own. When the British went away these magazines ceased to be available. (Milion Mutinies)

Most of the marriages in India are still being arranged. Nonetheless, the number of "love" marriages is mounting. Foreign marriages also become common or at least more frequent in contemporary Indian environment. Although the living conditions, the position of women in the society and the economic situation are still not equal to developed countries, India slowly but surely follows their direction.

Religion and Social Structure

As Indian society is deeply religious, Hinduism cannot be considered merely as a religion in India, it is rather a lifestyle. It determines and transfuses into every aspect of Indian life and, in its traditional form, it has put an obstacle on the Indian way to progress. Therefore, as I have already stated earlier, the traditional religious and social principles of the Indian society have gone through radical changes. Although Hindu religion cannot be completely diminished, which is not even necessary, it becomes more fitted to the needs of the contemporary economic development of the Indian society.

> Everybody tries to change things to suit himself. [...] [The rituals] were being adapted all the time (Million Mutinies). Some of the old traditions and rituals perished and those, which survived, were transformed to better serve the needs of the individuals. From the previous two books it is clear that most of the rituals practised in India are not fully understood by Indians themselves and with every new generation they are losing their meaning.

> It might have seemed then that Hindu India was on the verge of extinction, something to be divided between Christian Europe and the Muslim world, and all its religious symbols and difficult theology rendered as meaningless as the Aztec gods in Mexico, or the symbolism of Hindu Angkor. But it hadn't been like that. [...] a Hindu India had grown again, more complete and unified than any India in the past. (Million Mutinies)

The caste system as a social order in India is still prevailing, but, as in the case of religion, in its reduced forms. Many protests run through the whole country and the new attitudes are shaped. Naipaul broadly describes the Dravidian movement against Brahmins and their traditions initiated by Periyar:

> Other middle castes began to produce their own prominent personalities. Many of these middle-caste people were well-to-do [...] many were landlords; some could send their sons to Oxford and Cambridge. As soon as such people had emerged from the middle castes, the antique Brahmin caste restrictions would not have been

easy to maintain. What Periyar did was to take this mood of rejection to the non-Brahmin masses. (Million Mutinies)

This movement took form of "braking idols, cutting of Brahmins' churkis and sacred threads, and rubbing of the religious marks on the forehead" (Milion Mutinies). Vegetarian restaurants were known as "Brahmin hotels", whereas non-Brahmin restaurants were called "military hotels". The Brahmin side of Naipaul is revealed when he indicates that in the "military hotels" the conditions are very poor and unclean.

Caste system is still defining people's position in the country. Indians are not able to completely withdraw from their long ago established caste system. It became too much part of their identity. Though, the approach of individuals slightly modified, caste is still determining for certain positions and functions.

Caste was the first thing of importance. A man looking for office or a political career would have to be of a suitable caste. That meant belonging to the dominant caste of the area. He would also, of course, have to be someone who could get the support of his caste; that meant he would have to be of some standing in the community, well connected and well known. (Million Mutinies)

Yet there appears a remarkable shift in their caste system organisation. Middle-class people grow in importance not only economically, but intellectually as well, whereas, the members of the highest castes are subsequently losing their stable position in the Indian society. The new stratification of the society is evident from Naipaul's interviews. The new Indian elite springs out of these transformations.

Synopsis

This is the third book in V S Naipaul's acclaimed "Indian Trilogy". Much has changed since V.S. Naipaul's first trip to India and this fascinating account of his return journey focuses on India's development since independence. Taking an anti-clockwise journey around the metropolises of India — including Bombay, Madras, Calcutta, and Delhi — Naipaul offers a kaleidoscopic, layered travelogue, encompassing a wide collage of religions, castes, and classes at a time when the percolating ideas of freedom threatened to shake loose the old ways. The brilliance of the book lies in Naipaul's decision to approach this shifting, changing land from a variety of perspectives: the author humbly recedes, allowing the Indians to tell the stories of their own lives, and a dynamic oral history of India emerges before our eyes. "India: A Million Mutinies Now" is a truly perceptive work whose insights continue to inform travellers of all generations to India.

Summary

"India a Million Mutinies Now" is a fascinating journey through India, of the late 1980s and early 1990's, showcasing its on-going struggles, triumphs, and upheavals through the stories of common people. It is a travelogue by the noble prizewinning, Trinidad-born Indian author V.S Naipaul. The book is a compilation of interviews or conversations with the people of India, from different walks of life. He meets with Hindu and Muslim extremists, with Atheists, rationalists- anti-Brahmin rebels, Gangsters, Sikh terrorists, communist leaders and with former Naxalite rebels. Ordinary people like government officials, filmmakers, stockbrokers, and holy men.

Naipaul succeeds in bringing a common thread to all the interviews; he goes on from one to another almost seamlessly. He sees things with a rational point of view, does not romanticise, or sugarcoat facts for the sake of political correctness. He doesn't hesitate in talking about the sorry state of affairs in the country, accusations made are sometimes harsh and he has no qualms in expressing them. Naipaul crisscrossed the nation, from the West, Bombay to the East, Calcutta, and from Kashmir in the North to Madras in South. Throughout his journey he keeps reverting back to his life in Trinidad. The customs and rituals he performed then, without thinking or involuntarily were given meaning and reason in India.

Like eating off banana leaves after a special religious occasion in his grandmother's house was just a ritual, but in Madras he finds out that it is Brahminically (Brahmins are upper class Hindus) more correct than plates. He found out that, people in India felt the need to hold on to smaller ideas of who and what they were and found stability in the smaller groupings of region, clan, caste, family, much like in Trinidad where people held on, tightly to their community to feel a sense of belonging. It is a mildly satirical composition, full of sardonic wit, but behind this facade, comes a feeling of love for the land and its people. The individuals who represent the "Million Mutinies" were given faces and identities in Naipaul's descriptive narrative. He tells us about their revolt, sometimes silent, sometimes raucous. The unpredictable Indian scenario is has been very meticulously captured in this striking, comprehensive, and unforgettable book.

Analysis

Independence had come to India like a kind of revolution," V. S. Naipaul says in the introductory chapter of his elegant account of a journey around the world's largest democracy. "Now there were many revolutions within that revolution. ...All over India scores of particularities that had been frozen by foreign rule, or by poverty or lack of opportunity or abjectness had begun to flow again." From winter to spring: it is a comforting image, reassuring, suggestive of natural cycles and an inevitable movement towards warmth and light. The ground thaws, the sap flows, then comes the leaf, the bud, the full flowering of national and individual entitlements, an unstoppable surge towards the glorious fruition promised by the idea of independence. And yet blight intrudes: "Disruptive, lesser loyalties — of region, caste, and clan — now played on the surface of Indian life."

Democracy, after the first exciting flush of its birth struggle, is often fractious, frequently inefficient and unstable, a maelstrom of "disruptive lesser loyalties." Its great strength lies in its willingness to tolerate this messiness in the service of an ideal of fair government. Democracy's toughest test case is India, with its population of 800 million, with more than a dozen major languages and hundreds of dialects, with many faiths and religious traditions in conflict and symbiosis. In "India: A Million Mutinies Now," V. S. Naipaul is an erudite and sensitive guide at a time when the strain of accommodating the revolutions within the revolution — the growth of that internalised awareness of the *meaning* of independence, the sometimes violent clash of competing rights and entitlements, the "million mutinies now" — is particularly intense.

Born in Trinidad in 1932, 15 years before the independence of India, Mr. Naipaul grew up with the knowledge of the subcontinent as ancestral land, his forefathers having emigrated as indentured labourers in the 1880's. On the Caribbean island, Indian emigres like the Naipauls — whether they were Hindu or Muslim, whether their caste was high or low — were disadvantaged and isolated. Drawn together by shared exile, they had a communal sense of Indian identity.

Mr. Naipaul left Trinidad to study at Oxford, and has made England his primary residence ever since. He was 30 years old before he finally visited India. By then he had published four novels of life in Trinidad, "The Mystic Masseur" (1957); "The Suffrage of Elvira" (1958); "Miguel Street" (1959), and "A House for Mr. Biswas" (1961), as well as a non-fiction account of his first visit home to the Caribbean, "The Middle Passage" (1962).

He arrived in Bombay in 1962. His father had died while Mr. Naipaul was a student; now he was looking for his father's roots. On that first visit, Mr. Naipaul was running from Trinidad, rather than towards India, but he has been drawn back repeatedly since, leaving non-fiction records of his journeys: "An Area of Darkness" (an account of the first visit in 1962); "India: A Wounded Civilization" (documenting a 1975-76 stay during Indira Gandhi's "emergency rule"). Now in this new book, as he explores the India of the late 1980's, he recalls the shock and alienation he experienced on that first trip nearly 30 years ago.

Mr. Naipaul discovered that the baggage he had carried with him then, that Trinidadian sense of an Indian community, "had no meaning in India." There, "people needed to hold on to smaller ideas of who and what they were; they found stability in the smaller groupings of region, clan, caste, family." Looking back, Mr. Naipaul notes that such splintering made no sense to him in 1962 ("with my idea of an Indian identity, I couldn't be reconciled to it"), and the visit ended in personal confusion, "in futility and impatience . . . self-reproach and flight."

Now Mr. Naipaul sees pattern and meaning in the fragmentation. During his latest visit, which began in December 1988, Mr. Naipaul crisscrossed India from Bombay to Calcutta, from Kashmir in the North to Madras in the South. He sought out many of the people he met on his first trip, examining the changes in their lives and attitudes, at the same time scrutinising his own memories and changed reactions. He has also sought out the more explosive "revolutions within the revolution," meeting with individuals who are representatives of the "million mutinies" now fermenting.

The tone of Mr. Naipaul's first two books about India was intensely personal and often intensely angry. This time he is altogether gentler, more compassionate, an observer who has made private peace with his ancestral land and is moved both to humility and to celebration by its diversity. What is extraordinary is the sheer exuberance and catholicity of his curiosity.

He meets with a criminal gang leader in Bombay, with Hindu and Muslim extremists, with a leader of the Dalit Panthers (the aggressive political arm of the untouchable caste), with Maoist anti-Brahmin rebels and their police torturers in Madras. He meets with Sikh terrorists and with a former Naxalite rebel who had belonged to a splinter group of Communist peasants. But there are ordinary people too — government clerks, film-makers, stockbrokers, holy men.

Voices on all sides tell Mr. Naipaul that "India had changed; it was not the good and stable country it had once been." They maintain that "the great investment in development over three or four decades had led only to this: to 'corruption,' to the 'criminalisation of politics.' In seeking to rise, India had undone itself. No one could be sure of anything now; all was fluid."

Independence, that heady celebration of Aug. 15, 1947, is recalled by many as a brief and shining moment, a joyous birth, only to be followed by betrayals and rivalries, Camelot tragically undoing itself. But there was no "good and stable country" at the time of independence. There was chaos.

India was bloodily partitioned, its east and west flanks were lopped off to form the two halves of Pakistan, and millions of Hindus and Muslims were resettled on a redrawn map. Of roughly 10 million people exchanged by the two new countries, at least half a million were slaughtered. The new nation was in fact an abattoir. Yet Mr. Naipaul understands the yearning for utopia, the evocation of a world that was once whole.

The search for the unfragmented ideal is the most urgent and consistent theme in all of his writing. It is an idea at the core of both his personal and his literary survival. And the threat of losing that unified world has haunted him. "To see the possibility, the certainty, of ruin, even at the moment of creation: it was my temperament," he wrote in "The Enigma of Arrival" (1987), a brilliant work that he called a novel but which is really in the tradition of St. Augustine's "Confessions," an inner voyage of discovery. "The history I carried with me, together with the self-awareness that had come with my education and ambition, had sent me into the world with a sense of glory dead."

> "I dreaded change," Mr. Naipaul explained, "and that was why, meeting distress halfway, I cultivated old, possibly ancestral ways of feeling, the ways of glory dead, and held on to the idea of a world in flux; the drum of creation in the god's right hand, the flame of destruction in his left."

It is at the moment of loss, in Mr. Naipaul's experience, that the *darshan* comes, the moment of glory revealed, that moment in Hindu temple ritual when the devotee is given a glimpse of the deity. It was not until he left Trinidad and was living in London that Mr. Naipaul recognised the wholeness, the perfection of his own childhood. He enshrined it in "Miguel Street," but almost as soon as he found that glory, it was gone. He returned to Trinidad and nothing was the same. He fled, wrote the story of his father's life in "A House for Mr. Biswas," then fled again — to India — and again to Britain.

Flight, and return, and flight, and literary reconstruction: this is what the quest for wholeness has entailed, this is how past glory has been kept alive. But now Mr. Naipaul no longer seems to dread change. The world may be in flux, but the drum of creation is more powerful than the flame of destruction. Past glories return in new and more hopeful incarnations in every city in India, in every village, in every life.

In one of many memorable encounters, Mr. Naipaul visits a high official of the Shiv Sena, a militant Hindu fundamentalist sect that has had much to do with the current turbulence of Bombay politics. The Shiv Sena official, despite position, power and increased income, still lives with his family in two rooms in the Bombay chawl (tenement) where he grew up. Were it not for the encouragement of his young Brahmin guide, Charu, Mr. Naipaul notes, "I don't think I would have made it even to the internal staircase of the place — I was so demoralised, so choked, driven so near to a stomach-heave, by the smell at the entrance, with wet mangled garbage and scavenging cats... and then, in the suddenly dark passage, by the thick warm smell, catching at my throat, of blocked drains. It was Charu, with his Brahmin's sense of duty ...who (constantly looking back at me, and sometimes even stretching out a hand, like a father leading his child from sand to sea for the first time) led me on and on, up the chawl steps, past open doors giving glimpses of family living spaces."

The documentary method is comprehensive and organic. No sensory detail, no sign or symbol, is too small for Mr. Naipaul's attention, too slight for significance. Behind the immaculate prose rhythms shimmer allusions and echoes — Virgil reaching back to encourage the timid Dante; Homeric similes. Those charged sensory images of decay explain why, even when the details are forgotten, the aura of a Naipaul book remains clear, encoded within the same kind of complex bodily memory by which we recall our first schoolyard.

When Mr. Naipaul questions Mr. Ghate, the Shiv Sena official, about the filth and the overcrowding of the chawl, Mr. Ghate responds with a paean to chawl life. There had in fact been a time when Mr. Ghate and his wife had moved to a modern apartment ("after 100 square feet for 10 people in the chawl, they had 300 square feet for three people in the new apartment"). And Mrs. Ghate had come close to a nervous breakdown from claustrophobia and isolation, so they had returned to the chawl. Mr. Ghate rhapsodises: "In a chawl, you always know what's happening everywhere.... There is no *life* in an apartment." There is no overcrowding as far as Mr. Ghate is concerned. He does not notice the stench or the filth.

In this elucidation of disparities, this revelation that what is seen by the Trinidadian/British eye is precisely what is *not* seen by the Bombay eye, lies Mr. Naipaul's particular brilliance as a cultural analyst. There is a constant interplay of dualities of vision, so that the culture being examined grows ever sharper in focus, gains an ever greater depth. There is not only what Mr. Ghate sees and what Mr. Naipaul sees (which we confidently expect is what the Western reader would also see), there is also the afterimage of the "glory dead," that aura that throws the present into high and ghastly relief. Mr. Naipaul insists on the simultaneity of these perspectives; he refuses to romanticise, to suppress the ugly views for false reasons of political sentimentality.

This truth-telling has not always endeared him to Indians. India's newspapers may be filled with outraged revelations about civic inefficiency and corruption. India's self-accusations may often be as harsh as any Mr. Naipaul has made. But there is, however, a tacit agreement that this is not for outside dissemination, that Western stereotypes of India as a backward country should not be pandered to. Thus Mr. Naipaul is regarded as the outsider with inside information, the man who betrays. Lonely then, but unassailable, Mr. Naipaul gazes into every shadowy corner of the society, giving us a picture that is both harsh and beautiful, familiar and strange.

One has only one major reservation. Because Mr. Naipaul's portraits are careful and illuminating, I was disappointed that there were so few of women, and only one of these was other than cursory. The interview with Mallika, wife of the Dalit Panther poet Namdeo Dhasal, is superb. Mallika, married at 16 by her own defiant choice to the radical untouchable poet, had later written a sensational best-selling feminist autobiography, "I Want to Destroy Myself," the first part of which ended: "Male ego is the most hideous thing in our present society. Women find quite a pleasure in boosting it.... I do not believe that for anybody called Namdeo I should surrender my entire life." Mr. Naipaul talks with Mallika about her book, her life, her husband, in a vivid extended conversation.

But why is there only this solitary, detailed study? Of course, it is inordinately difficult for an unrelated male to converse at all with a woman in India. But even in instances where such a discussion was clearly possible, for example, with Arati, the wife of Dipanjan, a physicist, Mr. Naipaul never really presents her directly. From her husband, we know that Arati, who also teaches physics, cried for days when the couple returned to India from his study leave abroad. Being in England "altered her world," Dipanjan tells Mr. Naipaul. "Because she found for the first time that a woman was not merely or at all the appendage of some man." Clearly, Mr. Naipaul did talk to her at some length. Yet he hardly quotes her, as he does Mallika and his many male interviewees.

Perhaps the explanation for the relative absence of women lies in Mr. Naipaul's comment about a Kashmiri hotel steward. "I wondered why in 1962 I had asked Aziz so little about himself. Shyness, perhaps; a wish not to intrude." Was he restrained by shyness and a certain reticence about prying into women's lives? These are honourable reasons. But I do look forward to a future book in which Mr. Naipaul will direct his unsparing but compassionate outsider's eye towards the women of India.

For now, we can be thankful for the rich and detailed analysis, and perhaps for the sense of hope Mr. Naipaul leaves us with in his concluding pages. I say perhaps, because it's a conclusion that at first seems at odds with much of his book's own evidence, and with what many of the interviewees see in the future. "I am sure there's going to be a revolution," predicts Papu, a Jain stockbroker, gloomily. "In a generation or two. It cannot last, the inequalities of income. I shudder when I think of that.... It will be totally chaos."

Some people think the descent into chaos has begun. A journalist for The Indian Express was stabbed outside the Golden Temple by Sikh terrorists, who, Mr. Naipaul said, "lived hectically, going out to kill again and again." "It's madness, it's fanaticism," another journalist cried. "It can't really be explained." Yet Mr. Naipaul sees some pattern in the mutinies: "The idea of freedom has gone everywhere in India. ...There was ...now what didn't exist 200 years before: a central will, a central intellect, a national idea." He goes on, "The Indian Union was greater than the sum of its parts; and many of these movements of excess strengthened the Indian state, defining it as the source of law and civility and reasonableness."

This sounds, on first reading, so benign as to suggest that Mr. Naipaul has been overtaken by "the sentimental conviction that India is eternal and forever revives" that he has so trenchantly criticised in earlier books. But Mr. Naipaul's is a carefuliy considered optimism. Yes, he acknowledges, there is corruption and violence and excess, but, he says: "Excess was now felt to be excess in India. What the mutinies were also helping to define was the strength of the general intellectual life, and the wholeness and humanism of the values to which all Indians now felt they could appeal. And — strange irony — the mutinies were not to be wished away. They were part of the beginning of a new way for many millions, part of India's growth, part of its restoration."

This is entirely compatible with V. S. Naipaul's vision of "a world in flux: the drum of creation in the god's right hand, the flame of destruction in his left." It is an important vision at a time when much of the globe seems poised at this same delicate point where freedom vies with chaos: South Africa, the new Germany, Poland, Czechoslovakia, Romania, the Soviet Union. Is the democratic process of factional entitlement always a sign of hope? Hardly. Consider Ireland. Consider the Middle East.

The violent Hindu-Muslim clashes at Ayodhya and the fall of V. P. Singh's Government make Mr. Naipaul's optimism seem a little wistful. One thing is certain. Whatever India's future holds, its volatile present has been richly captured in this intricate, splendid and utterly memorable book.

10 The Middle Passage

The Middle Passage: Impressions of Five Societies — British, French and Dutch in the West Indies and South America is a 1962 book-length essay / travelogue by V.S. Naipaul. It is his first book-length work of non-fiction. The book covers a yearlong trip through Trinidad, British Guiana, Suriname, Martinique, and Jamaica in 1961. As well as giving his own impressions, Naipaul refers to the work of earlier travellers such as Patrick Leigh Fermor who described a similar itinerary in "The Traveller's Tree". Naipaul addresses a range of topics including the legacy of slavery and colonialism, race relations, the roles of South Asian immigrants in the various countries, and differences in language, culture, and economics.

Introduction

The Middle Passage is a book essentially about that perennial conjunction of historical misconduct with present and intrinsic human weakness: the colonial legacy. Mr. V. S. Naipaul describes and explains with controlled, one might say tolerant, despair the spiritual chaos and material shortcomings of modern life in some post-slaveholding societies. In form, the book is the account of what must have been on the whole a rather depressing Caribbean journey: Trinidad revisited, where the author, himself of

Hindu descent, was born and bred; British Guiana, Surinam, Jamaica, Martinique. *The Middle Passage* is a travel book. If writing is inseparable from the writer's quality of mind, travel writing is inseparable also from his tastes, his idiosyncrasies, his general temperament—it is what happens to him when confronted by a column, a bird, a sage, a cheat, a riot; wine, fruit, dirt; the delay in the dust, the failing aeroplane. Mr. Naipaul is a novelist (*The House of Mr. Biswas*); he is—undoubtedly—a good writer.

His values are sane, his reactions kind; when he is repelled, as he often has cause to be, his weapons are ironical exposition and resigned analysis; in fact, he is very civilized. He writes well; he can be wonderfully visual; he has a nice sense of comedy which is at ease with the odd characters he meets on boats and trains, and he is brilliant nailing down cat's-cradle conversations. He is not, on the evidence of this book, an inveterate traveller. As he puts it himself, "Travelling is often glamorous only in retrospect and at times would be insupportable without the many kindnesses encountered on the way." True enough.

But that exact sentence could not have been written by Norman Douglas or Patrick Leigh-Fermor; D. H. Lawrence (to whose travel writings Mr. Naipaul's have also been compared) would not have so acknowledged the kindnesses encountered; and all three impart to their travelling a sense of vigour, discovery, pleasure, significance, sheer life, while V. S. Naipaul's gently stoic progress hardly becomes lustrous even in retrospect. They are infectious travellers, he is not. He is adult though young, a little detached, fair and sad. He does not enjoy *himself*. He smokes too much and takes a little whiskey, mainly, one feels, to soothe his nerves; there is no fun in it. The reader is not exhilarated into longing to have been *there*; he is perfectly content to find himself at home reading such an intelligent book about it all.

The opening part, the voyage out, is full of pace and colour, a joy to read and promising great things. The author arrives at Trinidad, Port of Spain, the noisiest city in the world, ablaze with neons, throbbing with a "slightly flawed modernity,"

> ...as soon as anyone starts to talk the radio is turned on. It must be loud, loud. If there are more than three, dancing will begin. Sweat-sweat-dance-dance-sweat. Loud, loud, louder. If the radio isn't powerful enough, a passing steel band will be invited in. Jump-jump-sweat-sweat-jump.

Fear besets him, the fear of return. For years in England, falling asleep with the electric fire on, he used to be awakened by the nightmare that he was back in tropical Trinidad, back in the picaroon immigrant society with its ebullience and irresponsibility and tolerance, the tolerance "which is more than tolerance—an indifference to virtue as well as vice," with its taste for corruption and violence, its lack of respect for the person, its brutality: where people watching Belsen camp scenes at the cinema "will roar with derisive laughter," and the popular calypso sings *The old-time Cat-o'-nine!*, where contempt for the public lingers on in political administration, and "the public, obliged to beg favours, continues to hold authority in dread and contempt."

> ...the most successful people were commission agents, bank managers and members of the distributive trades. Power was recognised, but dignity was allowed to no one. Every person of eminence was held to be crooked and contemptible ...generosity—the admiration of equal for equal—was therefore unknown: it was a quality I only knew from books and found only in England...

There is the old West Indian craving for the new, the up-to-date, the imported. Trollope noted it in 1829: "They will give you oxtail soup when turtle would be much cheaper.... When yams, avocado pears, the mountain cabbage, plantains, and twenty other delicious vegetables may be had for the gathering, people will insist on eating bad English potatoes." Today it is not so much a matter of bad English potatoes as of mass-produced and magazine-advertised food, whiskey against local rum, Nescafe and Maxwell House against—excellent—home-grown coffee which is only touched by middle-class expatriates and the very poor.

Modernity, then, turns out to be the extreme susceptibility of people who are unsure of themselves and, having no taste or style of their own, are eager for instruction...in Trinidad instruction is now provided by advertising agencies...welcomed by the people...because the advertising agency is itself a modern thing...If curiosity is a characteristic of the cosmopolitan, the cosmopolitanism on which Trinidad prides itself is fraudulent. In the immigrant colonial society...subjected for years to the second-rate in newspapers, radio and cinema, minds are tightly closed and Trinidadians of all races and classes are remaking themselves in the image of the Hollywood B-man.

Political immaturity, destructive, aping modernity, wherever Mr. Naipaul went, in British Guiana, in Surinam, Jamaica, he was confronted by these and other elements of the colonial legacy: poverty, racial conflict, rootlessness. Here are some of his analyses. The prejudices of race which he found in nearly every West Indian were in his view generated by self-contempt, and self-contempt had first been taught by the missionaries:

> It is the basis of the faith of the heathen convert: And in these...territories, Christianity must be regarded as part of the colonial conditioning. It was the religion of the slave-owners and at first an exclusive racial faith. It bestowed righteousness on its possessors. It enabled the Dutch in Guiana to divide their (coloured) population into Christians and Negroes...

And from this division, this fostering of competing sectional interests, derived an absence of community sense, an absence of pride and ultimately cynicism. There is, for instance,

> ...little concern about the West Indian emigration to Britain. It was a lower-class thing: it was a black thing;...at another level, it was regarded with malicious pleasure as a means of embarrassing the British people, a form of revenge: and in this pleasure there was no thought for the emigrants or the dignity of the nation about which so much was being said and which was said to be "emergent."

And Mr. Naipaul has this to say about the state of political judgement in British Guiana:

> Wherever ministers go they are met with trivial complaints... surrounded by people who have favours to ask. That the government is elected does not matter, the people require it to be as paternalistic as before, if a little more benevolently; and a popular government must respond. "The people" have learnt their power, and the sensation is still so new that every new voter regards himself as a pressure group. In this way the people...beg, bribe and bully because this is the way they got things in the past...in this way the people are a threat to responsible government and a threat, finally, to their own leaders....

And this on the menace of the "protest" leader as contrasted with the "creative" leader in post-colonial societies:

> For the uneducated masses, quick to respond to racial stirrings and childishly pleased with destructive gestures, the protest leader will always be a hero. The West Indies will never have a shortage of such leaders, and the danger of mob rule and authoritarianism will never cease to be real. The paternalism of colonial rule will have been replaced by the jungle politics of rewards and revenge, the text-book condition for chaos.

And a last note. While in Surinam Mr. Naipaul had gone in search of a legend: He wanted to see the Lazy Negroes of Coronie, the idlest people in the colony, who, when slavery was abolished and the planters abandoned their land, settled down to a remote, detached existence, chasing out all newcomers of other races whose energy might disturb their calm. He found no idyll. He found flatness, mosquitos, neglect, a few coconuts, children in the mud, an old man pleased to see a visitor.

A derelict man in a derelict land...lost in a landscape which had never ceased to be unreal because the scene of an enforced and always temporary residence: the slaves kidnapped from one continent and abandoned on the unprofitable plantations of another, from which there could never more be escape. I was glad to leave Coronie, for, more than lazy Negroes, it held the full desolation that came to those who made the middle passage.

Summary

In The Middle Passage, Naipaul watches a Trinidadian movie audience greeting Humphrey Bogart's appearance with cries of "That is man!" He ventures into a Trinidad slum so insalubrious that the locals call it the Gaza Strip. He follows a racially charged election campaign in British Guiana (now Guyana) and marvels at the Gallic pretension of Martinique society, which maintains the fiction that its roads are extensions of France's routes nationales. And throughout he relates the ghastly episodes of the region's colonial past and shows how they continue to inform its language, politics, and values. The result is a work of novelistic vividness and dazzling perspicacity that displays Naipaul at the peak of his powers. The Middle Passage catches the Caribbean world at a critical moment; a world by turn sad, earnest and hilarious — indeed, a perfect subject for the understanding and comedy of the great writer V S Naipaul.

This book is a brilliant exposition of five colonial societies — Trinidad, British Guiana, Surinam, Martinique and Jamaica by the celebrated writer V S Naipaul. He undertook the Caribbean journey at the invitation, in 1960, of Dr. Eric Williams, the first Prime Minister of independent Trinidad, the author's birth place. At that time the plantation colonies of the region were formed, culturally, in the image of the metropolis. Racial and political assertions had yet to catch up with them in various ways. In Trinidad, African racialism found itself at odds with old colonial mimicry: forty years on, the racial issue will not be between black and white but between black and Asian. Guyana was Marxist but with the same racial divisions: forty years on, the country will be so ruined that a newspaper will be regarded almost as a luxury. In Surinam, a movement was afoot to replace the Dutch language with a pidgin English called talkie-talkie; Forty years on, that racial sentiment will have led to military dictatorship and an exodus of the locals to Holland. Whereas Martinique, defying geography, saw itself as France. And in Jamaica, such rejectionism took the form of Rastafarianism — which, absurdly, turn out to have been the invention of Italian black propaganda during the Abyssinian War of the 1930s. The Middle Passage catches this poor topsy-turvy world at a critical moment: a world by turns sad, earnest and hilarious — indeed, a perfect subject for the understanding and comedy of the celebrated writer V.S. Naipaul.

Synopsis

In this masterpiece of travel writing first published in 1962, V. S. Naipaul returned to Trinidad, his country of origin, and explored four adjacent societies. Naipaul ventures into a Trinidad slum so insalubrious that the locals call it the Gaza Strip. He follows a racially charged election campaign in British Guiana (now Guyana) and marvels at the Gallic pretension of Martinique society, which maintains the fiction that its roads are extensions of France's routes nationales. He relates the ghastly episodes of the region's colonial past and shows how they continue to inform its language, politics, and values. The result is a work of novelistic vividness and dazzling perspicacity that displays Naipaul at the peak of his powers.

11 An Area of Darkness

An Area of Darkness is a book authored by V.S. Naipaul in 1964. It is a travelogue detailing Naipaul's trip through India in the early sixties. It was the first of Naipaul's acclaimed Indian trilogy which includes *India: A Wounded Civilization* and *India: A Million Mutinics Now*. A deeply pessimistic work, *An Area of Darkness* conveys the acute sense of disillusionment which the author experiences on his first visit to his native land. True to his style, the narration is anecdotal and descriptive.

Introduction

In 1947, after a long period of English supremacy, India gained its independence, but had not managed to enjoy its "triumph" as the new obstruction appeared: the "internal discord" of the country caused by the conflicts between the Hindus and the Muslims led to the division of India and the new country of Pakistan was created (Keay 509). The independent India proved enormously incompetent in terms of governing its own nation and of economic development.

Naipaul comes to India, which is adrift by its social and political crises. The economic situation is shattering due to a high extent of corruption and ineffective governance. His reactions to the country of his origins were shock and despair. The picture of India, which he describes during his first visit, was too severe and cruel for him to be able to maintain an objective eye. Instead, he let all his emotions burst out of him. He could not stand to look at all the squatting people in the dusty streets, ragged, scruffy beggars, and pervasive dirt in the ruins of the long-ago burnt-out glory.

Even larger desperateness grows in Naipaul with the sad realisation that the real India and the India of his childhood are completely different places. His memories of the practices of Indian customs and traditions, which he experienced in the Hindu community in Trinidad, differ considerably from what he experiences later in India. That is also one of the principal reasons for his depression and melancholy that he feels in the Indian environment. The real India fails to fulfil the vision of India of his imagination.

Naipaul often compares India and Trinidad in terms of their colonial past. Both countries are bound by the same fate as former British colonies. England has a very important role within the book, not only as a place of Naipaul's contemporary residence, but mainly as a former colonial ruler over India and Trinidad. Naipaul examines the Indian colonial past and its influence on contemporary Indian situation. He sees the colonial experience of India as the source of all the inadequacies that are described in the book.

He also evaluates the Hindu principles that shape the core of the Indian society and affects the overall behaviour of Indian people. The most significant and influential Indian spiritual leader Mahatma Gandhi has a very specific role within the whole trilogy. His description and the attitude of Naipaul towards him go through considerable changes. In An Area of Darkness, he serves mainly as a representative of the western ideas and visions of the world and stands in contrast to the rest of Indian society. The overall mood of the book elucidates in the last chapter, where Naipaul provides the reader with a very personal declaration:

India had not worked its magic on me. It remained the land of my childhood, an area of darkness; like the Himalayan passes, it was closing up again, as fast as I withdrew from it, into a land of myth; it seemed to exist in just the timelessness which I had imagined as a child, into which, for all that I walked on Indian earth, I knew I could not penetrate. (Darkness)

Poverty in the Cities vs. Peaceful Kashmir

The most striking to the eye for Naipaul, before he could penetrate into the psyche of India, was its visual aspect. He sees the country full of dirt, dust, starved and sick people and poor beggars. Indian poverty, commented on throughout the travelogue, is for Naipaul an enormously painful experience. His vivid descriptions of people squatting in the streets and of dirty, decrepit beggars craving for alms create a typical picture of Indian environment. For Naipaul, "India is the poorest country in the world" (Darkness).

As Naipaul highlights, beggary has its special position in India and cannot be judged from a European perspectives. Beggars have a secure position within the society. It is an inseparable element of India. Beggary has its "function", because every act of "giving to the beggar" is seen as "the automatic act of charity, which is an automatic reverence to God" (Darkness).

Defecating belongs to India in the same way as beggary. It became almost a ritual. People walk in the streets full of excrements they do not notice, or even see. Although latrines and toilets are still not commonplace in India, the only reason for this situation is that Indians prefer defecating in an open air. It has become their daily routine and habit. For the westerner it is altogether incomprehensible as Naipaul asserts.

Indians defecate everywhere. They defecate, mostly, beside the railway tracks. But they also defecate on the beaches; they defecate on the hills; they defecate on the river banks; they defecate on the streets; they never look for cover. [...] These squatting figures [...] are never spoken of; they are never written about; they are not mentioned in novels or stories; they do not appear in feature films or documentaries. [...] The truth is that Indians do not see these squatters and might even, with complete sincerity, deny that they exist. (Darkness)

The Indian part of Naipaul's identity is completely repressed by his western self. He cannot stay blind to the obvious and he becomes extremely disgusted by the visual aspect of India. His severe indictments and accusations of Indian people, being blind to what for the western people is striking to the eye, are full of his own despair.

The only place of comfort for Naipaul is Kashmir. It has a sanative effect on the irritated author. After the disillusion and frustration that he suffers when he comes to India, Kashmir serves as a place of rest and peace to him.

Kashmir was coolness and colour: the yellow mustard fields, the mountains, snowcapped, the milky blue sky in which we rediscovered the drama of clouds. It was men wrapped in brown blankets against the morning mist, and barefooted shepherd boys with caps and covered ears on steep wet rocky slopes. (Darkness)

It is also the place where he "recaptures the idyllic world of his childhood" (Rai). He remembers the pictures of the Himalayas that he saw in his grandmother's house in Trinidad. The Himalayas belong to the India of his "fantasy" world. They serve as his jumping-off point in the world of chaos and twists. It is something static and peaceful; his only childhood vision that has been fulfilled.

Yet a special joy had been with me throughout the pilgrimage and during all my time in Kashmir. It was the joy of being among mountains; it was the special joy of being among the Himalayas. [...] In so many of the brightly coloured religious pictures in my grandmother's house I had seen these mountains, cones of white against simple, cold blue. They had become part of the India of my fantasy. (Darkness)

Indian Colonial Past

The Indo-British encounter was abortive; it ended in a double fantasy. Their new self-awareness makes it impossible for Indians to go back; their cherishing of Indianness makes it difficult for them to go ahead. [...] In the concept of Indianness the sense of continuity was bound to be lost. The creative urge failed. Instead of continuity we have the static. [...] Shiva has ceased to dance. (Darkness)

India is far from the glory it used to be known for; the country of glamour, magnificent temples and mosques, beauty and wealth. It is the glamour of the Indian past. The past of this country has completely overshadowed its present conditions. For most people over the world India is still the synonym for ancient India with its erstwhile grandeur. It is an attractive country with its dharma, karma, yoga lifestyle and vegetarianism, ignoring the fact that contemporary India is not equal to India of the past. It is not the same country any more. It looks like a ridiculous caricature of ancient India. It has stagnated in a desperate imitation of its past and cannot move ahead. In the opinion of Naipaul, India "regards the progress of the rest of the world with the tired tolerance of one who has been through it all before" (Darkness).

In ancient times India was one of the most developed countries, where medicine, science and high technologies amazed the whole world. As Naipaul claims, "democracy flourished in ancient India. Every village was a republic, self-sufficient, ordered, controlling its own affairs" (Darkness). It has been a long time since India was at the peak of its development. Indian people keep turning back to their past, but its greatness is irrecoverably gone. There is no "growth and development" of India these days (Darkness). Indian colonial past serves as a certain justification of its position. Indian people do not feel the necessity to continue, develop and change. They got to the sticking point.

One of the reasons that Naipaul gives for the Indian stagnation is that India is a country that cannot be independent, because Indians cannot cope with independence. It had stayed under foreign control too long to be able to stay on its own. Indians under the rule of England lost their identity and were given the new, artificial identity. The new sense of nationalism was imposed on them. After England's withdrawal, India never recovered, never established a sovereign, self-reliant state with its full nationalist feeling and cultural uniqueness. There are always remains of the past, which are given prominence. English supremacy severed the continuity of advancement and progression of Indian society. But none of it would have happened if India had not permitted that.

As Naipaul suggests, one of the greatest problems of Indian inability to develop and to create a worthwhile nation is the way in which India accepted the English rule. He claims that "no other country was more fitted to welcome a conqueror; no other conqueror was more welcome than the British" (Darkness). India did not show any resistance to the British Empire, because it has always been conquered and dominated by someone else. It too voluntarily gave up all its oneness and submitted to the English rule.

The English, on the other hand, failed in India as well, because "the 'affectation' existed among the officials, at about the same time, 'of being very English, of knowing nothing at all about India, of eschewing Indian words and customs'" (Darkness). Englishmen strictly imposed their culture on India and denied any interaction. They failed to benefit from their position in India, which, as Naipaul stresses, was too distinctive to be simply refashioned. The imposition of foreign architecture, language and culture did not fit to the place like India, although India was too weak and incompetent to resist.

With one part of myself I felt the coming together of England and India as a violation; with the other I saw it as ridiculous, resulting in a comic mixture of costumes and the widespread use of an imperfectly understood language. (Darkness)

India had always been under control of someone else. The ability to maintain its own identity was completely lost. In India "everything is inherited, nothing is abolished; everything grows out of something else" (Darkness). Naipaul observes that the English rule in Trinidad was completely different from that in India. While in Trinidad the English colonial supremacy was not regarded as "oppressive", because "every child new that [Trinidad] was only a dot on the map of the world, and it was therefore important to be British: that at least anchored [Trinidadians] within a wider system", in India the English dominance "remained an incongruous imposition" (Darkness). The Indian colonial past results in Indian failure in terms of selfhood and self-sufficiency. Out of the inability of Indians to run their country as an independent state arises in inclination to imitate not only their long ago established norms and customs but also their colonial rulers and western countries.

Indian mimicry is both less and more than a colonial mimicry. It is the special mimicry of an old country which has been without a native aristocracy for a thousand years and has learned to make room for outsiders, but only at the top. The mimicry changes, the inner world remains constant: this is the secret of survival. (Darkness)

The mimicry of the past and especially of the colonial times is typical of the higher level of the Indian society. It has the base in Indian inability to exist without the guidance of someone else. Indian people feel the need to be subdued to something larger, which gives them the reason for their existence. The concept of mimicry changes with the changes of the sovereign element that serves as the pillar of the society. "Yesterday the mimicry was Mogul; tomorrow it might be Russian or American; today it is English" (Darkness). Indian mimicry is rich and occurs in many aspects of Indian life. Naipaul gives an example of Indian art, which turns back to ancient times. Artists and craftsmen imitate the ancient styles and techniques of paintings, architecture and traditional craft industry. India simply cannot untie itself from its past. What used to be deemed as a piece of superb artwork may seem in the environment of the new world as a ridiculous caricature of itself. It has no sense to build ancient temples; they have no purpose in contemporary world. The building looks like a pathetic attempt to resurrect bygone Indian glory.

Indians also imitate the English. They have borrowed their language, traditions and customs, although it does not really make sense to Indians. They do not care about a deeper meaning of these practices. The Indian command of English is imperfect as all other borrowed tendencies, customs and ideas. Mimicry of the western cultures constantly appears in India with the pressure of the present times, especially in the domains where the country is incapable of offering its own device. India is not willing to develop its own devices; it is not intellectually equipped for such a development, it is simply used to being guided and unconsciously longs for guidance.

The strongest irritation arouses in Naipaul when he meets Indians who are blind to their true conditions and the real situation of the country and tend to retreat to their inner world. This is the result of long colonial past. The outside reality is not relevant. They see neither the awful dirt and poverty nor the unbearable vulnerability of the nation incapable of progress with regard to its future. This Indian inability to objectively pass a judgement on their true existence was induced by their deep-rooted incompetence to understand their history. The history of Indians is a fantastic world of myths and false conceptions. Naipaul, for example, mentions tourist guides giving very insufficient versions of the past events such as the establishments of Indian cities: "So he went to Delhi and he built a big city there" (Darkness). This is a sufficient and precise commentary on a historical event for Indians.

They do not need any further explanation of "creation and decay" (Darkness).

It is well that Indians are unable to look at their country directly, for the distress they would see would drive them mad. And it is well that they have no sense of history, for how then would they be able to continue to squat amid their ruins, and which Indian would be able to read the history of his country for the last thousand years without anger and pain? It is better to retreat into fantasy and fatalism, to trust to the stars in which the fortunes are all written. (Darkness)

Indians seem to be captured in their own fantasy world. The ability of misperception of the reality provides them with the ability to go on. They live in their own imaginary world where time and space do not play any role. In Naipaul's view, "Indians have their own fantasies with which they protect themselves from the painful awareness of present distress and past degradation" (Nightingale).

Religion and Social Structure

The substance of the Indian character lies in the deeply rooted Hindu tradition and the caste system, which determines the social structure in India. Hinduism is the major Indian religion apart from Buddhism and Islam. The Hindu-Muslim conflict is many times evoked in the trilogy. The clashes and the mutual misunderstanding between the devotees of the two religious groups are usually shown on the way people are living. Naipaul writes about the Muslim ghettos placed out of the rest of the Hindu society. In the encounter of Naipaul, as a representative of Hindu, with Aziz, a representative of Muslim, we can trace a considerable misunderstanding between those two religions. Naipaul himself confesses that despite the fact that his relationship to Aziz was more or less warm and on friendly terms, there occurred some moments of misapprehension. Naipaul realises that Muslims "were somewhat more different than others", because "they were not to be trusted; they would always do you down" (Rai).

Yet the author does not focus on these relations that much as he focuses on Hinduism itself. It stands at the background to every aspect of life portrayed in his books. Naipaul himself has a very ambiguous position in terms of religious affiliation. Though he clearly states that he is not a believer that he "remained almost totally ignorant of Hinduism" (Darkness) and that his Hindu upbringing evoked only "that sense of the difference of people, [...], a vaguer sense of caste, and a horror of the unclean" (Darkness), there was evidently "Hindu-traditional, Brahmin side of him" (Rai). It appears in the way he is accepting the people practising their rituals, in the way he is sympathising with the Brahmin family and their eating habits and in his ability to "separate the pleasant from the unpleasant" (Darkness).

Hindu people tend to escape to their inner world instead of facing the reality. In case of any conflict, they are known for their inactivity. The outer world does not really matter. They live in purity, frugality and non-violence. Poverty is regarded as the part of the Hindu lifestyle. It goes hand in hand with Hinduism, because Hindus are not focused on materialistic aspects of life. It is almost romanticised into something worth adulation. The individual spiritual elevation is superior to the prosperity of the whole nation. The only unit that matters in terms of Hindu lifestyle is caste, clan and family. This deeply established social structure is the base of the Indian social hierarchy. Everyone is predetermined by birth to play a certain role in his life. There is no tolerance of social mobility within caste system. Caste is what primarily defines each person within the society. Class is a system of rewards. Caste imprisons a man in his function. From this it follows, since there are no rewards, that duties and responsibilities become irrelevant to position. A man is his proclaimed function. There is little subtlety to India. The poor are thin; the rich are fat. (Darkness)

On the other hand, Naipaul does not deplore the caste system as such. He believes that it had a very important role in shaping the nation in the past and it worked well. Yet, he sees the failure of this system as it prevailed into present. The modern society cannot be based on such principles as is caste system and he regards this lasting, deep-rooted social structure as the obstacle on the way to India's transformation and development. He asserts that "in the beginning" caste system was "useful division of labour in a rural society", but "it has now divorced function from social obligation, position from duties. It is inefficient and destructive; it has created a psychology which will frustrate all improving plans" (Darkness).

Naipaul devotes his deepest interest to Mahatma Gandhi, the most significant and reputable Indian spiritual leader and famous representative of Hinduism. Gandhi has a very specific role in An Area of Darkness, because of his western experience. The author uses Gandhi to show the contrast of western vision of India and the Indian perception of reality. Like Naipaul, Gandhi acquired a capability to see India with a western eye through his long residence abroad. The whole Indian society is centred on Gandhi. The observer, the failed reformer, is of course Mohandas Gandhi. Mahatma, great-souled, father of the nation, deified, his name is given to streets and parks and squares, honoured everywhere by statues and mandaps [...], he is nevertheless the least Indian of Indian leaders. (Darkness)

In An Area of Darkness, Naipaul's description of Gandhi is mostly positive. He sees him as the greatest Indian reformer, who, having gained a western experience, could objectively perceive the reality in

India and who felt a strong need for a change. The first thing Gandhi noticed is the filth all around India. He was not blind to the poverty and dirt like other Indian people. He asserts that

> Instead of having graceful hamlets dotting the land, we have dung-heaps. [...] By our bad habits we spoil our sacred river banks and furnish excellent breeding grounds for flies. [...] Leaving night-soil, cleaning the nose, or spitting on the road is a sin against God as well as humanity, and betrays a sad want of consideration for others. The man who does not cover his waste deserves a heavy penalty even if he lives in a forest. (Darkness)

Gandhi's position in India is unique at least at the same level as is Naipaul's. As a young man Gandhi went to England to study at University and before he finally came back and settled in India, he spent twenty years in South Africa. His African experience is "regarded as crucial in moulding Gandhi's identity in positive fashion" (Rai). Therefore, "he looked at India as no Indian was able to; his vision was direct, and this directness, was, and is, revolutionary" (Darkness). He was able to see Indian inadequacies and also felt the need to reform India to be able to endure in modern world, because he "never [lost] the critical comparing South African eye" (Darkness). Gandhi supported many ideas that are typical of European countries and Naipaul praises him for this attitude, describing him as if he was not an Indian but "a colonial blend of East and West" (Darkness).

> [Gandhi] sees exactly what the visitor sees; he does not ignore the obvious. He sees the beggars and the shameless pundits and the filth of Banaras; he sees the atrocious sanitary habits of doctors, lawyers and journalists. He sees the Indian callousness, the Indian refusal to see. No Indian attitude escapes him, no Indian problem; he looks down to the roots of the static decayed society. (Darkness)

Summary

The book emerging out of that visit, *An Area of Darkness*, remains a valuable record of an India in transition — an India losing, under a weak and exhausted Nehru, a war with China, and losing along with it its flush of post-independence idealism and innocence. Indeed, each one of Naipaul's trilogy of books on India has come to stand as a historical document of India's post-colonial evolution. Published just after Mrs Gandhi's Emergency, India: a wounded civilization (1977) captures the post-Nehru years of drift and aimlessness, "the simplicity of a country ruled by slogans". In India: a million mutinies now (1990) Naipaul correctly intuited, and made his theme, the rise of long-suppressed identities that radically altered Indian society in this decade.

Many different ideas and expectations prompted Naipaul's first visit to India. He left Trinidad, where he was born in 1932, when he was 18 to study at Oxford. He had wanted to be a writer and had travelled to England, which was then the centre of the world for English-speaking colonials everywhere. It had taken him much time to sort out his writerly ambition, and even after a brilliant start as a writer — five books in just seven years, one of which was the considerable achievement of A House for Mr. Biswas — the value of his work was slow to be recognised.

Published at a time when "Indian" novels were an oddity, particularly Indian novels from the West Indies, Naipaul's books suffered critical and commercial neglect. There were other disappointments. The life in London to which he had looked forward had turned out to be "sterile" and "mean". But what were the alternatives? What were the places he could think of as "home", as the centre of his world? He had been back to Trinidad; the visit — described in The Middle Passage — had merely vindicated an early childhood vow to distance himself from the island. There remained only India, the land of his Brahmin ancestors.

On his first visit, Naipaul took with him the conventional ideas of India — the India people then knew as the land of Gandhi and Nehru, the India of the glittering classical past, which had been meticulously dredged up by European Indologists in the 19th century. He took with him his own childhood memories of an old India, the Brahmanic world of rituals and myths that had been carefully preserved in Trinidad. This past held an emotional charge for Naipaul. His ancestors had come to Trinidad as indentured labourers in the last quarter of the 19th century. The regions of North India they lived in were systematically rendered destitute by the British in the post-mutiny period. Brahmins had been a special target. The long sea voyages to the "Great Unknown" — the Caribbean, Fiji, Mauritius — violated caste rules but were made necessary by the surrounding dereliction.

The history of these Brahmins was one of great poverty and wretchedness; and to the generations that followed the first arrivals in Trinidad those early traumas were fresh in the memory. Naipaul, a third-generation Indian, had just begun to outgrow this painful past when he went to India. But India, poor and abject, was to revive in the most unexpected way all the fears and insecurities he had known as a child.

"It was a journey that ought not to have been made; it had broken my life in two," Naipaul wrote on the penultimate page of An Area of Darkness — a record of intense fear and anguish. But if this book was only about a lacerated sensibility, similar to books by certain kinds of western travellers to India, it would not be read any more. Remarkably, for a travel book published in 1964, it has outlasted its time; and it has done so because of literary virtues that sound simple but are hardest to achieve: honesty and directness.

Consider this moment towards the end of the book. Naipaul is winding up an awkward visit to his ancestral village; a boy asks for a lift back to town with him. Naipaul says, "Let the idler walk". The trip ends in "futility and impatience, a gratuitous act of cruelty, self-reproach and flight". Elsewhere, Naipaul first shows himself growing angry; and then examines the event with the writer's later detachment and serenity: "It was brutal; it was ludicrous; it was pointless and infantile. But the moment of anger is a moment of exalted shrinking lucidity, from which recovery is slow and shattering."

Anger and fear made Naipaul see things other travellers miss. Few writers had ever said as many incisive things about the cultural encounter between India and Britain as found in the chapter titled "Fantasy and Ruins". The work abounds in startling new perceptions, and for many writers and intellectuals in India, it became a crucial part of their self-education — Naipaul's radical interpretation of Gandhi, among other things, disturbed.

Serious-minded travellers to India continue to read Darkness as a guide to a range of bewildering Indian attitudes. Others cherish it for Naipaul's descriptions of places — particularly of Kashmir — which are precise and lyrical, without ever relying on the heavy vocabulary deployed by, for instance, Jan Morris. And in Naipaul's own intellectual journey, it is an important landmark. The Middle Passage, Naipaul's first travel book, is largely conventional in form and content. The unique mingling of social enquiry and autobiography that marks Naipaul's later non-fiction (and indeed his fiction) first occurred in An Area of Darkness. It is where you can see him developing his special ways of seeing and working towards new kinds of knowledge about himself, about India, about the "half-made societies" that would become his subject in later books. It is where he began to find that elusive centre of his world — the centre that lay not in any particular place but in the many areas of darkness of his own richly diverse past.

Plot

The story is a semi-autobiographical account given by Naipaul of a year he spent in India in 1964. The opening section entitled Travellers Prelude deals with the difficulties surrounding bureaucracy in the country. Naipaul speaks about how he made many difficult efforts to recover alcohol that was confiscated from him. The book is divided into three parts. Part one is entitled A Resting Place for the Imagination. He speaks about his ancestors coming to India as indentured labourers. He also deals with his first experiences on the issue of race, of Muslims and Hindus. Naipaul was born an unbeliever. He grew up in an orthodox Hindu family. In India he explains how caste comes to mean the brutal division of labour and this was an unpleasant concept. While he was an unbeliever he was still saddened at the decay of old customs and rituals. Naipaul talks about the poverty in India and how it is one of the poorest countries in the world. When he moves to London he find himself as one more face in the midst of Industrialised England.

Naipaul speaks about the Indian English mimicry and how this is just like fantasy. He goes on to speak about the custom of defecating everywhere and how they refuse to acknowledge this fact. The approach to many villages is not a pleasant experience therefore. Naipaul speaks about Mahatma Gandhi and how he was able to look at India squarely and see its problems in a totally objective manner.

Part Two opens with the image of a Doll's House on the Dal Lake. This is in fact a hotel called Hotel Liward, which is situated in Kashmir. He speaks about his relationships with the various people who worked in the hotel and the ensuing conflicts, which occurred. We learn about the function of the Indian Civil Service. He is encouraged to join a pilgrimage to the Cave of Amarnath the Eternal Lord, which is ninety miles north of Srinagar. He, speaks about his joy and that of the other pilgrims as they climb the Himalayas and try to get inside a cave. Even though they are on a pilgrimage Naipaul states how as soon as they got inside the cave it was like a typical Indian bazaar. Naipaul recounts many anecdotes among them one about a young couple called Rafiq and Laraine. Rafiq is a poor musician. They spend a good deal of time fighting but eventually they get married. They split up however as she is unable to bear the poverty in India. She returns home to America.

Part Three is entitled Fantasy and Ruins. This section deals with how the British possessed the country completely. Their withdrawal was irrevocable. He speaks about the English of the raj how they swaggered and had mannerisms and spoke a jargon. He mentions Kipling and how he is a good chronicler of Anglo-India. He talks about how the Taj Mahal is a great building without a function. He goes on to speak about writers and how Indian attempts at the novel reveal the Indian confusion further.

Naipaul moves on to speak about Indian railways and how he befriended a Sikh while travelling by train in the south of India. He comes to the conclusion however that India for him remains an area of darkness. He has learned over the years his separateness his contentment with being a colonial without a past and without ancestors. At the conclusion of the novel he tells us about his encounter with an emaciated man called Ramachandra. This man wants help to start litigation and get some land, which formerly belonged to Naipaul's grandfather. Naipaul is disgusted at this incident and leaves in a mood of self-reproach. He talks about his flight home and how it was made up of anxiety and frustration. He admits that the journey to India should not have been made as it broke his life in two.

Genre

This novel is in part autobiography and in part travel genre. Naipaul writes about his experiences in India over a span of one year. It is written in the first person narrative voice and Naipaul uses descriptive passages very well to outline his themes.

General Vision or Viewpoint

The general vision given in this novel of India is somber and dark. The title An Area of Darkness refers to India. Many of the negative aspects of Indian culture are highlighted and Naipaul seems to see the whole bleakness of the culture at every stage. Colonialism is an important issue in the story and again this is treated with a good deal of ironic detachment. Towards the conclusion of the story Naipaul acknowledges that he should never really have returned to the country.

Cultural Context

Colonial India in the twentieth century forms the cultural context of this novel. Naipaul gives the reader a vivid insight into the various sects and cultural systems dominating this country. In Part Two of the novel Naipaul analyses the whole colonial process. There are copious references to Hinduism and Muslims and Buddhism and he paints some vivid pictures of the various customs, which these people engage in. Poverty is a key aspect of this culture ad contributes a good deal to the reason why he chose such a title for the novel.

Themes

Poverty

The story abounds with descriptions of the extreme poverty of India. Naipaul describes India as 'the poorest country in the world.' The Indians defecate everywhere but fail to face up to this fact according to Naipaul. He analyses in a very logical way the reasons why he thinks Poverty exists in such a real way in India. He mentions at one stage how 'divorce of the intellect from body labour has made of us the most resource less and most exploited nation on earth.' The concluding section abounds in grim and rather depressing images of poverty. When Naipaul pays a trip to the village and meets the emaciated Ramachandra who is surrounded in dire poverty he is appalled and simply wants to leave the country at once. Poverty is seen as a self-defeating and destructive reality in this country.

Caste System

Naipaul speaks a good deal about the caste system in India. He describes it as the 'brutal division of labour' and something, which is unpleasant. He mentions how the cast system only imprisons a man 'in his function' and makes so many people anonymous and faceless. Indians who are born overseas are not accepted by the system and have no identity. Naipaul devotes one section of his book to speaking about the work that Gandhi tried to carry out for his country. He tried to attack the psychology underlying the caste system and to show that there was dignity in man and a need to clean and have proper sanitation methods. Naipaul feels that Gandhi failed to get this message across.

Colonialism

One section of the novel is devoted to this theme. He mentions at one stage how the country only pretends to be colonial,' yesterday the country's mimicry was Mogul, tomorrow it could be Russian or American.' He concludes by stating that the Indian English mimicry is like fantasy. When the British withdrew completely from India something of fantasy remained attached to their presence there. He draws a comparison between colonial India and colonial Trinidad. Trinidad is a British colony but in size it is only a dot on the map and therefore it is important to be British. Naipaul states that the England of India was different 'an incongruous imposition' in his words. He goes on to state the negativity of colonialism and how he felt the coming together of India and England as 'a violation, buildings were too grand, too big for the puniness, poverty and defeat in which they were set. He mentions how these buildings strove to impose attitudes on people from both within and without. Overall the impression given in this book of colonialism in India is extremely negative.

Analysis

The themes of the first four chapters can be summarised in the words poverty, caste, defecation, and failure. But Naipaul being Naipaul manages to transform the squalor of the world he observes into clean, cold and lucid prose. His language is, for the most part, that of a surgeon who feels neither contempt nor pity when he dissects. Naipaul writes that the "sweetness and sadness which can be found in Indian writing and Indian films are a turning away from a too overwhelming reality; they reduce the horror to a warm, virtuous emotion. Indian sentimentality is the opposite of concern." This explains why Naipaul's apparent detachment is so misleading: for Naipaul unsentimental description is — quite unexpectedly for the reader — a way of showing concern.

Naipaul is most effective when he is sarcastic. His book sparkles with rhetoric fervour when he quotes Gandhi on the squalor and shortcomings of India and points out that Gandhi's observations are still valid today. Chapter 3, "The Colonial," depicts the colonial's view of India. Incidentally, the colonial happens to be Mahatma Gandhi, and Naipaul quotes extensively from Gandhi's early writing. It starts with a quote just below the Chapter heading: "Well, India is a country of nonsense." Naipaul effectively turns one of the founding fathers against his successors who, in Naipaul's opinion, let the country rot in its stagnancy. Naipaul feels that India undid Gandhi: "He became a mahatma. He was to be reverenced for what he was; his message was irrelevant"; and that "his failure is there, in his writings: he is still the best guide to India. It is as if, in England, Florence Nightingale had become a saint, honoured by statues, everywhere, her name on every lip; and the hospitals had remained as she had described them."

When Naipaul writes about Gandhi, he also characterises his own way of seeing and writing: "He looked at India as no Indian was able to; his vision was direct and the directness was, and is, revolutionary. He sees exactly what the visitor sees; he does not ignore the obvious. He sees the beggars and the shameless pundits and the filth of Banaras; he sees the atrocious sanitary habits of doctors, lawyers and journalists. He sees the Indian callousness, the Indian refusal to see. No Indian attitude escapes him, no Indian problem; he looks down to the roots of the static, decayed society. And the picture of India which comes out of his writings and exhortations over more than thirty years still holds: this is the measure of his failure."

Bottom-line: opinionated and brilliant as most of Naipaul's writing, surely not a balanced portrait of India in the early 1960s, but definitely a must-read for anyone trying to understand Naipaul, and a good case-study how easy it is to misunderstand the intentions of a writer or how easy it is to use quotations out of context to malign someone.

An Area of Darkness, he wrote about the year that he spent in the country and his experiences interacting with the people of India. In the case of the current book, he has less time and ability to speak to people and so supplements his analysis in what is a brief but brilliant exposition with his criticism of literature and politics in that extraordinary country. His results are memorable and fuller of insight than any number of much more extensive economic and political treatises.

The central image or emblem of the book is a phrase uttered by a young woman at a dinner party. Living outside India with a foreign husband but returning to her home when possible to spend time with her family, Naipaul overhears her discussing what she saw on her various visits, when she was not actually looking at her family members and engaged directly in the relationships that required. I see, she is reported to have said, 'people experiencing their being' — Naipaul seizes on this and expounds upon it. The visitor to India is likely to be struck by the enormous variety of people living cheek by jowl by each other but capable, it seems, of completely ignoring each other's presence. So, in the urban environment especially, smartly dressed executives walk past homeless beggars while a group of swaddled

Muslim women are driven past migrant worker families living in the dust-ridden building sites they are responsible for building at dreadfully low wages. How can people do this? Is it a form of total heartlessness? In Naipaul's view, it is the 'being experience' that shapes the way that people think and act.

For an Indian, every single moment of the day is characterised by the extensive and complex clan and tribal connections that require constant attention. Paying proper attention to these duties and requirements occupies a great deal of time and effort and, by experiencing this form of being, the Indian person simply does not notice other things going on around (it also indicates the ruinous degree of loss suffered by a person suddenly plucked from that milieu). For additional verification, Naipaul turns to the memoirs of Mahatma Gandhi. As a young man, Gandhi was possessed with the idea of moving to Britain to study the law. Against the odds, he succeeded in this task and he records his maritime trip to the imperial centre and his studies in the approach to the bar. Yet, as Naipaul observes, Gandhi seems to notice nothing going on around him (and this continues when he is elsewhere) and his focus is almost entirely internal. He, Gandhi, is also experiencing his being. He does not notice as important those events occurring outside of him when there is so much going on inside his consciousness. Major Indian religions and philosophies emphasise the importance of cultivating the inner being, after all.

Indian society has in some ways changed enormously since the mid 1970s, what with the rapid economic development of some industrial sectors in Bangalore and New Delhi and the emergence of a transforming middle class. Yet in India's population of something like 1.4 billion people (the likelihood of ever having an accurate estimate is fairly slim), the vast majority have scarcely been affected directly. Indeed, the inequalities separating the villages from those benefiting from globalisation have increased. These are the people living in generational debts to the village Patels so ably described by Naipaul and for whom no future prospects are yet in view.

12 A Wounded Civilization

India: A Wounded Civilization, by V. S. Naipaul, is the second book of his "India" trilogy, after *An Area of Darkness*, and before *India: A Million Mutinies Now*.

It was on his third visit to India, prompted by the Emergency of 1975, that Naipaul came to write this book. In this work he casts a more analytical eye than before on Indian attitudes while recapitulating and probing the feelings previously aroused in him by this vast, mysterious and agonised continent. What he saw and heard on this visit reinforced his conviction that India, wounded by many centuries of foreign rule, has not yet found an ideology of regeneration. Reviewers have described it as a work of fierce candour and precision.

Mr. Naipaul, born in Trinidad (an island in West Indies just off the northeastern coast of Venezuela), is a descendant of Hindus who emigrated from India. Hence at a personal level the book is a description of one man's complicated relationship with the country of his ancestors, which has withdrawn into itself as a result of long years of foreign rule. Mr. Naipaul wishes that his ancient homeland would come to terms with the past and move on towards the future.

Introduction

India: A Wounded Civilization is the second book of the trilogy describing Naipaul's journey to India in 1975. It is evident from the very first chapter that Naipaul's attitudes as well as the style of his narration have changed. It is less about the sorrowful recognition of the difference between the imaginary world and the real one; it is more concentrated on the true description of India. Whereas An Area of Darkness deals with the nostalgia over India, which will never be the India of Naipaul's dreams, the second book is more emotionally well-balanced, descriptive, analytical and with the sense of hope in Indian future. The author examines India in more details; his thoughts and descriptions seem to be more integrated and less emotive. This may be ascribed to the fact that he had enough time to cope with his feelings about India since his first visit to the country and had gone through a certain development as an author. He himself comments on his writing:

One can't be entirely sympathetic; one must have views; one must do more than merely respond emotionally. I can get angry, impatient, like anyone else; I can be irritated, bored – but you can't turn any of that into writing. So you have to make a conscious effort to render your emotions into something which is more logical, which makes more sense, but which is more, and not less, true. Naipaul still sees the inefficiencies in Indian political system as well as in the social establishment and cultural background of India. Yet in comparison with An Area of Darkness, the second book of his trilogy is more complex and the general mood is less pessimistic.

The author goes back to his first visit to India to re-evaluate and recapitulate the most important ideas expressed in his first volume. He refers to all the main points of his perceptions of India without emotions, which, to a certain extent, makes his descriptions even crueller. In contrast to An Area of Darkness, he is able to see India from a detached position and with an objective eye. In comparison with An Area of Darkness, where the issues of politics played a minor role, here he largely focuses on the political changes in India, responding, for example, to the political situation at the time of the Emergency imposed by the Prime Minister Indira Gandhi. Nevertheless, he basically concentrates on the social impact of the Emergency and examines historical and social background of these changes.

He regenerates his study of Mahatma Gandhi, the man of Naipaul's special interest within the whole trilogy. It is obvious that now his approach to this Indian spiritual leader is different from how he portrayed him in An Area of Darkness. In Naipaul's eyes, Gandhi and his teachings failed in the time of the Emergency, they did not prepare Indian people to cope with the changes that were inevitable for India to maintain its integrity within a modern world and to be able to transform the country.

The optimistic mood of the book can be seen in Naipaul's frequent references to the transformations of urban landscape and agricultural amendments. Although he still regards most of the Indian practices somewhat defective, he evaluates the future perspective of Indian civilization. At the end of his book, Naipaul is more or less positive about Indian development and future, although he visited the country during great Indian disturbances when India was shaking in its foundations. Naipaul regards the political instability and the present uncertainty of India as a possibility for the new start. He realises that the present situation of India is necessary for Indian people to wake up from their long lasting slumber and indifference.

Period of Emergency

The period of the Emergency, imposed by the Prime Minister Indira Gandhi, is usually regarded as one of the most controversial periods of independent India. It was a turbulent time of instability, political and social feuds and strives, terror and dismay. The new independent India, still working on its old principles, was not competent enough to master this situation.

The reforms on the basis of the overall re-establishment of the society were needed. The basic aims of the Emergency were to suppress the poverty and illiteracy and to make industry and agriculture more effective and productive. For the opposition, Indira's "rule by decree" in India did not work on democratic principles, because she had an absolute power and control over the nation. "The strong-arm methods" were used "in the promotion of slum clearance and birth control." Thousands of innocent people were "gaoled without trial". The press was subjected to censorship and "the courts silenced" (Keay 528). The legacy of the Emergency and Indira's governance of the country is highly disputable and "Mrs. Gandhi comes out looking bad for having violated Western democratic rights". Yet "by implication she emerges as India's possible saviour, because Mohandas Gandhi and Gandhianism come out looking worse, for having imposed on India an allegedly archaic, retrogressive set of values" (Van Praagh 317).

Naipaul again invokes the idea of Indian incompetence to develop a stable, prosperous nation. Indian people look back to their past with the sentimental feelings. They worship the ancient India; they still live on its glory. While the whole world goes forward India is static, looking back to the past, living out of their memories and traditions, though their traditions have already lost their sense.

In the midst of the world change, India, even during this Emergency, was unchanging: to return to India was to return to a knowledge of the world's deeper order, everything fixed, sanctified, everyone secure. (Wounded Civilization) According to Naipaul, the predisposition of India's incapacity to move ahead is the fact that the country had been under control of someone else for too long and is absolutely unprepared for independence. In India: A Wounded Civilization he further develops his idea of the Indian vulnerability towards foreign invasion and its tolerant acceptation of the supremacy of other nations mentioned in An Area of Darkness and claims that India had to overcome numerous conquests and recover from its different defeats. Indians take the recovery of their nation for granted and have developed a strong inclination to fatalism. They do not feel the need to fight for their country and regard the future development with Hindu passivity and resignation. Out of a superficial reading of the past, then, out of the sentimental conviction that India is eternal and forever revives, there comes not a fear of further defeat and destruction, but an indifference to it. India will somehow look after itself; the individual is freed of all responsibility. (Wounded Civilization)

Naipaul suggests that India can no longer hide and stay indifferent to its current affairs like in the times under foreign control. It can no longer blame the others for the deficiencies within its own organisation. It is forced by the circumstances to open its eyes towards what is long evident to the rest of the world. India cannot exist on its ancient Hindu principles any more. For Naipaul, this is the time of the decay of the "wounded old civilization". The crisis of India is not only political or economic. The larger crisis is of a wounded old civilization that has at last become aware of its inadequacies and is without the intellectual means to move ahead. (Wounded Civilization)

The change of Naipaul's attitudes to the country of his ancestors can be clearly traced in the above extract. He no longer has such a pessimistic and ironical approach as he had in his first book. He still writes about the inadequacies of India but on the other hand, and on the contrary to An Area of Darkness, he describes Indian people as being aware of these inadequacies. He notices a significant transformation in Indian perception of their conditions. They are not blind to the poverty and dirt, the archaic order and inefficient economy any more. They long for reform. They cannot look back to their past, moreover they cannot sink into their past like every time when India was in crises in previous ages of its existence. After a long lasting period of indifference to the political situation and deep-rooted social establishment of their country Indian people finally feel the need to change. Indians are no longer able to continue in their well-trodden paths. The circumstances and the outer world with its pressures are not bearable any more. Indians imagine that to be able to keep up with the rest of the modern world, there have to be radical transformations of their political, economic and social structures. Naipaul sees that "new pressures on the society are creating new movements" (Nightingale).

With advancing industrialisation and improved farming techniques, many peasants are being pushed off the land and into the cities, loosening ties by which individuals have defined themselves and which have limited their ability to appraise outside reality. Suddenly, Indians recognise the fact of Indian poverty and human distress as a cause for political protest rather than as a reinforcement of the concept of karma." (Nightingale) Nevertheless, it is clear that Naipaul sees these transformations as a very slow process and he knows it will take time till the new order will be established in India. India is still a "wounded old civilization", which is captured in its dreadful past and is unable to develop.

The concept of mimicry can also be traced in India: A Wounded Civilization. Naipaul again comments on the unsuitability of the importation of foreign ideas, strategies and tendencies to the country. India has always been vulnerable towards foreign influences and has always borrowed outside practices and traditions. All the disciplines and skills that India now seeks to exercise are borrowed. Even the ideas Indians have of the achievements of their civilization are essentially the ideas given them by European scholars in the nineteenth century. (Wounded Civilization)

The problem of the borrowing is that Indian people do not properly understand the outside practices which usually mutate in Indian environment into meaningless and purposeless acts of mere imitations that have no larger concepts. In Naipaul's words they are "sterile, divorced from reality and usefulness" (Wounded Civilization). There are no bases in India for such practices and ideas and no background for the unforced development of the imported ideas. These ideas are pulled out of context and do not fit to Indian needs. It is "mimicry within mimicry, imperfectly understood idea within imperfectly understood idea" (Wounded Civilization).

Complex imported ideas, forced through the retort of Indian sensibility, often come out cleansed of content, and harmless; they seem so regularly to lead back, through religion and now science, to the past and nullity. (Wounded Civilization) In the time of Indian industrial and agricultural revolution Naipaul uses the imported technical practices as an example of his theory of mimicry. The new technologies brought from the western developed cultures cannot be used properly in India. People use it only for the purpose of using it. Indians are not intellectually elevated enough to cope with such technologies and they do not understand them. These technologies were not designed. to fit to the Indian environment, which even highlights their absurdity. India in Naipaul's vision did not manage to completely break from its past yet and still has too much of the Old India. To match technology to the needs of a poor country calls for the highest skills, the clearest vision. Old India, with all its encouragements to the instinctive, non-intellectual life, limits vision. (Wounded Civilization)

Poverty and Conditions of Living

In the village I went to, only one family out of four had land; only one child out of four went to school; only one man out of four had work. For a wage calculated to keep him only in food for the day he worked, the employed man, hardly exercising a skill, using the simplest tools and sometimes no tools at all, did the simplest agricultural labour. Child's work; and children, being cheaper than men, were preferred; (Wounded Civilization)

Naipaul again describes very poor conditions of living in India and the ever-present poverty of Indian people. He writes about the poor sheds, the dirt and the starved people; about children forced to work from their eighth year of age to maintain money for their family and about other aspects of Indian life absolutely irreconcilable with the principles of the modern developed countries. He is perhaps even much crueller in his descriptions than in An Area of Darkness, because his narration lost the emotive aspect. The thousand years established caste system was one of the deficiencies of the society that makes the Indian people unable to transform their situation. Everyone has his own predispositions for living. The position within the society is inborn and any attempt to improve living conditions and to circumvent the long established caste system is regarded as the serious disruption of the fundamental principles of the Indian society and often leads to the expulsion from the community, because "every man [knows] his caste, his place; each group [lives] in its own immemorially defined area; and the pariahs, the scavengers, [live] at the end of the village" (Wounded Civilization).

It is still somehow clear that Naipaul does not provide the reader with such horrific descriptions for the sake of condemning the Indian society or rejecting it. His depictions serve for the purpose of giving the reasonable background to the events he is willing to describe further on in his narration. He also advocates the posture that it is not possible to look at India from the perspective of a westerner, outsider or simply foreigner. He perhaps has the gift of seeing India from within as Indians do, because of his origins. He claims that "India is not to be judged. India is only to be experienced, in the Indian way" (Wounded Civilization).

Religion and Social Structure

Naipaul emphasises again that the traditional Hindu attitudes "subvert the cause of progress" (Nightingale 197). The Hindu principles work on the individual's withdrawal into his inner world; meditation and non-violence are the only ways of resistance. "The outer world matters only so far as it affects the inner. It is the Indian way of experiencing" (Wounded Civilization). It is the Hindu way of protection and the way of coping with the difficulties of outer world. They believe that to stay passive and to withdraw into their inner world every time when some trouble occurs is the best thing to do to be able to survive.

This is exactly what Indians do instead of facing the discrepancies in their own country. Instead of trying to find the reasonable solution, they shut away in their inner world.

While his world holds and he is secure, the Indian is a man simply having his being; and he is surrounded by other people having their being. But when the props of family, clan, and caste go, chaos and blankness come. (Wounded Civilization)

India is not a nation; it is the country of individuals. For Indian being an Indian does not have the same meaning as for Americans being Americans or for British being British. 'Indian' is just an empty word. What matters in India is the caste, family or clan. People's identities are shaped by these smaller units; Indians do not perceive themselves as being the members of some larger entity on the basis of the whole nation. Naipaul calls this phenomenon the "underdeveloped ego". It is "created by the detailed social organisation" (Wounded Civilization).

Caste and clan are more than brotherhoods; they define the individual completely. The individual is never on his own; he is always fundamentally a member of his group, with a complex apparatus of rules, rituals, taboos. (Wounded Civilization) The concept of the "underdeveloped ego" is the reason why Indian people are so difficult to be understood by the rest of the world. Their mental and intellectual capacities operate in a way that is absolutely incomprehensible for 'outsiders'. This is the reason why Indians look at India from a different perspective, why they are blind to many aspects that are striking for many non-Indians and why their behaviour in some particular situations is regarded, to say the least, bizarre. They are simply being misunderstood. Naipaul regards the lack of the meaning of Indian identity as one of the basic grounds for Indian "defect of vision" and for their passivity and fatalism. (Wounded Civilization)

Identity was related to a set of beliefs and rituals, a knowledge of the gods, a code, an entire civilization. The loss of the past meant the loss of that civilization, the loss of a fundamental idea of India, and the loss therefore, to a nationalist-minded man, of a motive for action. It was part of the feeling of purposelessness of which many Indians spoke, part of the longing for Gandhian days, when the idea of India was real and seemed full of promise, and the 'moral issues' clear. (Wounded Civilization)

In India: A Wounded Civilization Naipaul's attitude towards the doctrine of Mahatma Gandhi and his role in the forming of the modern Indian nation considerably changes. The author no more sees Gandhi as overall positive. He is more critical about Gandhi's actions and reforms and finally, he regards Gandhi's influence in India as a complete failure. As far as Naipaul's attitude is concerned, it almost seems that India: A Wounded Civilization stands in straight contrast to An Area of Darkness. Whereas in An Area of Darkness Naipaul praises Gandhi for his ability to see India and Indian people from a European point of view and evaluates his aptitude of proper judgements, in India: A Wounded Civilization this idea is not applied any more. On the contrary, Naipaul blames Gandhi for having a "defect of vision" (Wounded Civilization 97). Moreover, Naipaul claims that Ganghi completely failed to understand the needs of India and that he led India to an even much greater retreat.

When quoting from Gandhi's autobiography, Naipaul criticises his deficiencies in the description of foreign countries. In Naipaul's eyes, Gandhi failed as an observer and instead concentrated on his own situation and problems:

> I did not feel at all sea-sick. ... I was innocent of the use of knives and forks ... I therefore never took meals at table but always had them in my cabin, and they consisted principally of sweets and fruits I had brought with me ... We entered the Bay of Biscay, but I did not begin to feel the need either of meat or liquor ... However, we reached Southampton, as far as I remember, on a Saturday. On the boat I had worn a black suit, the white flannel one, which my friends had got me, having been kept especially for wearing when I landed. I had thought that white clothes would suit me better when I stepped ashore, and therefore I did so in white flannels. Those were the last days of September, and I found I was the only person wearing such clothes. (Wounded Civilization)

Naipaul criticises Mahatma Gandhi for not paying attention either to the description of the landscape and the cities of these countries he had visited, or to the characterisation of the people he had met during his travels. On the other hand, we may trace the Hindu principles in Gandhi's behaviour. His isolation in his inner world is typical of Hinduism. Gandhi saw the inadequacies of the Indian nation; moreover, he felt the need to do something about it. He knew the reform was inevitable in order to readjust India to the conditions of the outer world and modern civilization but he could not deny his deeply rooted Hindu temperament. Above all he was a Hindu.

Gandhian non-violence has degenerated into something very like the opposite of what Gandhi intended. [...] non-violence isn't a form of action, a quickener of social conscience. It is only a means of securing an undisturbed calm; it is non-doing, non-interference, social indifference. (Wounded Civilization)

Naipaul shows the failure of Gandhi and the inadequacy of his ideas and lifestyle in modern world through his successor Vinoba Bhave, who is considered to be the only "moral reference" to Gandhi by continual imitation of his lifestyle, the "authorised version of Gandhi" (Wounded Civilization). It is clear from Naipaul's descriptions that he is more a caricature of Gandhi than a real Gandhian successor.

By a life of strenuous parody Bhave has swallowed his master. Gandhi took the vow of sexual abstinence when he was thirty-seven, after a great struggle. Bhave took the same vow when he was a child. (Wounded Civilization)

What might have seemed a good ideology and might have been an effective way of resistance and protest in the times of Gandhi, does not imply the same level of respectability, adequacy and productivity these days. For Naipaul, Bhave is a ridiculous figure accentuating the failure of Gandhianism. Naipaul concludes that

Bhave, even if he understood Gandhi's stress on the need for social reform, was incapable of undermining Hindu India; he was too much part of it. The perfect disciple, obeying without always knowing why, he invariably distorted his master's massage. (Wounded Civilization)

Summary

Book starts with Vijayanagar kingdom's plunder and ends with Vinoba Bhave and Mahatma Gandhi's spiritualism. Between this two extreme point Naipaul oscillates his thoughts under the Indian Idea force. He tries to dissect Indian psyche as like skilful surgeon raises question with ingenuous curiosity and carries high force of intellectual aptitude with him to understand the phenomenon called: Indian Civilization.

He argues that Indian civilization is wounded one and satisfies reader very convincingly. India always been under change but irony is that change not driven by convictions and confidence but it just swept by the conditions of time and space.

Indian always believed in karma. And this karma never let them to self-contemplation. When tragedy occurres people finds refuge in karma (action) and thinks of moksha (release). Indian never believed in self, but reacted to time and space.

India's intellectual life was short and now its under depletion. It borrowed every idea "from Parliament to press" from alien place. It never tries to work honestly and continuously for refinement of these ideas. It just took it casual and now don't know how to proceed.

During emergency people were up against PM Indira without any idea of revolution. All protesters were under the illusion of Karma and Dharma. They thought this revolution will mark new beginning but they did not know about invisible curtain on reality. Naipaul writes " the revolution is an expression of rage and rejection but this was a revolution without ideas. It was an emotional outburst, a wallow".

13 Among the Believers

Among the Believers: An Islamic Journey is a book by the Nobel laureate V.S. Naipaul. Published in 1981, the book was based on a six month journey across the Asian continent. V.S. Naipaul explores the culture and the explosive situation in countries where Islamic fundamentalism was growing. His travels (and travails) start with Iran, on to Pakistan, Malaysia and end in Indonesia, with a short stop in Pakistan and Iran on the return to the UK.

An Overview

Published in the year 1981, "Among the Believers: An Islamic Journey" is based on six month long journey undertaken by the author across the Asian continent. On the journey, Naipaul explored the explosive situation and culture in those countries where Islamic Fundamentalism was known to be growing. He covers four countries; Iran, Pakistan, Malaysia and, finally, Indonesia. The purpose of this long journey, according to Naipaul, was that he wanted to study the cultures of those countries-which have some amount of pre-Islamic history and are attempting to establish a country based on Islam. Naipaul also added that he did not visit Arabian countries because he was only interested in people who converted from other religions to Islam.

Summary

In sixteen works of fiction and non-fiction written over a period of some 20 years, V.S. Naipaul has been taking his readers to remote, inaccessible places in the third world. "Among the Believers," his new book, is the chronicle of a seven-month journey he made in 1979 and 1980 to Iran, Pakistan, Malaysia and Indonesia in search of Islam. It displays all of Naipaul's major themes, his great talent as a writer and his increasing limitation of vision.

We can see in this book, perhaps more than in Naipaul's previous writings, the dilemma of a gifted author led by his obsessive feelings regarding the people he is writing about to a difficult intellectual and moral bind. He expressed this dilemma in "Conrad's Darkness," the concluding essay in his last book, "The Return of Eva Peron":

> "It came to me that the great novelists wrote about highly organised societies. I had no such society; I couldn't share the assumptions of the writers; I didn't see my world reflected in theirs. My colonial world was more mixed and second-hand, and more restricted. The time came when I began to ponder the mystery — Conradian word — of my own background: that island in the mouth of a great South American river, the Orinoco, one of the Conradian dark places of the earth, where my father had conceived literary ambitions for himself and then for me, but from which, in my mind, I had stripped all romance and perhaps even reality; preferring to set (Conrad's) 'The Lagoon,' when it was read to me, not on the island I knew, with its muddy rivers, mangrove and swamps, but somewhere far away."

No romantic illusions brought to those dark places — "half-made societies that seemed doomed to remain half-made" — could satisfy Mr. Naipaul, for he knew from experience the bleak landscape and petty ways of "the bush" — his favourite metaphor for the third world. In an interview last year, he said that his dark vision of third-world people on the margins of society "came from living in the bush. It came from a fear of being swallowed up by the bush, and it's a fear I haven't altogether lost. They are the enemies of the civilization I cherish."

But he has repeatedly travelled back into the bush from London, his adopted home, and the restrictions of the third world have continued to torment and limit him. He feels that those dark places cannot sustain vision or produce great art, yet they remain the major subject of his work.

Naipaul's concern with his fellow colonials has taken him from the West Indies, the setting of most of his books, to India ("An Area of Darkness," "India: A Wounded Civilization"), Africa ("A Bend in the River"), Argentina ("The Return of Eva Peron"), and now Iran, Pakistan, Malaysia and Indonesia. He doesn't, however, go to those places to "meditate" on them — a Conradian term — but increasingly to express his bewilderment and "rage" — a Naipaulian word — at what he finds there.

In his brief foreword to "The Return of Eva Peron," he spoke of the "obsessional nature" of the essays in the book and admitted that his "themes repeat." Those themes have by now become Naipaul trademarks: third-world revolutionaries who rant about cultural "authenticity" but who at bottom are really "hustlers," their heritage a "bogus past," their causes nothing but "jargon" and "borrowed ideas" and "sentimental hoax," their Western admirers either media people looking for "jesters" or "revolutionaries who visit centres of revolution with return air tickets."

He has written again and again about the "frenzy" that drives third-world people to undo their world and brings them face to face with their own limits and mediocrity. In regard to his subject matter, Naipaul has been in his own words "at once too close and too far." The consoling detachment enjoyed by someone less threatened by what he writes about, like Conrad, has been denied Naipaul. On the other hand, he cannot achieve real proximity to the places he depicts. There is, increasingly, in his work more of the "political panic" he says in the Conrad essay he carried with him from Trinidad to London.

His travels have become not journeys to other places but journeys into himself — bleak re-enactments of the fear of the bush he experienced in childhood. He has become more and more predictable, too, with serious cost to his great gift as a writer. The books set in the West Indies have always demonstrated a masterly grasp of the material, and his work about India has at least been inspired by his ancestry, but in "Among the Believers" Naipaul is on considerably less familiar ground, and because the book seems to have no central theme, readers must depend on the testimony of the witnesses Naipaul picks to interview.

As always, in Naipaul's writing, there are passages that soar. He can show in a few sentences the anxiety caused in Moslem believers in Indonesia by a threatening outside civilization they can neither master nor dismiss:

> "Islam was pure and perfect; the secular, dying West was to be rejected: that was the message. But the West was taking a long time to die. And more and more people were being drawn into the new world. In this new world, whose centre seemed so far away, so beyond control, newly evolved men like the President of the Jakarta youth organisation felt only their inadequacies. These men were not peasants or pesantren boys. They aspired to high Western skills; they took encouragement from, they needed, Western witness. It was part of their great dependence. This dependence provoked the anguish which (like adolescents) they sought to assuage in the daily severities of their new religious practice: the five-times-a-day prayers, the unnecessary fasts....
>
> "Rejection and dependence: it was hard for the half-evolved to break out of the circle." And here is one of his favourite themes, the redeemer who leads men into calamity — in this case Iran's Ayatollah Ruholla Khomeini: "Interpreter of God's will, leader of the faithful, he expressed all the confusion of his people and made it appear like glory, like the familiar faith: the confusion of a people of high medieval culture awakening to oil and money, a sense of power and violation, and a knowledge of a great new encircling civilization. That civilization couldn't be mastered. It was to be rejected; at the same time it was to be depended on."

Ever the gifted novelist, Naipaul tells the story best when he lets some of his characters open up and reveal themselves. In Iran, for example, the tension in the twin revolutions against the Shah — that of Khomeini and the mullahs and that of Abolhassan Bani-Sadr and the secular nationalists — is illuminated through Behzad, a young leftist from a provincial town who is a science student in Teheran.

In spite of the mullahs, Behzad says, he initially wanted to claim the revolution as his own. He wanted to believe that the mullahs could be pacified and handled, and that he and his fellows would inherit the new world. But the two revolutions went their separate ways, and young people like Behzad discovered that one form of tyranny can be replaced by another. "For the third time in this century the people of Iran have been broken," he says.

Malaysia comes together in Shafi, a 32-year-old Malay in Kuala Lumpur. At one time a building contractor in a village to the north, he now works for ABIM, a major Moslem youth movement. In Pakistan there is Ahmed, a high civil servant, a man of Sind, a devout Muslim with a feel for history.

For Ahmed, as for so many others in Pakistan, the dream of a Moslem state has gone bad. But faith, somehow, survives. "If the state failed, it wasn't because the dream was flawed, or the faith flawed; it could only be because men had failed the faith." In Indonesia, Muhammad Imaduddin Abdul Rahim represents the new Islam. Imaddudin (an Arab name meaning "pillar of the faith") would like Islam to cleanse the country, so he offers it in the form of "mental training courses" to members of Indonesia's young middle class.

All four of them, like so many others they stand for, bring to their religion and tradition modern demands and anxieties. This creates pressures, for today's needs are great. The outside world at once tempts and threatens Moslems. Many of them enter that world, but they can enter it only partly. When they fail to deal with it, they retreat into their shell. When they surrender to it, guilt seizes them. In Naipaul's words: "In the fundamentalist scheme the world constantly decays and has constantly to be re-created. The only function of intellect is to assist that re-creation. It reinterprets the texts; it re-establishes divine precedent. So history has to serve theology, law is separated from the idea of equity. ..."

This theme comes close to being Naipaul's central theme, and in dealing with it he lets his personal feelings get in the way of his presentation. He chides Moslems for being "made" by the Western world they reject. Instead of trying to understand these people, Naipaul is ready to judge them. In his desire to discover their hidden vulnerabilities and point out their contradictions, their need for outside goods and outside approval, he tends to miss the drama and the real meaning of their situation. He forgets that it is part of the painful process of history that people are always made by the world they reject and that the rage at it they express is in large measure rage at themselves.

In addition to this limitation of vision, one gets the distinct feeling of superficiality in this book. Of the holy city of Qom, Naipaul writes: "Qom's life remained hidden." It is probably fair to say that much of the territory he covered remained hidden to him. The places he went to confused and eluded him, denied him entry. He was in a hurry; he wanted to see "Islam in action."

But the people he wanted to comprehend were ambiguous and guarded, and under no obligation to reveal themselves to a traveller. Inside the large international hotels, visitors came to talk with him, but his questions frequently seem rigged and their answers canned. He wanted them to explain to him the secrets of their motivations, the cause of their rage. Over and over again he asked them for blueprints — how would they build an economy? keep a state together? — and repeatedly they had no blueprints to come up with, but only the confusions of their certainties, their reliance on metaphysics, the belief that all the answers could be found in sacred texts.

"We read," Naipaul says in his Conrad essay, "to find out what we already know." Most Naipaul readers will take to this book an image of Islam as a world of anarchy and rage, partly because of recent developments in the Middle East — so dramatically revealed in the assassination of President Anwar el-Sadat of Egypt — but partly also because that is the image of the third world that they have been taking away from Mr. Naipaul's work for some time now. This time his generalisations are sweeping. In the section on Malaysia, he says:

> "The new men of the villages, who feel they have already lost so much, find their path blocked at every turn. Money, development, education have awakened them only to the knowledge that the world is not like their village, that the world is not their own. Their rage — the rage of pastoral people with limited skills, limited money, and a limited

> grasp of the world — is comprehensive. Now they have a weapon: Islam. It is their way of getting even with the world. It serves their grief, their feeling of inadequacy, their social rage and racial hate."

In the section on Indonesia he says: "Islam sanctified rage — rage about the faith, political rage: one could be like the other. And more than once on this journey I had met sensitive men who were ready to contemplate great convulsions."

Naipaul's third-world interpretations have acquired the prestige they have in the West because he is so gifted a writer and also because he has often presented a believable image of places most writers before him were able to see only through the mists of illusion. Timing, too, had something to do with his success; he made his appearance at a point when there was great disillusionment in the West with the affairs of the third world. So many revolutions had failed; so much jargon had been discredited; so much of the modern veneer on third-world countries had cracked. Eventually, no one who really wanted to come to terms with the third world felt he could dismiss Naipaul or slight his work. But he has continued to depict the same thing over and over: a world where the oppressed often turn out to be as vicious as their oppressors; where the promises of redemption lead into blind alleys of fear and terror.

Some third-world critics have blamed Naipaul for not being a real crusader or revolutionary himself, but it is, as he would say, not the task of writers to remake societies. Where I do fault Naipaul, however, is on the depth of his material, and for me "Among the Believers" is his thinnest and least impressive book. What he has said of Conrad must surely apply to himself as well: "Conrad's experience was too scattered; he knew many societies by their externals, but he knew none in depth."

It has been a Naipaulian assumption that only men who live in remote, dark places are "denied a clear vision of the world." This is the major theme of much of his work. And many men who have left the third world to settle in other places have a tendency to think this way as well. (My own country, Lebanon, for instance, is not unlike Naipaul's birthplace). Their intellectual vocations often allow them to look at their own countries and similar ones with a critical eye, and to feel that they have a right to judge and interpret the places they have broken with. But these same men usually approach the civilization of the West with awe and leave it unexamined. Were Naipaul to want really to come to terms with his own past, and to determine whether any men have a clear vision of the world, he would have to set his work (as he once had to set his imagination in order to appreciate Conrad) somewhere far away from the third world, somewhere in the West perhaps.

At one point in his later years, Joseph Conrad returned for a brief visit to Poland, where he felt, as he said, the shadows "crowding upon" him and understood that his art had all along depended on his keeping a distance from his past. His Polish past had always remained with him, but in order to see what he had seen and write what he had written he had to open up a whole different world.

The shadows have been "crowding upon" Naipaul, too, obscuring his vision. More and more the women and men in his fiction and political essays appear to be unsupported by anything of value, diminished and disfigured, vain, insincere, crazed, dishonest.

Surely, as Conrad would tell us, this is too simple a view of things, for "a man is much more like the sea whose movements are complicated to explain, and whose depths may bring up God only knows what at any moment." Were Naipaul to meditate on places less haunted for him by old ghosts, he might come to realise some of the truths that Conrad learned; that darkness is not only there but here as well; that all men and societies are haunted by their own demons; that all of us are denied a clear vision of the world.

Objectives

The proposed aim of the author was to study cultures which have a long pre-Islamic history and their modern attempts to establish a religious state. Naipaul does not include Arab countries as he is interested in "converted peoples".

Travels

Iran: He went to Iran just after the revolution and could listen to all the mixed voices, guided around the holy places like Qom by a communist, Behzad. Ayatollah Sadegh Khalkhali is interviewed.

Pakistan: It is a country based on Islam, at the same time with strong Indian-English tradition. Being of Indian origin, Naipaul has strong views on Pakistan, and gives a controversial portrait of the country.

Malaysia: Naipaul meets with the famous Anwar Ibrahim, when he is a rising star. Anwar had been to Iran and met Ayatollah Khomeini, and he wanted to awake Malaysian people.

Indonesia: He describes the Indonesian history, how the Japanese "liberated" them and how they later fought the Dutch until free. Islam in Indonesia is mixed with former beliefs and there are forces that want to make Islam more pure. He meet poets in Jakarta and he make a trip to visit the Koranic schools. All in all he does a very deep portrait of Indonesia.

Naipaul further argues that contrary to the contention of the Islamic fundamentalists, there is no scope for Islam prescribing an institutionalised method of cratering to people's political and social needs while taking their civilization forward. Because:

> The Islamic fundamentalist wish is to work back to such a whole, for them a God-given whole, but with the tool of faith alone—belief, religious practices and rituals. It is like a wish—with intellect suppressed or limited, the historical sense falsified—to work back from the abstract to the concrete, and to set up the tribal walls again. It is to seek to re-create something like a tribal or a city-state that—except in theological fantasy—never was. The Koran is not the statute book of a settled golden age; it is the mystical or oracular record of an extended upheaval, widening out from the Prophet to his tribe to Arabia.

Thus, his conclusion is two-fold: Islam was used by aggrieved people who do not know where to look for solutions; Islam, in an intrinsic and structural way, provides no *political* solution to these people.

This conclusion cannot be dismissed as shallow opinions of a man who is hostile to Islam and ignorant of its key tenets, but rather can be countered (if at all) only by equally keen and perceptive arguments.

Analysis

It is dizzying to read of recent Indonesian history. And to look at it in the life of one man is to wonder how, with so little to hold on to in the way of law or country, anyone could withstand so many assaults on his personality. Suryadi was in his mid fifties. He was small, dark-brown, frail-looking. He was born in East Java and he described himself as one of the "statistical Muṣlims" of Indonesia. He had received no religious training; such religion as he had was what was in the air around him. He wasn't sure whether he believed in the afterlife; and he didn't know that belief was fundamental to the Muslim faith.

He belonged to the nobility, but in Java that meant only that he was not of the peasantry. The Dutch ruled Java through the old feudal courts of the country. But Java was only an agricultural colony, and the skills required of the nobility in the Dutch time were not high. Suryadi's grandfather, as a noble, had a modest white-collar job; Suryadi's father was a bookkeeper in a bank. It was possible for Suryadi, as a noble, to go to a Dutch school.

The fees were low; and Suryadi, in fact, didn't have to pay. The education was good. Just how good it was shown by the excellent English Suryadi spoke. And recently, wishing to take up German again and enrolling in the German cultural centre in Jakarta, the Goethe Institute, Suryadi found that, with his Dutch-taught German of forty years before, he was put in the middle class, and he was later able without trouble to get a certificate in an examination marked in Germany.

Early in 1942 the Japanese occupied Java. The message from Radio Tokyo was that the Japanese would give Indonesia its independence, and there were many people willing to welcome the Japanese as liberators. Suryadi was in the final year of his school. The Dutch teachers were replaced by Indonesians, and the headmaster or supervisor was Japanese.

For six months classes continued as they would have done under the Dutch. Then — and it is amazing how things go on, even during an upheaval — Suryadi went to the university. The lecturers and professors there were now Japanese. But the Japanese simply couldn't manage foreign languages. They recognised this themselves, and after a time they appointed Indonesians, who worked under Japanese supervisors.

The Indonesians used the classes to preach nationalism. Already much of the good will towards the Japanese had gone. It was clear to Suryadi that the whole economy was being subverted to assist the Japanese war effort. Thousands of Indonesians were sent to work on the Burma Railway (and there is still a community of Indonesians in Thailand, from the enforced migration of that time). Radios were sealed; the radios that had once brought the good news from Radio Tokyo could no longer be listened to,

Two incidents occurred at this time which made Suryadi declare his opposition to the Japanese. The university authorities decreed that all students were to shave their heads. It was the discipline of the Zen monastery. And Suryadi felt it as he was meant to feel it: an assault on his personality. And then one day on the parade ground — students were given military training — a student was slapped by a Japanese officer. All the Indonesians felt humiliated, and Suryadi and his friends held a protest demonstration in the university. Thirty of them, teachers as well as students, were arrested by the Japanese secret police and taken to jail.

In the jail they heard people being tortured for anti-Japanese offences and even for listening to the radio. But Suryadi's group were treated like political prisoners; and they continued to be disciplined in the way of the Zen monastery. They were beaten with bamboo staves, but it was only a ritual humiliation. The bamboo staves were split at the end; they didn't hurt, they only made a loud cracking noise. After a month of this Suryadi and his friends were released. But they were expelled from the university. So Suryadi never completed his education.

They had got off lightly because the Indonesian nationalism leaders were still cooperating with the Japanese. Sukarno never believed that Japan was going to lose the war, Suryadi said. Sukarno didn't even believe that the atom bomb had been dropped on Japan. It was only after the Japanese surrender that Sukarno and the nationalists proclaimed the independence of Indonesia. And four years of fighting against the Dutch followed.

What events to have lived through, in one's first twenty-six years! But Suryadi was without rancour. The events had been too big; there was no one to blame. He had no ill-feeling towards either Dutch or Japanese. He did business now with both; and he respected both as people who honoured a bargain. The Japanese had the reputation in South East Asia of being hard bargainers (there had been anti-Japanese riots in Jakarta because of the Japanese domination of the Indonesian market); but Suryadi had found the Japanese more generous, if anything, than the Dutch.

Suryadi was without rancour, and it could be said that he had won through. But there was an Indonesian sadness in him, and it was the sadness of a man who felt he had been left alone, and was now — after the Dutch time, the Japanese time, the four years of the war against the Dutch, the twenty years of Sukarno — without a cause. More than once the world had seemed about to open out for him as an Indonesian, but then had closed up again.

He had lain low during the later Sukarno years. Army rule after that had appeared to revive the country. But now something else was happening. A kind of Javanese culture was being asserted. Suryadi was Javanese; the Javanese dance and the Javanese epics and puppet plays were part of his being. But he felt that Javanese culture was being misused; it was encouraging a revival of feudal attitudes, with the army taking the place of the old courts. Suryadi had the Javanese eye for feudal courtesies. He saw that nowadays the soldier's salute to an officer was more than an army salute; it also contained a feudal bow. It was a twisted kind of retrogression. It wasn't what Suryadi had wanted for his country.

And he had lost his daughter. She had become a convert to the new Muslim cause — the Malaysian disease, some people called it here. At school and then at the university she had been a lively girl. She had done Javanese dancing; she was a diver; she liked to go camping. But then, at the university, she had met a new Muslim, a born-again Muslim, and she had begun to change. She went out with her hair covered; she wore drab long gowns; and her mind began correspondingly to dull.

Suryadi and his wife had done the unforgivable one day. They had gone among the girl's papers, and they had come upon a pledge she had signed. She had pledged to be ruled in everything by a particular Muslim teacher; he was to be her guide to paradise. She, who would have been a statistical Muslim like Suryadi and his wife, was now being instructed in the pure faith.

Suryadi didn't take it well. He thought now he should have been calmer in the beginning; by making his dismay too apparent he had probably pushed the girl further away from him. He said to her one day, "Suppose someone asks you to go out camping now, will you say, 'I can't go, because I have no assurance there will be water for my ablutions before my prayers'?" He had spoken with irritation and irony. But later she came back to him and said, "I have checked. In the Koran there is nothing that says it is obligatory if you are travelling." And Suryadi understood that she had become impervious to irony.

Review

When V. S. Naipaul's Among the Believers: An Islamic Journey was first published in 1981, the world barely took any notice of it. Presumably, the world was least interested in one man's travel across relatively unknown and inconsequential corners of Asia and his ramblings about the alleged precariousness of the Islamic revolution. But the world has changed since 1981; especially after the horrendous rise of religious fundamentalism.

The horrific happenings of the last decades have forced people to see and appreciate what Naipaul confronted in this travelogue two decades ago. The book – which records Naipaul's journeys through Iran, Pakistan, Malaysia and Indonesia – which was once considered delirious, is now widely regarded as prophetic for it gives acutely insightful accounts of the rift between the east and the west.

Naipaul journeys the four countries between summer of 1979 and the winter of 1981 when each of the four countries was in someway or the other experiencing turbulent times: Iran had just overthrown the regime of Shah Pahlavi and instated an Islamic state; Pakistan and Indonesia were under military rule; and in Malaysia (to some extent in Indonesia also), a slow racist storm was brewing against the immigrant Chinese.

But what was common to all these nations was that the ideology of Islam was extending itself from its original realm of religion and culture into the realm of politics and governance. Naipaul in his eloquent and compelling way scrutinises the inherent flaw of allowing the religious mullahs to take the helm of the government (as exactly what had happened in Iran, where the Ayatollah Khomeini ruled after the Islamic revolution as the representative of the twelfth Imam or the regent of god). The Islamic revolutionaries seek to bring the golden rule of prophet back, where governance will be conducted by the rule of the holy book Quran. But is this the right way forward?

The reasons for the instinctive move towards the glory of the past, as Naipaul elicits, are multi-layered and confounding. In Iran, the people desperate and desolate under the oppressive regime of the Shah, believe that Islamic rule will be the panacea for wide spread corruption in the system. In Pakistan too, the military rule promised the Islamic rule to the deprived people. It is almost like people wanted a one-time quick fix solution to all the ills of the society; something that can solve people's problems for eternity so that they can live happily ever after.

In Malaysia and Indonesia, the oppressed people were the destitute natives overwhelmed by the immigrant and prosperous Chinese. The native peasants who struggle to find their place in the world seek solace in Islam, which seems to give them a sense of identity and a purpose in their life. Consequently, the call for the rejection of materialism (and in turn the rejection of anything that is ideologically west) and the embracing of universal justice and equity takes deep roots in their minds in the form of Islamic allegiance.

But this rejection is not entirely possible, as these civilizations increasingly find themselves dependent upon western technology to sustain them; and in the end, caught in a state of incertitude that will split them between their allegiance and the inevitable betrayal and cause even more anguish.

Naipaul handles the enigmatic subject with a facile clarity and inimitable style. With a novel like characterisation, he creates the exquisite landscapes with his lucid prose. He effortlessly transforms the reader to places with his sense for detail and acumen for historical accounts. But people are the most important part of his travel.

Naipaul is constantly striving to reach out to the humans that ultimately everyone is. Even though he is cynical towards their ideologies, he views them with compassion. He travels to unknown corners of the world and converses with people from all walks of life; he transforms us into their worlds, painting their portraits with his poignant prose. Naipaul finally might be the agent of the west; his vision slightly blurred by its influences. But his compassion for people is finally what that allows him to delve deep into their lives and discern better.

Far ahead of its time, the book was more than just a prophecy. It was a portentous warning of what religious fundamentalism was capable of; a warning the world sadly missed. But what the book fails to acknowledge (though implicitly it does at places) is the root cause of the ideological rejection of the west: the rampant exploitation and oppression in the era of colonisation which created the need for alternative ideologies. This leaves a disturbing void, almost like an unconfessed guilt nagging the inside of our minds. But Among the Believers is Naipaul's intimate affair with the east; an affair that is as compassionate as it is enlightening.

14 Beyond Belief

Beyond Belief: Islamic Excursions among the Converted Peoples is a non-fiction book by V. S. Naipaul published by Vintage Books in 1998. It was written as a sequel to Naipaul's *Among the Believers: An Islamic Journey* (1979). Naipaul draws a distinction between Arab countries and the countries of "converted peoples" where the adoption of Islam involves to some extent the adoption of Arabic culture. The book describes his five-month journey in 1995 revisiting four Muslim countries: Indonesia, Iran, Pakistan and Malaysia.

Introduction

V.S. Naipaul's writings about the Muslim world have become increasingly influential in mainstream western culture. Since the publication of his travel narratives, Among the Believers and Beyond Belief, in which he offered an account of his travels in Indonesia, Iran, Pakistan and Malaysia, Naipaul has established himself as an authority on "Islam in action." With specific reference to his "Islamic journeys," critics have commended Naipaul for his "moral integrity," "fearless truth-telling," and loyalty to the "proof of evidence."

The favourable critical reception that Among the Believers and Beyond Belief elicited has given rise to the inclusion of Naipaul's work in books that promise "new levels of understanding about Islam." Critical acclaim has been matched by official recognition: In 1990, Naipaul received a knighthood for his services to literature and, in 2001, was awarded the Nobel Prize for Literature.

However, in contrast to this impressive resume, critics beyond the periphery of mainstream western culture have referred to him as a man "incapable of restraining his loathing for the Islamic world and its people." Concerns about Naipaul's hatred of Islam, as voiced by Eqbal Ahmad, Amin Malak, Caryl Phillips, and even Salman Rushdie, give Naipaul's prominent status in mainstream western culture a rather more sinister aspect.

In this article, I shall expose how his Islamophobia has been interpreted as expertise by offering a revisionist reading of Beyond Belief. Focusing on three main literary themes in Naipaul's most recent "Islamic excursion," namely, nineteenth-century literary conventions, the gothic genre, and neurosis, I shall argue that his standing as an authority on the Muslim world needs to be reconsidered.

Literary Conventions and Restricted Passages

Although literary critics overwhelmingly accept that there is an ambivalent relationship between travel writing and fiction, travel writing is still largely referred to as non-fictional literature. This label is misleading, for it detracts from the fact that travel writing is an established literary genre full of narrative conventions and fictional devices. Travel writing and fiction frequently overlap and intertwine. However, while critics celebrate Naipaul for his "moral integrity" and "commitment to truth," it is not surprising that Beyond Belief has been predominantly read as an informative, factual text. We are repeatedly promised that Naipaul's travel writing will "enable" western readers to gain an "insight" into the life of Muslims.

Naipaul does everything possible to reinforce this sort of reading. In the prologue to Beyond Belief, the narrative voice assures us that "This is a book about people. It is not a book of opinions." We are guaranteed that "the truth" will be presented to us in an undistorted manner. Sensitive to the ways in which an obtrusive narrator can undermine the authority of a "non-fictional" text, Naipaul promises that the "writer will be less present, less of an enquirer"; instead, he will be "in the background, trusting to his instinct." Modelling himself on a figure esteemed by nineteenth century English romantics, Naipaul claims to be a pure, natural, and instinctive artist. In this manner, he assures us that we can rely on his objectivity.

Nineteenth-century literary conventions do not only provide Naipaul with inspiration regarding the narrator's role. During this literary period, the English novel as a genre had not yet found a narrative device that could provide the illusion that the reader could enter into the character's mind. Modernist conventions such as the "stream of consciousness" were yet to emerge. Consequently, the "internal" drama was displaced onto an excessively responsive physical body or environment. Nineteenth-century literature twitches with hysterical characters prone to excessive blushing, hyperventilation, trembling, and faints. For example, in Wilkie Collins' novel The Woman in White, "womanish tears," shivering skin, and severe bouts of "nervousness" besiege the main characters. All of the characters' doubts and concerns are played out on the skin's surface.

Similarly, in a novel such as Charlotte Bronte's Jane Eyre, we know when the central character is angry or frustrated, because at these moments of crisis, a sudden backdrop of scarlet-coloured soft furnishings and violent rainstorms appear. This sort of narrative displacement is a technique that Naipaul employs to great effect when encountering Muslims in Beyond Belief.

Writing himself into the role of the central character, Naipaul displaces his emotions onto both his physical body and the local environment. However, the symptoms that he exhibits are not the typical shivers, faints, or sweats of the nineteenth-century hero or heroine. Rather, Naipaul's internal anxiety and, in some cases, clear disgust manifest themselves in a very specific manner. On encountering practising Muslims, Naipaul begins to suffer from severe breathing restrictions. He also experiences an accompanying change in air quality.

The first incident occurs when he visits Imaduddin's office. Imaduddin, who lives in Indonesia, is referred to as an "unusual man" because he is "a man of science" and "a dedicated man of the faith." Naipaul is uncomfortable with this "contradiction" (despite their long and intertwined history, science and Islam are, in Naipaul's view, incompatible). It is clear that he also considers Imaduddin to be a hypocrite: He takes exception to Imaduddin's wealth, preferring "his" Muslims to be pious and poor. Despite the kindness that Imaduddin shows to his guest, his "Muslimness" causes Naipaul to suffer from unpleasant physical reactions.

Naipaul enters the office and, loyal to nineteenth-century realism, begins to make his inventory of the room:

> On one side of the laptop was a well-handled Koran; on the other side was a pile of shoddily produced paperback books, perhaps a foot high, of similar size and in electric blue covers, which had been published in Egypt and might have been a very long commentary on the Koran: no doubt like meat and drink to Imaduddin.

Naipaul is safe while Imaduddin remains in the room. But when he answers the *Adhan* (call to prayer) and deserts Naipaul, the very presence of what Naipaul suspects to be a set of "Islamic books" (he cannot read Arabic and is therefore forced to hazard a guess at the books' contents) is enough to provoke serious health implications. We are informed that,

> ... without the man himself [...] his missionary paraphernalia felt oppressive [...]. It was only someone like Imaduddin who could give point and life to the electric-blue Egyptian paperbacks on the glass-topped desk.

In his heightened state of anxiety, Naipaul transforms Imaduddin's private reading material into "dangerous missionary paraphernalia" with awesome powers. They are the "meat and drink," the life-blood upon which Imaduddin apparently survives. The "electric-blue" covers suggest that these books are made of hazardous, explosive materials and, being only "shoddily produced," they are set in stark contrast to the laptop computer and glass-desk upon which they rest. Naipaul prefers not to ask Imaduddin about the content of these books, for doing so would deflate the passage's tension.

Rather, he reassures himself with the thought that this possible "commentary on the Koran is something that only a man like Imaduddin could give point and life to." However, mere proximity to these potentially "Muslim" books causes him to suffer from the "oppressive" atmosphere that they generate. This episode offers a foretaste of what is to come, and Naipaul endures far more severe reactions when he is exposed to the material presence of Islamic literature in Pakistan.

The second change in atmospheric quality occurs when Naipaul visits Mohammed Akram Ranjha at a commune run by, in Naipaul's words, "the most important of the fundamentalist groups: Jamaat-i-Islami." Imprisoned for kidnapping and possibly helping to murder his brother's wife (Naipaul's choice of Muslim "interviewees" are far from being, as he claims, "representative"), Mohammed is imprisoned and shares a cell with a "political prisoner." This leads to his "jailhouse conversion." Eventually, a lawyer who we are told is "crazed with religion" helps Mohammed get into law college. While practising law, Mohammed becomes politically active on behalf of Jamaat-i-Islami.

His son Saleem, a 34-year-old senior customs officer, agrees to drive Naipaul to the commune on the edge of Lahore. This is when Naipaul realises that he has made his first major mistake: He failed to accept Saleem's "offer of air-conditioning." Naipaul refused the offer because he feared that he might catch a "chill." He comes to regret this decision because the closer he gets to the commune, the more "choked" he becomes. Significantly, Naipaul's breathing restrictions once again coincide with the call to prayer (like Imaduddin before him, Saleem deserts the afflicted Naipaul in order to go to the mosque). When Saleem returns, he takes Naipaul to his study and library.

At this point in the journey, Naipaul encounters yet another set of "Islamic books":

> Half the wall facing the door carried those Islamic sets in decorated binding [...]. I soon stopped looking at the books. I began to choke in the stale, enclosed air. I felt I was becoming ill.

This room of "Islamic learning" appears to be drained of oxygen. We are told that it is "entirely sealed" (by this, Naipaul later clarifies that he meant that the window was closed). Naipaul tries to rectify this and demands that someone open the window and switch on the "air-cleaner." Sitting on the only chair in the room, one that has been brought up for him at his specific request, he sits by the window, inhales some slightly less polluted air, and begins to recover.

But the relief that he enjoys is short-lived. Having survived the stifling atmosphere produced by the *Adhan*, the mosque, Islamic literature, and Muslim households, Naipaul's breathing restriction returns during the following dialogue, in which Saleem proudly introduces his young son:

> Saleem said, 'He is going to learn the whole Koran by heart.'
>
> 'The whole Koran,' the old man said, picking up the duet with his son.
>
> I asked, 'How long will that take?'
>
> Saleem said, 'Five or six years.'
>
> I couldn't stay. My breathing had become very bad. Downstairs, the servants, thin and dark and dingy, behind the sacks with the split golden paddy.

Outside, the fumes and grit of the Multan road. Saleem's driver drove me back to the hotel. Saleem didn't come with me. Naipaul's reaction to the tradition of learning to recite the Qur'an is so violent that he flees back to the relative safety of his hotel in Lahore without delay. The little boy is left unheard.

As one can see from these passages, Naipaul's fear of Islamic literature, mosques, or indeed any form of Muslim worship are clearly reflected in both his environment and his physical ailments. In Beyond Belief, poor air-quality is an indicator of the Islamic faith, and Naipaul's asthmatic responses are symptomatic of the emotions that he experiences during close encounters with Muslims. In her study of Naipaul, Fawzia Mustafa observes that he uses "physical discomfort" as "a gauge for reading the functioning, or completeness, or societal health of the place in which he finds himself." This is correct, but she fails to mention that Naipaul's physical discomfort is most acute when he is in the presence of "the believers."

Muslims of various races, traditions, and character induce violent physical responses from this narrator of supposed "moral integrity." His dislike of Islam is so intense that he is compelled to rush out of "interviews," escape an "oppressive" atmosphere, reach for "air-cleaners," and struggle to open windows when in the presence of practising Muslims. Although Naipaul may well have a sensitive physical disposition, his commitment to literary conventions in nineteenth-century fiction helps to explain both his recurrent breathing restrictions and the faith-dependent air quality that he "discovers" in Indonesia, Pakistan, Malaysia, and Iran.

Gothic Realism

One of the main nineteenth-century genres that Naipaul mobilises in his "Islamic" travelogue is a style called "gothic realism." Occasionally, he abandons himself to its dictates so completely that he produces rather humorous results. The typical plot of the nineteenth-century gothic novel is that of the delicate but curious heroine who is lured into the ancestral home of a seemingly innocent but fearsomely dangerous count or aristocrat.

Naipaul recycles this plot, placing himself at the centre. It goes like this. The inquisitive Naipaul visits Imaduddin's house in order to "hear a little more about his past – his ancestry." But Naipaul arrives late and, to his disdain, is left to wait in an empty room. Once again he fulfils the familiar role of the "realist observer" and describes the objects in the room:

> On the pillars of the sitting room there were two or three decorative little flower pieces and, surprisingly, a picture of a sailing ship. About the sitting room were small mementoes of foreign travel, tourist souvenirs, showing a softer side of Imaduddin (or his wife), a side not connected with mental training, if indeed the house was theirs, and if their mementoes had truly tugged at their hearts (and did not, rather, preserve the memory of some pious giver).

As the description develops, the language becomes increasingly gothic in style. Superficially, the room has the appearance of familiarity, even comfort, but there is the suggestion that this might just be a sinister and deceptive cover. In Naipaul's view, Islamic education ("mental training") is incompatible with a love of travel, sentimentality, or a liking for nautical scenes. Therefore, the collection of "sentimental objects" becomes suspicious and Naipaul doubts whether the house actually belongs to Imaduddin and his wife. The implication is that these comforting objects are being displayed in order to lure him into a false sense of security. Naipaul's nerves get the better of him as he waits for Imaduddin, and he begins to experience a deep sense of panic:

> ... how long [...] should I stay where I was, violating the house, and how when the time came [...] might I get away from the curious trap I had appeared to have fallen into.

This passage could have been lifted straight out of Jane Austen's *Northanger Abbey* or Brahm Stoker's *Dracula*. Naipaul, in his loyalty to the gothic narrative, has written himself into the role of the vulnerable, innocent heroine at the mercy of the dark lord. As if aware of the narrative trap into which he has fallen, as well as of the weak narrative position that he has inadvertently adopted, he attempts to recover his narratorial authority by means of a well-used Naipaulian weapon: a toilet joke.

Once he discovers that Imaduddin was doing nothing more menacing than having a massage, he claims that he had suspected that Imaduddin's "bathroom problems" were the cause of his wait all along. However, Naipaul's use of the gothic genre is usually rather more disturbing. Naipaul uses gothic language to portray both Islam and Muslims throughout *Beyond Belief*, and its powers of political manipulation are alarming. In the section on Indonesia, Islam is described as having spread in a Dracula-like fashion:

Islam had come here not long before Europe. It had not been the towering force it had been in other converted places. [...] It had not completely possessed the souls of people. According to Naipaul, Indonesia only narrowly escaped this ghoulish fate. We need only study his description of Muslims (or "possessed souls") answering the *adhan* in order to see the importance of the gothic genre in his narration,

> ... within the office, no doubt from the carpeted and rumpled open space at the end of the corridor, hesitant scraping sounds developed into a shy chant. [...] The chanting from the corridor became more confident.
>
> It couldn't be denied now. I could see that Imaduddin wanted to be out there, with the chanters and the prayers. The chanting now filled the corridor [...] he couldn't be held back.

This passage is infused with gothic tension: the "hesitant scraping sounds" and rising "chants" suggest the actions of a frightening and possibly subhuman sect, rather than a group of Muslims at prayer. Muslims do not chant before beginning the main prayer. If a Muslim arrives early, he or she might do two *rak'ats*, that is, salutations to the mosque, but this is always done in silence. It does not involve "hesitant scraping sounds." In Naipaul's view, by merely answering the call to prayer, Imaduddin reveals himself to be one of the walking dead, a mindless being seduced against his will, for "he couldn't be held back." (Notably, those who are not Muslims in *Beyond Belief* are repeatedly referred to as being "their own men.") As in numerous instances in the text, Naipaul's use of gothic imagery tells us more about his own fears and prejudices than about reality.

This can also be seen in Naipaul's description of Saleem. When Saleem hears the *Adhan*, he is described as responding in a spasmodic and zombie-like fashion. We are told that "in sudden haste" he "took off his tie and threw his jacket on the car seat and went to join in the prayers." That Muslims are captured souls at the mercy of a mind-numbing and unstoppable force is a persistent theme in Naipaul's text. According to Naipaul, "cultural depression" causes "religious teaching and a knowledge of Islam" to flourish.

He goes on to assert that learning how to recite the Qur'an, "how to have ablution," and "how to do the right prayers" involves an "isolating and beating down and stunning of the mind," a "kind of pain." Once again, Naipaul suggests that Muslims are like the living dead, their brains anaesthetised by pain and suffering. This theme is extended when he describes the theological school of Qom, Iran.

Naipaul's translator, Mehrdad, informs him that "special night prayers involve a lot of bowing and rubbing of the forehead against the earth." Naipaul describes these "very pious people" as having "something like a scorch mark on their forehead; this was because they heated the cakes of earth for their prayers." The underlying references have a powerful impact. Muslims answer the call to prayer in zombie-like fashion and have scorched foreheads, as if marked by the Anti-Christ.

The women who walk through the streets of this centre of learning are described in an equally hellish manner. Like enslaved creatures, they "held the chador over their face with their hands or bit an end of it between their teeth; they looked like people who were muzzling themselves." Though it is traditional in a number of cultures for women (especially those of the older generation) to hold their headscarf between their teeth, he uses this as "evidence" that these "subhuman" women have given up their souls and are suffering torturous consequences. These hellish images echo Dante's *Inferno*. Naipaul uses the gothic genre to give credence to his opinion that political Islam is "a complete form of control" that "deform[s] people's lives."

Naipaul fails to comment on the fact that in the same areas in which he identifies this monstrous "complete form of control," non-Islamic practices are rife. For example, he encounters brothels, the caste system, local superstitions, fast-breakers, scantily clad women, military dictatorships, and so on. In response to his earlier travelogue, Amin Malak remarks:

> ... two of the four countries – Pakistan and Indonesia – are under military dictatorships, the third (Iran) is undergoing a revolutionary process, and the fourth (Malaysia) is suffering from racial tension [...]. No wonder then that his search for Islamic institutions or Islamic law in practice becomes an exercise in futility. It would be hard to imagine stable and legitimate social structures existing, let alone functioning, in the political climates of the four countries visited.

Despite the fact that Naipaul details non-Islamic practices at length, he persists in his claim that all the ills of the people whom he meets have their origin in Islam. The text's message is clear: non-Arab Muslims are to be pitied because they have given away their souls. It is no accident that *Beyond Belief* frequently reads like a gothic novel. The gothic genre is dominated by vulnerable characters who submit their will, often subconsciously, to a higher demonic force that feeds off their life blood and leaves them void. In Naipaul's view, the men who are "unable to resist" the call to prayer and the women who "muzzle themselves" have signed such a contract of submission and have agreed to abolish "the self." At a reading of his book *Half a Life* at Queen Elizabeth Hall in October 2001, Naipaul claimed that Islam demanded an "abolition of the self" that "was worse than the similar colonial abolition of identity [...] much, much worse in fact." In *Beyond Belief*, he asserts that:

> ...converted peoples have to strip themselves of their past; of converted peoples nothing is required but the purest faith (if such a thing can be arrived at), Islam, submission. It is the most uncompromising kind of imperialism.

Naipaul repeatedly asserts that Islam demands that people annul their individuality. With regards to Pakistan, he argues that "the fundamentalists wanted people to be transparent, pure, to be empty vessels for the faith. It was an impossibility: human beings could never be blanks in that way." Yet, according to him, such people exist. Those who are "empty," those who are suffering from cultural depression and an ignorance about their past are identified as being those most "at risk" of conversion.

In his view, certain people or cultures are more vulnerable to Islam than others. For example, he states that Indonesians are susceptible to conversion because "they have no idea of themselves." A vacuum of identity is stipulated as being the ideal environment in which Islam can prosper. Like the weak and vulnerable women that faint and submit to blood-sucking vampires in the gothic novel, Naipaul's text suggests that non-Arab Muslims, with their delicate mental Constitutions, have inadvertently become the living dead.

Author and Neurosis

Naipaul's evident concern with the mental health of Muslims constitutes another area of similarity between *Beyond Belief* and nineteenth-century literature. Although not a genre as such, mental instability became a preoccupation in nineteenth-century fiction, reaching its peak towards the latter part of the century. Instead of locking madness in the attic (such is the fate of Bertha Mason, the "madwoman" in *Jane Eyre*), *fin-de-siècle* novels brought madness downstairs to be "analysed." Central characters become increasingly "unstable," and even those marginal characters who are included in order to "cure" the afflicted begin to show signs of insanity.

For example, one of the doctors of psychiatry in *Dracula* becomes slowly addicted to drugs, while the other one is prone to alarming bouts of hysteria. This ambiguous line between madness and sanity can also be seen in Joseph Conrad's *The Heart of Darkness* and Wilkie Collins' *The Woman in White.*

The readiness to address the causes, symptoms, and fluidity of madness in literature ran parallel to the increasingly influential academic discipline of psychiatry. During this period, the language of such psychiatrists as Andrew Wynter (*The Borderlands of Insanity*, 1875), Henry Maudsley (*The Pathology of the Mind*, 1895) and Sigmund Freud entered into popular discourse.

Reflecting contemporary cultures' anxieties, characters regularly slip in and out of madness, experiencing hysteria, degeneration, insanity, and other newly defined (or redefined) psychological states.

In much *fin-de-siècle* literature, characters and narrators utilise the discourse of psychiatry in order to authoritatively "define" and explain the psychological states of others. Such "mental assessments" are not confined to those "qualified" to offer opinions. Madness is such a pervasive discourse that everyone, including the patients, is eager to practice amateur psychology. For example, in *Dracula,* Dr. Seward classifies the character Renfield as a "zoophagous patient" (explained by his penchant for eating flies). However, between fly-eating episodes the "pet lunatic" Renfield asserts:

> Since I myself have been an inmate of a lunatic asylum, I cannot help but notice that the sophistic tendencies of some of its inmates lean towards the errors of *non causæ* and *ignoration elenchi.*

In *fin-de-siècle* literature, authors eagerly experiment with this new authoritative discourse of the mind, and narrators and characters alike define and classify the liberal spread of madness with "scientific" enthusiasm. Yet again, Naipaul does not fail in his allegiance to nineteenth-century fiction. While travelling in the "Muslim world," he is regularly faced with what he perceives to be "irrational behaviour" and is quick to offer his diagnosis regarding the mental health of the "converted peoples." He writes:

Islam is in its origins an Arab religion. Everyone not an Arab who is a Muslim is a convert. Islam is not simply a matter of conscience or private belief. It makes imperial demands. A convert's world view alters. His holy places are in Arab lands; his sacred language is Arabic. His idea of history alters. He rejects his own; he becomes, whether he likes it or not, a part of the Arab story. The convert has to turn away from everything that is his. The disturbance for societies is immense, and even after a thousand years can remain unresolved; the turning away has to be done again and again. People develop fantasies about who and what they are; and in the Islam of converted countries there is an element of neurosis and nihilism. These countries can be easily set on the boil.

Neurosis, a tendency towards nihilism, self-delusions, latent aggression and fantasy lives are, according to Naipaul, characteristics of these simmering Muslims. Of Pakistan, Naipaul writes:

> The local people would hardly be there, in their own land, or would be there only as ciphers swept aside by the agents of the faith. It is a dreadful mangling of history. It is a convert's view; that is all that can be said for it. History has become a kind of neurosis. Too much has to be ignored or angled; there is too much fantasy. This fantasy isn't in the books alone; it affects people's lives.

Islam is found guilty of inducing mental illness on a national scale because it is an "Arab" religion with sacred places in Arab lands. According to this peculiar thesis, Arabs do not suffer from neurosis because they are not "converts." Naipaul fails to mention that Arabs were generally polytheists at the time of Prophet Muhammad and, in order to become Muslims, necessarily "converted." Perhaps he dismisses this factor because he believes that the "sacred places" of Arabs are "in their own lands"?

Assuming that this is Naipaul's reasoning, it would follow that European and American Christians and Jews suffer from a similar "neurosis" because their "sacred places" are abroad. However, it is clear that Naipaul regards western Christians and Jews as mentally sound. The logic behind his argument is impossible to follow. As Eqbal Ahmed asks:

> Who is not a convert? By Naipaul's definition, if Iranians are converted Muslims, then Americans are converted Christians, the Japanese are converted Buddhists, and the Chinese, large numbers of them, are converted Buddhists as well. Everybody is converted because at the beginning every religion had only a few followers.

> Christianity, Islam, Buddhism, Judaism, all prophetic religions developed through conversion. In that sense, his organising thesis should not exclude anyone.

Michael Gilsenan dismisses Naipaul's claim that non-Arab Muslims suffer from "neurosis" with the rebuff that his line of reasoning is made of "shallow stuff." Naipaul's attempts to identify and explain what he refers to as "the irrational energies of the faith" are poorly reasoned, and his pains to assume the role of psychiatrist are far less convincing than those of his literary predecessors.

Summary

When the former Indonesian leader Suharto sought spiritual advice, he apparently consulted the dukun of his native Java. They are village healers and fortune-tellers, and they told him that his *wahyu* — his power — came from God. Islam conquered the islands of Indonesia centuries ago, but the power of the dukun endures. As Jakarta smoulders, it would be interesting to know what the dukun are saying to the old man now.

"Beyond Belief," V. S. Naipaul's journey through the Islamic lands of Indonesia, Iran, Pakistan and Malaya, is an incomparable guide to the complex of animist and Islamic belief with which Indonesians confront the collapse of their economic miracle and the breakdown of the Suharto regime.

It is equally useful as a guide to the religious and nationalist emotions at play in the arms race on the Indian subcontinent. Two "God-intoxicated" elites there can now make nuclear weapons, and their continued hold on power depends on diverting their electorates from their discontents with displays of nationalist and religious brinkmanship.

Naipaul did not anticipate any of these events, yet "Beyond Belief" provides an essential guide to their deeper context. For five months in 1995, Naipaul retraced the itinerary of an earlier book, "Among the Believers," which appeared in 1979. Then he was trying to understand the fundamentalism that seemed to be sweeping the region. Now he is asking what happens when fundamentalism fails and when its dreams of purity encounter global economic change. Sometimes the contrast between 1979 and 1995 is dramatic. In 1979, six months into the Iranian revolution, he visited the "hanging judge" from Qom, Ayatollah Sadegh Khalkhali, a publicity-seeking clown in clerical black, who boasted that he condemned as many as 30 people a week.

In 1995, Naipaul returned and found the hanging judge edged out of power, alone and sick, "completely bald, baby-faced without his turban, head held down against his chest, looking up from below his forehead, eyes without mischief now and seemingly close to tears, as though he wished to dramatise his situation and needed pity." The exaltation of revolutionary terror had given way to a routine authoritarianism, and the old executioner was no longer needed.

These returns across time give unusual depth to Naipaul's encounters. Existential lightness afflicts most travel writing. In many other examples of the genre, the writer never spends enough time with his informants to give them life and human dimension. Naipaul seems to spend days with the people he meets, learning their family histories, their intimate secrets, and letting them talk. His informants have the vividness of characters in a good novel.

This is a book of stories, not a book of argument, but there are arguments aplenty in it. The principal one is that Islam is an imperialism, at war not only with the capitalist West but also with the spiritual traditions of the region. It is not native to Pakistan, Iran, Malaya and Indonesia but was an Arab imperial incursion, beginning in the seventh century:

> "There probably has been no imperialism like that of Islam and the Arabs. The Gauls, after 500 years of Roman rule, could recover their old gods and reverences; those beliefs hadn't died; they lay just below the Roman surface. But Islam seeks as an article of the faith to erase the past; the believers in the end honour Arabia alone; they have nothing to return to."

Islam is still at war with all of the impulses that divert people from keeping their eyes firmly fixed on Mecca. "For the new fundamentalists of Indonesia," Naipaul writes, "the greatest war was to be made on their own past and everything that linked them to their own earth." Even secular Indonesians remain close to their animist traditions.

Naipaul journeys back to the village where one of Jakarta's most respected economic commentators grew up and learns that before the Muslim Ulema (scholars who are religious authorities) arrived to officiate at her wedding in her family's ancestral house, raw meat was thrown out into the jungle to keep the spirits sated and benign on her wedding day.

The book's essential theme is how faith struggles with globalism, with the "steady grinding down of the old world." Ancient customs survive but both capitalist modernity and Islam alike are devouring them, leaving people without a home either in the purist dreams of fundamentalist Islam or in the rootless cosmopolitanism of capitalism.

When the old customs do endure, they are uprooted from the context that gave them sense: "Before the rice harvest you went out to the ripe field and cut seven stalks. You hung these up on your house. Only then you could start the full cutting. No one knew why. The original prompting had vanished somewhere down the centuries."

"Beyond Belief" can be read as a phenomenology of globalism: how ordinary people, born in primitive and tribal worlds, undergo the spiritual dislocations of economic revolution. But Naipaul doesn't like big words — globalisation and fundamentalism — and he refuses to play the analyst.

He prefers instead to be a storyteller or at least a manager of other people's narratives. This can be irritating occasionally — one wants a summary, a large idea, a conclusion, but he is stubbornly against getting in the way of ordinary people's stories. If the result is confusing and contradictory, shot through with a sense of dislocation, that is because, Naipaul seems to be saying, loss is the dominant emotion of global economic revolution.

As a writer of complex and divided loyalties — an Indian of Brahmin origin who underwent the loss of caste and status that accompanied his family's emigration to Trinidad — he seems to have a special understanding for people living on the cusp of ancient faith and late-modern economic reality: an Indonesian poet and a Roman Catholic, obsessively chronicling the decline of the village dukun; a computer programmer in high-tech Bandung who seeks solace from the pressure and loneliness of his work by following a religious guru; young Pakistanis watching their own lives slip by as the state collapses,

Karachi sunders into gang warfare and intellectual freedom is throttled by Islamic obscurantism.

Devout Muslim readers will reject Naipaul's picture of Islam as an imperialism more disruptive than the British Raj. And some may be distressed by Naipaul's unsparing portrait of Iran as an Islamic theocracy gone sour. But "Beyond Belief" is not anti-Islamic in any easy way, and it is unfailingly perceptive about how true believers handle the discordance between their dreams of godly life and ungodly reality. Sometimes they mourn the death of their dreams; sometimes they barely perceive that a problem exists.

He is especially sharp about the breezy fundamentalist intellectuals of Indonesia who served both the Suharto regime and its hubristic dreams of technological takeoff: "The perfection of the value system of his Islam," he writes of one of them, "was curiously circular. It was — adapting his preacher's analogy — like a very smooth and easy treadmill, rather than a car; it kept him busy and went nowhere."

The title "Beyond Belief" implies an ironic distance towards faith. But Naipaul's irony is tempered by compassion and also by his own nostalgia for the sacred. In one revealing passage, he says that he realised after he left his native Trinidad that he had been uneasy because it was "unhallowed." At first, he thought this was because no great literature had transformed the Trinidad experience into myth.

Then he realised it had been a plantation economy built on the bones of an aboriginal people whose sacred places had been plowed under to make the sugar-cane fields. "Perhaps it is this absence of the sense of sacredness," he writes, "that is the curse of the New World." As the new global economy grinds down the Old World, the people of Indonesia, Pakistan, Malaya and Iran cling to the sacred to keep their balance, to tell themselves, if they are successful, that God intended their success, and if they are ground under, to tell them that He has not forgotten them in their misery.

Naipaul is an incomparable chronicler of sacred survivals and the desperation the sacred has to keep at bay. In one remarkable passage, he watches the wealthy Indonesian and Chinese families who flee the smog and stress of Jakarta every weekend for five-star resort sanctuaries in the countryside. They belong to an American evangelical faith, named the Bethany Successful Families, and they gather in the hotel ballrooms, clapping hands and praying for the luck to last: "It felt like luck, this wealth that could bless even the uneducated, because the technologies and the factories that produced it had been imported whole. For that reason, too, it felt like plunder, something that had to end."

When they pack up and return to Jakarta on Sunday night, Naipaul notices the stickers on the rear bumpers of their limousines — Bethany Successful Families — like an amulet to ward off the evil eye. As this elite drives back now, through burned-out shopping malls and gutted apartment buildings, they must wonder, as Suharto used to, which combination of ancient and modern gods, which sacred power, will protect them.

Conclusion

In *Beyond Belief,* Naipaul plunders the nineteenth-century novel in order to present a disturbing image of the Muslim world. Having striven to establish himself as a reliable and trustworthy narrator, he presents a landscape in which mosques, the *Adhan,* Islamic literature, Islamic dress, and Muslim households combine to generate an oppressive atmosphere in which he cannot breathe. Naipaul's use of this nineteenth-century literary convention is rhetorically powerful: The narrative encourages the reader to feel stifled in oxygen-drained Muslim environments and relieved by the free flow of air in non-Muslim spaces.

But the manipulation does not stop there. Naipaul goes on to mobilise the gothic genre – a genre designed to terrify its readers. Bloodthirsty vampires and immortal beasts take over the minds of their victims and threaten civilization, reason, modernity, and sanity. By studying Naipaul's depiction of eerie Muslim households, threatening Islamic artifacts, and brainwashed Muslims at prayer, one can see how his manipulation of the gothic genre culminates in a powerful piece of propaganda.

The final nineteenth-century narrative strand that pervades *Beyond Belief* is that of madness. Followers of Islam are repeatedly referred to as violent, irrational, void, confused, numbed by pain, and prey to a nihilistic form of neurosis. For this reason, those who share his hatred of Islam regard *Beyond Belief* as a "first-rate humanist study" of "contemporary Islamic converts." However, the prestigious awards and critical acclaim that Naipaul has received suggest that his Islamophobic worldview is disturbingly widespread, confirming Edward Said's fear that "malicious generalisations about Islam have become the last acceptable form of denigration of foreign culture in the West."

At a time when Muslims and non-Muslims need to find grounds for mutual respect and understanding, it is essential that the twisted vision presented in *Beyond Belief* is not read as a reliable account of the Muslim world. Naipaul exploits the nineteenth-century novel in order to reinforce his bigoted, Islamophobic worldview. It is, therefore, vital that his place in mainstream western culture be both challenged and revised.

Bibliography

Akhtar Jamal Khan: *V.S. Naipaul: A Critical Study,* Creative Books, New Delhi, 1998.

Bala, Suman: *V.S. Naipaul: A Literary Response to the Nobel Laureate,* Khosla Publication House, New Delhi, 2003.

Ball, John Clement: *Satire and the Postcolonial Novel: V.S. Naipaul,* Chinua Achebe, Salman Rushdie, New York, 2003.

Barnouw, Dagmar: *Naipaul's Strangers,* Indiana University Press, Bloomington, 2003.

Bruce King: *V.S. Naipaul,* Palgrave MacMillan, Basingstoke, 2003.

Cavanagh, John: *British Theatre: A Bibliography, 1901 to 1985,* Motley, Hampshire, 1989.

Clifford, Leech and T. W. Craik: *The Revels History of Drama in English,* Harper and Row, New York, 1975.

Dagmar Barnouw: *Naipaul's Strangers,* Indiana University Press, New York, 2003.

Dissanayake, Wimal and Carmen Wickramagamage: *Self and Colonial Desire: Travel Writings of V.S. Naipual,* Peter Lang, New York, 1993.

Dissanayake, Wimal: *Self and Colonial Desire: Travel Writings of V.S. Naipaul,* P. Lang, New York, 1993.

Dolly Hassan, Z.: *V.S. Naipaul and the West Indies,* Peter Lang, New York, 1989.

Dooley, Gillian: *V.S. Naipaul, Man and Writer,* University of South Carolina Press, Columbia, 2006.

Drabble, Margaret: *The Oxford Companion to English Literature,* Oxford University Press, New York, 1995.

Dyson, A. E.: *The English Novel: Select Bibliographical Guides,* Oxford University Press, London, 1974.

F.W. Bateson and H.T. Meserole: *A Guide to English and American Literature,* Longman, London, 1976.

Fawzia Mustafa: *V. S. Naipaul,* Cambridge University Press, 1995.

Feroza Jussawalla: *Conversations with V.S. Naipaul,* University Press of Mississippi, New York, 1997.

Fordyce, Rachel: *Caroline Drama : A Bibliographic History of Criticism,* G.K. Hall, Toronto, 1992.

French, Patrick: *The World is What it is the Authorized Biography of V.S. Naipaul,* Picador, London, 2008.

G. Watson: *The New Cambridge Bibliography of English Literature,* Cambridge University Press, Cambridge, 1969.

Gillian Dooley: *V.S. Naipaul: Man and Writer,* University of South Carolina Press, New York, 2006.

Gillon Aitken: *Between Father and Son: Family Letters,* Alfred A. Knopf., New York, 2000.

Girdharry, Arnold: *The Wounds of Naipaul and the Women in his Indian Trilogy,* Copley, 2004.

Gorra, Michael: *After Empire: Scott, Naipaul, Rushdie,* University of Chicago, Chicago, 1997.

Gussow, Mel: *V.S. Naipaul in Search of Himself: A Conversation,* New York Times, New York, 1994.

Hamner, Robert, D.: *Critical Perspectives on V. S. Naipaul,* Three Continents Press, Washington, 1977.

———: *V.S. Naipaul,* Twayne, 1973.

Harbage, Alfred: *Annals of English Drama, 975-1700 : An Analytical Record of all Plays, Extant or Lost, Chronologically Arranged and Indexed by Authors, Titles, Dramatic Companies,* Routledge, New York, 1989.

Harmon, Willliam and Holman, C. Hugh: *A Handbook to Literature,* Prentice-Hall, New Jersey, 1996.

Harner, James L.: *Literary Research Guide : A Guide to Reference Sources for the Study of Literatures in English and Related Topics,* Modern Language Association of America, New York, 1993.

Hassan, Dolly Z.: *V. S. Naipaul and the West Indies,* Peter Lang, New York, 1989.

Hayward, Helen: *The Enigman of V. S. Naipaul: Sources and Contexts,* Palgrave MacMillan, London, 2002.

Helen, Hayward: *The Enigma of V.S. Naipaul: Sources and Contexts,* Palgrave MacMillan, New York, 2002.

Hughes, Peter: *V. S. Naipaul,* Routledge, London, 1988.

Ian, Ousby: *The Cambridge Guide to Literature in English,* Cambridge University Press, New York, 1993.

J.D. Hart: *The Oxford Companion to American Literature,* Oxford University Press, New York, 1995.

Jarvis Kelvin: *V.S. Naipaul: A Selective Bibliography with Annotations, 1957–1987,* Metuchen, New Jersey, 1989.

John Clement Ball: *Satire and the Postcolonial Novel: V. S. Naipaul,* Salman Rushdie, Routledge, 2003.

John Mellors: *Mimics into Puppets: The Fiction of V. S. Naipaul,* London Magazine, 1976.

John Thieme: *The Web of Tradition: Use of Allusion in. V.S. Naipaul's Fiction,* Fredericton, York Press, 1983.

Judith Levy: *V. S. Naipaul: Displacement and Autobiography,* Garland Publishing, New York, 1995.

Jussawalla, Feroza: *Conversations with V.S. Naipaul,* University Press of Mississippi, 1997.

Kamra Shashi: *The Novels of V.S. Naipaul: A Study in Theme and Form,* Prestige Books, New Delhi, 1990.

Kelly, Richard: *V. S. Naipaul,* Continum, New York, 1989.

Kelvin Jarvis: *V.S. Naipaul: A Selective Bibliography with Annotations, 1957-1987,* Scarecrow Press, New York, 1989.

Kimbahune, R.S.: *V.S. Naipaul's Travelogues: Indian Readings in Commonwealth Literature,* Sterling, New Delhi, 1985.

King, Bruce: *V.S. Naipaul,* MacMillan, New York, 1993.

Kramer, Jane: *From the Third World: An Assessment of Naipaul's Work,* New York Times Book Review, New York, 1980.

Kumar, Amitava: *The Humour & the Pity: Essays on V.S. Naipaul,* Buffalo Books, New Delhi, 2002.

Kuntz, Joseph Marshall: *Poetry Explication : A Checklist of Interpretation Since 1925 of British and American Poems Past and Present,* G. K. Hall, Boston, 1980.

Landeg White: *V.S. Naipaul: A Critical Introduction,* MacMillan, London, 1975.

Levy, Judith: *V.S. Naipaul: Displacement and Autobiography,* Garland Publishing, New York, 1995.

Mason, Nondita: *The Fiction of V. S. Naipaul,* The World Press, Calcutta, 1986.

McGuinness, Frank: *A Rough Game,* London Magazine, 1971.

McKerrow, Ronald Brunlees: *An Introduction to Bibliography for Literary Students,* Clarendon Press, Oxford, 1928.

McSweeney, Kerry: *V. S. Naipaul: Sensibility and Schemata,* Critical Quarterly, 1976.

McWatt, Mark: *The West Indian Writer and the Self: Recent 'Fictional Autobiography' by Naipaul and Harris,* Journal of West Indian Literature, 1989.

Mellors, John: *Mimics into Puppets: The Fiction of V. S. Naipaul,* London Magazine, 1976.

Michael Gorra: *After Empire: Scott, Naipaul, Rushdie,* University of Chicago Press, New York, 1997.

Morris, Robert K.: *Paradoxes of Order: Some Perspectives on the Fiction of V. S. Naipaul*, University of Missouri Press, Columbia, MO, 1975.

Mustafa, Fawzia: *V. S. Naipaul*, Cambridge University Press, Cambridge, 1995.

Nazareth, Peter: *The Mimic Men As a Study of Corruption*, East Africa Journal, 1970.

Nicoll, Allardyce: *A History of English Drama, 1660-1900*, University Press, Cambridge, 1952.

Nightingale, Peggy: *Journey through Darkness: The Writing of V.S. Naipaul*, University of Queensland Press, St. Lucia, 1987.

Nixon, Rob: *London Calling: V. S. Naipaul, Post-Colonial Mandarin*, Oxford University Press, New York, 1992.

Noel, Jesse A.: *Historicity and Homelessness in Naipaul*, Caribbean Studies, 1972.

Nokes, David: *An Annotated Critical Bibliography of Augustan Poetry*, St. Martin's Press, New York, 1989.

Nondita Mason: *The Fiction of V.S. Naipaul*, World Press, 1986.

Ousby: *The Cambridge Guide to Literature in English*, Cambridge University Press, Cambridge, 1993.

Panwar, Purabi: *V.S. Naipaul: An Anthology of Recent Criticism*, Pencraft International, Delhi, 2003.

Park, Jong-Seong: *An Exploration of the Outsider's Role in Selected Works of Joseph Conrad, Malcolm Lowry, and V.S. Naipaul*, University of London, 1996.

Patrick, French: *The World is what it is: The Authorized Biography of V.S. Naipaul* Random House, 2008.

Paul Theroux: *V. S. Naipaul*, Modern Fiction Studies, 1984.

Peggy Nightingale: *Journey Through Darkness: The Writing of V.S. Naipaul*, University of Queensland Press, 1987.

Perkins, David: *A History of Modern Poetry*, Belknap Press of Harvard University Press, Cambridge, 1976.

Peter Hughes: *V.S. Naipaul,* Routledge, London, 1988.

R.S. Kimbahune: *V. S. Naipaul's Travelogues: Indian Readings in Commonwealth Literature,* Sterling, New Delhi, 1985.

Rai, Sudha: *V.S. Naipaul: A Study in Expatriate Sensibility,* Arnold-Heinemann, New Delhi, 1982.

Ramadevi, N.: *The Novels of V.S. Naipaul Quest for Order and Identity,* Prestige Books, New Delhi, 1996.

Rao, Judy: *V. S. Naipaul and the Self-Destructive Novel,* Journal of West Indian Literature, 1989.

Richard I: *Experience As Drama in the Works of V. S. Naipaul,* Kunapipi, 1981.

Richard Kelly: *V.S. Naipaul,* Continum, New York, 1989.

Richmond, Angus: *V. S. Naipaul: The Mimic Man,* Race and Class, 1982.

Rob Nixon: *V.S. Naipaul: Postcolonial Mandarin,* Oxford University Press, London Calling, 1992.

Robert Boyers: *Atrocity and Amnesia: The Political Novel Since 1945,* Oxford University Press, Oxford, 1985.

Robert Hamner, D.: *Critical Perspectives on V.S. Naipaul,* Three Continents Press, 1977.

———: *V.S. Naipaul,* Twayne, New York, 1973.

Roger, Fowler: *A Dictionary of Modern Critical Terms,* Routledge & Kegan Paul, London, 1987.

Rohlehr, Gordon: *The Ironic Approach: The Novels of V. S. Naipaul,* Three Continents Press, Washington, 1977.

Rothfork, John: *V. S. Naipaul and the Third World,* Research Studies, 1981.

Said, Edward: *Intellectuals in the Post-Colonial World,* Salmagundi, 1986.

Salomon, Brownell: *Critical Analyses in English Renaissance Drama: A Bibliographic Guide,* Garland Pub., New York, 1991.

Samantrai, Ranu: *Claiming the Burden: Naipaul's Africa,* Research in African Literatures, 2000.

Schutte, Gillian: *Behind Sir Vidia's Masque: The Night the Naipauls Came to Supper,* Book Southern Africa, 2010.

Scott, Kilvert Ian and Michael Thorpe: *V. S. Naipaul. Harlow, Essex,* Longman Group, UK, 1976.

Selwyn Cudjoe, R.: *V.S. Naipaul: A Materialist Reading,* University of Massachusetts Press, New York, 1988.

Shashi Kamra: *The Novels of V.S. Naipaul: A Study in Theme and Form,* Prestige Books, 1990.

Singh, H.B.: *V.S. Naipaul: A Spokesman for New Colonialism,* Literature and Ideology, 1969.

Singh, Manjit Inder: *V. S. Naipaul,* Rawat Publications, Jaipur, 1998.

Smyer, Richard I.: *Experience As Drama in the Works of V. S. Naipaul,* MacMillan, New York, 1981.

St. Omer, Garth: *The Writer As Naive Colonial: V.S. Naipaul and Miguel Street,* Carib, 1979.

Stevenson, Lionel: *The History of the English Novel,* Barnes & Noble, New York, 1967.

Stuttaford, Genevieve: *India: A Million Mutinies Now,* Book Review, 1990.

Suman Bala: *V. S. Naipaul: A Literary Response to the Nobel Laureate,* Khosla Publishing House, New Delhi, 2003.

T. Riggs: *Reference Guide to American Literature,* St James Press, London, 2000.

Theroux, Paul: *Sir Vidia's Shadow: A Friendship Across Five Continents,* Hamish Hamilton, London, 1998.

———: *V.S. Naipaul: An Introduction to his Work,* Deutsch, London, 1972.

Thorpe, James Ernest: *Principles of Textual Criticism,* Huntington Library, San Marino, 1972.

Thorpe, Michael: *V. S. Naipaul. Harlow,* Longman Group, UK, 1976.

Timothy Weiss: *On the Margins: The Art of Exile in V.S. Naipaul,* University of Massachusetts Press, 1993.

Timothy, F.: *On the Margins: The Art of Exile in V.S. Naipaul,* University of Massachusetts Press, Amherst, 1992.

Tinkler Villani, Valeria: *Fact and Fiction in V. S. Naipaul's The Killings in Trinidad and Guerrillas,* Rodopi, Netherlands, 1993.

Trevor-Roper, Hugh: *Born Again,* Review of Books, New York, 1981.

Verghese, Abraham: *The Family Business,* Times Book Review, New York, 2000.

Walder, Dennis: *V. S. Naipaul and the Postcolonial Order: Reading in a Free State,* John Hopkings University Press, Baltimore, 1993.

Waller, A. R.: *A Dictionary of British and American Women Writers, 1660-1800,* Rowman & Allanheld, New Jersey, 1985.

Walsh, William: *V. S. Naipaul,* Oliver and Boyd, Edinburgh, 1973.

Weiss, Timothy, F.: *On the Margins: The Art of Exile in V.S. Naipaul,* University of Massachusetts Press, 1992.

White, Landeg: *V. S. Naipaul: A Critical Introduction,* MacMillan, London, 1975.

Whitley, David: *Cultural Identities Under Pressure,* Taylor and Francis, London, 1995.

William Walsh: *V.S. Naipaul,* Oliver & Boyd, Edinburgh, 1973.

Wimal, Dissanayake: *Self and Colonial Desire: Travel Writings of V.S. Naipaul,* P. Lang, 1993.

Woodcock, George: *V.S. Naipaul and the Politics of Fiction,* Queen's Quarterly, 1980.

Wright, Rachel: *V. S. Naipaul and Poet James Fenton,* Oxford University Press, Oxford, 1995.

Zapata, Varela J.: *V.S. Naipaul: El Retrato de la Sociedad Post-Colonial Desde la Literatura de la Commonwealth,* Universidad de Santiago de Compostela, Spain, 1998.